THE POETRY OF
JEAN DE LA CEPPÈDE

A Study in Text and Context

BY

PAUL A. CHILTON

OXFORD UNIVERSITY PRESS

1977

Oxford University Press, Walton Street, Oxford OX2 6DP

OXFORD LONDON GLASGOW NEW YORK
TORONTO MELBOURNE WELLINGTON CAPE TOWN
IBADAN NAIROBI DAR ES SALAAM LUSAKA ADDIS ABABA
KUALA LUMPUR SINGAPORE JAKARTA HONG KONG TOKYO
DELHI BOMBAY CALCUTTA MADRAS KARACHI

© *Oxford University Press 1977*

British Library Cataloguing in Publication Data
Chilton, Paul Anthony
    The poetry of Jean de la Ceppède: a study in
    text and context. – (Oxford modern languages
    and literature monographs)
    Bibl. – Index
    ISBN 0-19-815529-8
    1. Title   2. Series
    841'.3   PQ1628.L2/
    La Ceppède, Jean de – Criticism and interpretation

*Printed in Great Britain
at the University Press, Oxford
by Vivian Ridler
Printer to the University*

ACKNOWLEDGEMENTS

THIS book owes its largest debt to those who advised and assisted me during the preparation of the doctoral dissertation which, in spite of certain revisions, is still its basis. In particular my gratitude is due to Dr. R. A. Sayce, who made available to me his knowledge and his counsel. I should like to thank Professor A. J. Steele, and Professor I. D. McFarlane, whose examination of the original version has been of far-reaching value. I am grateful to Dr. D. C. Potts, who stimulated the initial discovery of the subject and its ramifications, and to Dr. A. W. Raitt, for his encouragement and support from the early stages to publication. I owe much, too, to the stimulus provided by the lectures and seminars of the late Professor Stephen Ullmann.

A study of this kind must draw on the work of many more scholars than could be acknowledged here, and to those who have furthered the understanding of Renaissance poetry and poetics, and on whose scholarship I have depended, I acknowledge my indebtedness. Needless to say, all remaining shortcomings are the author's responsibility.

CONTENTS

LIST OF ABBREVIATIONS

Arb.   Musée Arbaud, Aix-en-Provence
Ars.   Bibliothèque de l'Arsenal,
BN   Bibliothèque Nationale, Paris
Ing.   Bibliothèque Inguimbertine, Carpentras

BHR   *Bibliothèque d'humanisme et renaissance*
CAIEF *Cahiers de l'association internationale des études françaises*
DSS   *Dix-septième siècle*
FS   *French Studies*
MLN   *Modern Language Notes*
PMLA   *Publications of the Modern Language Society of America*

INTRODUCTION

THE earliest criticism of La Ceppède is contained by implication in the sonnet written by Malherbe for the first part of the *Théorèmes*, and in the following *sizain* written for the second part:[1]

> Muses, vous promettez en vain
> Au front de ce grand Escriuain
> Et du laurier et du lierre.
> Ses ouvrages trop precieux
> Pour les couronnes de la terre
> L'asseurent de celles des cieux.

It is conceivable that in the diplomatic ambiguity of these verses Malherbe is making an observation on the inherent incompatibility between his own requirements and poetry of religious inspiration. If this is so, it is not perhaps surprising that La Ceppède's work seems to have fallen almost immediately into neglect. Goujet merely recalls a few biographical details and concentrates attention on what he considers improved versification in Part II of the *Théorèmes*.[2] During the twentieth-century rehabilitation of the minor post-Pléiade poets, however, La Ceppède has been admired for a variety of reasons. Bremond was the first to acclaim him as a devout poet of genius possessing unusual powers of evocation and spiritual exaltation.[3] Critics in England have since pointed to the intellectual yet sensuous qualities of his work, while others associated with his native region have stressed his connections with Provence.[4]

This variety of criteria is in part related to the uncertainty of the literary-historical characterization of La Ceppède's poetry. It was inevitable that it should have been judged at the time of its

---

[1] *Théorèmes* I, facing title-page, and *Théorèmes* II, p. 647.

[2] *Bibliothèque françoise*, vol. xiv, pp. 320 ff.

[3] *Histoire littéraire du sentiment religieux en France*, vol. i, pp. 347 ff.

[4] e.g. Boase, 'Poètes anglais et français de l'époque baroque'; O. de Mourgues, *Metaphysical, Baroque and Précieux Poetry*, pp. 49 ff.; Clarac, 'Jean de La Ceppède, poète de la Passion'; Pingaud, 'La Ceppède, poète et magistrat aixois'.

publication by emerging classical standards. Inverting this bias, modern scholarship has most frequently approached the poetry through broad historical concepts such as 'baroque', 'metaphysical', and 'mannerist'.[5] Consequently, La Ceppède's text has tended to be utilized illustratively to support an *a priori* standpoint. While this approach has highlighted important features and yielded penetrating analyses of individual sonnets, its effectiveness as a method has been hampered by terminological inconsistency. Moreover, because it necessarily abstracted the elements appropriate to its own hypothesis, the method was not well equipped to provide comprehensive accounts of the origins and intrinsic character of works by individual writers.

An alternative approach to the religious poetry of the period, implicit in Bremond, sought a firm historical basis on which to relate poetry to the devotional movement of the sixteenth and seventeenth centuries, and in particular to the literature of systematic meditation.[6] Methodologically more sound, this approach has nevertheless been obliged to treat texts selectively in order to establish the existence of a historical movement. Only isolated areas of La Ceppède's poetry have been elucidated by it. In particular, no attempt has been made to assess the degree of importance of meditative method in comparison with other religious traditions. Arguments for the influence of meditative exercises have sometimes been based less on his acknowledged sources than on comparisons of formal arrangement, which, while not disturbing the structure of the alleged source, do appear to violate the unity of the poetic text. Textual investigations have not in any case always fully confirmed the hypothesis of meditative influence, but such investigations have themselves been selective.[7] Part I alone of the *Théorèmes* lists over 150 sources, and their significance remains to be considered.

---

[5] A complete survey of this approach is impracticable here, but cf. O. de Mourgues, op. cit., on La Ceppède as a 'metaphysical' poet; Buffum, *Studies in the Baroque*, ch. 3; Hatzfield's suggestion that La Ceppède is 'mannerist' in the review of Buffum, *MLN* 72 (1957), p. 631.

[6] Cf. Martz, *The Poetry of Meditation*; Cave, *Devotional Poetry in France*; also Lawrence, 'La Ceppède's *Théorèmes* and Ignation Meditation'; Nugent, 'La Ceppède's Poetry of Contemplation'; Wilson, 'Spanish and English Religious Poetry'.

[7] Cf. Wilson, 'Notes on a Sonnet by La Ceppède'; McCall Probes, 'La Ceppède's *Théorèmes* and Augustinian Sources', qualified by 'La Ceppède's Discriminatory Use of St. Augustine'.

There have, of course, also been important literary-critical syntheses of the facts concerning La Ceppède that have become available.[8] It is not the primary aim of the present study to rival these works in seeking to produce yet another, but more all-embracing, synthesis. In particular, the concept of the baroque and its congeners has been abandoned for the purpose of establishing the characteristics of the poetry. The method adopted is to examine not literary or religious currents prior to the poetry, but to seek relevant affiliations from the information contained in the text and from the available historical facts surrounding its genesis. The general schema of the study is determined by the desire to concentrate on two fundamentals: the historical facts of the environment and composition of the poetry; and the substance of its text and annotations. Consequently, the argument deals in the first instance with the immediate background, the genesis of the texts, and the analysis of their style and meaning structure, while historical consideration of pre-existing currents of literature and thought are introduced where relevant.

In the wider context La Ceppède's poetry poses a number of questions. It spans the contrasting periods of Pléiade and Malherbian literary conceptions; it spans a stretch of time in which far-reaching changes are occurring in thought and sensibility. Does his poetry throw light on these changes? How did La Ceppède, who was an admired friend of Malherbe, react to the movement away from the sixteenth-century outlook? And then, if his poetry is, as on its own terms it must be, characteristically Christian, do its particular religious qualities cause it to conflict with emergent classical taste? But what does 'characteristically Christian' mean? There is the broad question of the role of rhetoric and imagery in any religious expression, of the influence of sacred texts on language and symbolization. More specifically, may it not be the case that the Malherbian poetic is intrinsically incompatible with La Ceppède's type of religious vision, while the tradition mediated by the Pléiade has a close affinity with it? There are other sides to La Ceppède, however. It ought not to be forgotten that he was a magistrate who lived through a period of

---

[8] Ruchon, *Essai sur la vie et l'œuvre de Jean de La Ceppède*; Rousset, Préface to *Théorèmes;* idem, *L'Intérieur et l'extérieur,* pp. 13 ff.; Donaldson-Evans, *Poésie et méditation chez Jean de La Ceppède;* on particular aspects cf. Du Bruck, 'Descriptive Realism'; Evans, 'Figural Art'; Lawrence, 'Nature Imagery'.

conflict and social collapse. In the historical context does his poetry have any function beyond piety and asethetic pleasure? What were the fortunes of Provence during and after the religious wars, and how, if at all, are they reflected in La Ceppède's work?

NOTE ON THE TEXTS

FOR the *Imitation* of 1612 and the *Théorèmes* the text used is
the photographic reprint by Droz of the copy held by the
Bibliothèque de Marseille.[1] Reference to the *Imitation* is to
the 1612 edition, except where comparison of variants is made.
For the 1594 edition of the *Imitation* the copy used is that of
the Musée Arbaud, Aix-en-Provence. References to the Bible, including the Psalms, are to the Vulgate version unless otherwise
stated. In transcription of French texts the original spelling and
typographical arrangement are retained, except that contractions
for *m* and *n* are resolved.[2] Where modern editions of sixteenth-
and seventeenth-century works are used the editor's conventions
have been followed. In references to the *Imitation* the psalm
number and strophe number are given in arabic numerals in that
order; in references to the *Théorèmes* the part number (I or II) is
given first, followed by the book number (i, ii, iii, or iv), followed
by the sonnet number (1 to 100).

[1] See Bibliography.
[2] In the case of book titles where capitals have been transcribed as lower
case the modern distinction between *u* and *v* and *i* and *j* has been adopted.

sixteenth century. The University was formed in embryo in 1409 by Count Louis II, but lagged behind the early Renaissance burgeoning of universities. This meant that the essential material of the humanist expansion was absent: editions of ancient texts, commentaries, translations, literary theorizing, philosophical and theological speculation. The eventual emergence of Aix was intense and rapid, but it did not take place till after about 1550.[4] A further explanation of this delay may lie in the related linguistic and political development of the region.

The annexation of Provence to France was ratified by the États in 1487. Under the unifying policies of the French kings, Provençal society lost the feudal character it had had under the kings of Naples and counts of Anjou, and in the first decades of the sixteenth century saw the adaptation of its administration to the requirements of a central government. The Parlement of Provence was set up in 1501–2 on the model of the older Toulouse, Bordeaux, and Grenoble bodies to counterbalance the ancient Chambre des comptes of Aix. It was in this sphere of contact and conflict between the local and the centralized power that La Ceppède had his public career, as a *conseiller* from 1578 in the Parlement, as second president of the Chambre[5] from 1586, and as its first president from 1608. As in Toulouse, the administrative and legal milieu was of great significance for literary developments. Aix emerged at the end of the century as the governing capital of the province with a cultured French-speaking magistracy closely aligned with the central power of the monarch.

These political developments are mirrored on the linguistic and cultural level.[6] René d'Anjou had introduced French to the Provençal nobility, but its use was confined to court culture. Latin and the Provençal dialect continued to be used by the États and the *communautés* for administrative purposes, and even in communications with the king till around 1530. Although the use of the dialect declined after this date, and especially after the ordinances of Villers-Cotterêts of 1539, it was only in the last quarter of the century that the *parlementaires* sought to enhance their status through the cultivation of literary French. The progress of French

---

[4] Cf. Brun, *Bellaud de La Bellaudière*, pp. 27 ff.

[5] By that time renamed the Cour des comptes, aides et finances. For La Ceppède's career see Donaldson-Evans, 'Notice biographique'.

[6] See Brun, *Recherches historiques sur l'introduction du français dans les provinces du Midi*.

NOTE ON THE TEXTS

FOR the *Imitation* of 1612 and the *Théorèmes* the text used is the photographic reprint by Droz of the copy held by the Bibliothèque de Marseille.[1] Reference to the *Imitation* is to the 1612 edition, except where comparison of variants is made. For the 1594 edition of the *Imitation* the copy used is that of the Musée Arbaud, Aix-en-Provence. References to the Bible, including the Psalms, are to the Vulgate version unless otherwise stated. In transcription of French texts the original spelling and typographical arrangement are retained, except that contractions for *m* and *n* are resolved.[2] Where modern editions of sixteenth- and seventeenth-century works are used the editor's conventions have been followed. In references to the *Imitation* the psalm number and strophe number are given in arabic numerals in that order; in references to the *Théorèmes* the part number (I or II) is given first, followed by the book number (i, ii, iii, or iv), followed by the sonnet number (1 to 100).

[1] See Bibliography.
[2] In the case of book titles where capitals have been transcribed as lower case the modern distinction between *u* and *v* and *i* and *j* has been adopted.

I

PROVENCE AT THE END OF THE
SIXTEENTH CENTURY

THE Preface to the first part of La Ceppède's *Théorèmes* is entitled 'A la France'; in it he apologizes for the latent influence of his 'ramage natal'; the only other allusion to the historical milieu of his poetry, apart from the royal dedications, occurs in the *Imitation* and concerns the sufferings of Provence. In other words, La Ceppède's sparse references to his times touch on three crucial aspects: the relationship between Provence and France, the role of the regional language and culture, and, not unexpectedly, the civil wars. Now it must be a fundamental fact in considering his place in literary history that La Ceppède is a provincial poet in a period of increasing centralization. It will be necessary, therefore, before examining the genesis of his poetry, to trace the patterns of cultural consciousness in Provence at a time of upheaval and transition. Brun[1] and Lafont[2] have dealt with the sixteenth-century Provençal renaissance; Fromilhague[3] has shown the extent of Malherbe's debt to the province. But a different perspective is required for La Ceppède, who may be said to fall between the Provençal and central French extremes. Since he himself is relatively silent about his background, further clarification seems to be required, first of the changes in Provençal culture and self-awareness in general, and second of the particular phases in the development of the Aix poets during and after the wars of religion.

1. *Revival, Rebellion, and Repentance*

With two brief exceptions—the troubadour entourage of Raimond Béranger V in the thirteenth century, and the circle of poets drawn largely from outside the region by René I in the fifteenth—literary life in Aix remained undistinguished till the second half of the

---

[1] *Bellaud de La Bellaudière* and *Poètes provençaux du XVIᵉ siècle.*
[2] *Renaissance du Sud.*   [3] *Vie de Malherbe,* chs. 2 and 4.

sixteenth century. The University was formed in embryo in 1409 by Count Louis II, but lagged behind the early Renaissance burgeoning of universities. This meant that the essential material of the humanist expansion was absent: editions of ancient texts, commentaries, translations, literary theorizing, philosophical and theological speculation. The eventual emergence of Aix was intense and rapid, but it did not take place till after about 1550.[4] A further explanation of this delay may lie in the related linguistic and political development of the region.

The annexation of Provence to France was ratified by the États in 1487. Under the unifying policies of the French kings, Provençal society lost the feudal character it had had under the kings of Naples and counts of Anjou, and in the first decades of the sixteenth century saw the adaptation of its administration to the requirements of a central government. The Parlement of Provence was set up in 1501–2 on the model of the older Toulouse, Bordeaux, and Grenoble bodies to counterbalance the ancient Chambre des comptes of Aix. It was in this sphere of contact and conflict between the local and the centralized power that La Ceppède had his public career, as a *conseiller* from 1578 in the Parlement, as second president of the Chambre[5] from 1586, and as its first president from 1608. As in Toulouse, the administrative and legal milieu was of great significance for literary developments. Aix emerged at the end of the century as the governing capital of the province with a cultured French-speaking magistracy closely aligned with the central power of the monarch.

These political developments are mirrored on the linguistic and cultural level.[6] René d'Anjou had introduced French to the Provençal nobility, but its use was confined to court culture. Latin and the Provençal dialect continued to be used by the États and the *communautés* for administrative purposes, and even in communications with the king till around 1530. Although the use of the dialect declined after this date, and especially after the ordinances of Villers-Cotterêts of 1539, it was only in the last quarter of the century that the *parlementaires* sought to enhance their status through the cultivation of literary French. The progress of French

---

[4] Cf. Brun, *Bellaud de La Bellaudière*, pp. 27 ff.

[5] By that time renamed the Cour des comptes, aides et finances. For La Ceppède's career see Donaldson-Evans, 'Notice biographique'.

[6] See Brun, *Recherches historiques sur l'introduction du français dans les provinces du Midi*.

in Provence from the end of the fifteenth century is summarized by the Provençal lawyer Raimond de Soliers, who is well aware of the accompanying political changes:

Toutefois depuis que la Provence a été unie au royaume de France, on a commencé d'y parler à demi françois et sans doute qu'en peu de temps, on n'y parlera que françois, au lieu que sous le comte René, il n'estoit cogneu qu'entre quelques courtisans.[7]

But the bilingual situation concealed a conflict. As the medium primarily of the region's political institutions French was inevitably associated with royal power. Just as French was beginning to make headway, a Provençal reaction—or renaissance—set in, which led to a literary revival. This phenomenon, diverse in its manifestations, was primarily a revival of Provençal—not of the conventional literary language of the troubadours, but of the dialect as it had developed by the sixteenth century. In certain cases it was associated with a separatist tendency that coincided with the Ligue rebellion. Yet in other cases it stimulated a royalist literature that increasingly adhered to French literary norms.

From about 1570 there seems to have been an awakening of the interest in the Roman and medieval past of Provence. De Soliers's manuscript of his encyclopedic *Chronographia provinciae* was terminated in 1577,[8] and part was published in 1615 under the significant title *Les antiquitez de la ville de Marseille, où il est traicté de l'ancienne république des Marseillois*. But the key role was played by the Nostredame family. Michel de Nostredame (Nostradamus) was venerated amongst the poets of the region, and an apparently widespread belief in his prophetic quatrains may have played some part in the popular fervour of Aix under the Ligue.[9] The degree of invention which his brother Jean de Nostredame indulged in his *Vies des plus célèbres et anciens poètes provençaux* is an indication of the intensity of the need for a local historical identity.[10] Another motive for providing Provence with a unified mythic past was rivalry with the Italians, who from Dante to

---

[7] *Les antiquitez de la ville de Marseille*, trans. Fabrot, 1615, p. 109, cited by Brun, *Recherches*, p. 335.

[8] See Brun, *Bellaud de La Bellaudière*, p. 32.

[9] Cf. C. de Nostredame, *L'Histoire et chronique de Provence*, p. 879; Haitze, *Histoire de la ville d'Aix*, vol. iii, p. 154.

[10] The work was published in Lyons in 1575. For detailed accounts see Anglade, introduction to Nostredame, *Vies*; Lafont, *Renaissance*, pp. 123 ff.

Bembo had been familiar with Provençal poetry. The 'Proesme' of the work is a *deffence et illustration*, in which it is argued that the Italians themselves acknowledge the priority of Provençal culture, that in spite of its debased state the dialect remains the first among vernaculars precisely because of its very heterogeneity.[11] It is this emphasis on the value of the local forms of speech, illustrated by the author's own attempts to imitate troubadour models, that contributed to the atmosphere in which the diverse poetic school of Aix was able to develop.

Jean de Nostredame's immediate continuator was his nephew, César, whose *Histoire et chronique*, approved by the États assembled at Aix in 1603, and published at public expense in 1614, can be seen as an official expression of the Provençal revival. César's purpose is expressed in terms of the Renaissance commonplace of personal and national ambition, only the nation here is Provence. He desires, he says, 'd'acquerir quelque immortelle renommée, et d'illustrer ma patrie'. As a humanist he emphasizes the classical past of the Roman *provincia*, which was 'la bien aymée des vieux Romans, leur petite Italie'. More than this, it had a special part in divine history, for it is 'vne seconde Palestine, vne terre saincte et sacrée, heureusement enrichie de la pluspart des venerables et saincts restes de la famille de Dieu'.[12] Amongst the families of the region placed in this perspective is that of La Ceppède, whose connections Nostredame traces with symbolic appropriateness to Teresa of Avila,[13] whose family name was Cepeda. The book in general displays a sense of historical destiny in which Provence and its inhabitants are seen as part of a divine plan, and events are set in an ordered ritualistic pattern.

The writings of Jean and César de Nostredame constituted a continuous enterprise and represented the intense local patriotism that was channelled in varying directions during the late sixteenth and early seventeenth centuries. A further factor was the commitment of the region to the Catholic cause, and it is not surprising to find that at the height of the civil wars cultural self-awareness

---

[11] *Vies*, p. 12: ' . . . parce qu'elle [la langue provençale] est meslée en partie de termes françois, espagnols, gascons, tuscans et lombards, il est aisé à veoir qu'elle devoit estre l'une des plus parfaictes et meilleures langues de toutes les vulgueres . . .'

[12] *Histoire*, Preface. On C. de Nostredame's use of his uncle's *Vies* and MS. history of Provence of 1575 see Anglade, introduction to *Vies*, pp. 153 ff.

[13] *Histoire*, p. 732; cf. also Perrier, *Un Village provençal*, p. 67.

was transformed into an assertion of political independence that was closely allied with the Ligue. Signs that the major division in Provence was between royalist moderates and extreme Catholics supported by the local interest were already apparent when Henri d'Angoulême, Grand Prieur of the Knights of Malta in France, arrived in the region in 1576 to impose royal authority on the comte de Carcès, whose followers were in 1584 to join the Ligue in an attempt to establish an independent Marseilles. The literary academy, which the Grand Prieur instituted at Aix at this time, and which included Malherbe, La Ceppède, Louis de Gallaup, César de Nostredame, and the dialect poet Bellaud de La Bellaudière, can be seen as part of the policy to reinforce French prestige. After the assassination of Henri d'Angoulême in 1586, the Ligue under the leadership of Hubert de Vins gained control of the Parlement of Aix; Marseilles again attempted secession in 1591; and, to add to the confusion, the House of Savoy sought to gain control of the province.[14]

The allegiance during the rebellion of the poets who had surrounded Henri d'Angoulême is worth considering, since it may be relevant to the literature they produced. When de Vins recognized Mayenne as *lieutenant général*, a section of the royalist Parlement moved to Pertuis and subsequently Manosque. La Ceppède himself was detained in 1589, attempted to escape, and on recapture was well treated by de Vins.[15] His loyalty to Henry IV is hardly in doubt, although his letter[16] written from Avignon to the King in 1594 indicates that he felt some need to clear himself from suspicion, and it is conceivable on grounds to be discussed later, including the internal evidence of his poetry, that he shared a feeling of collective guilt for the situation in Aix. This is not surprising in view of the activities of his literary associates, the most symbolic of which was the coincidence of the publication of La Bellaudière's *Obros* with the Marseilles rebellion.

The printing and publication of this work in 1595 were financed by the separatist consul, Charles de Casaulx, and his *viguier* Louis d'Aix, who together attempted to realize the traditional aspirations of the city to autonomy. The title-page of the first issue ran: *Obros et rimos prouvenssalos de Loys de La Bellaudiero, gentilhomme*

---

[14] For this period see Haitze, *Histoire*, vol. iii.
[15] Haitze, vol. iii, pp. 118–19.
[16] BN, ancien petit fonds français 23194, fos. 445–6.

*prouvenssau . . . dedicados as vertuouzes et generouzes Seignours,
Louys d'Aix et Charles de Casaulx.* A number of the Aix circle appear
to have been implicated. Verse by Louis de Gallaup was included;
César de Nostredame contributed verse and a preface interpreting
the publication as the official restoration of the Provençal tradition,
and justifying the Marseilles revolt against the Crown. The assassination of Casaulx and the fall of Marseilles in 1596 were followed
by a wave of atonement and readjustment to royal power. Bellaud's
Obros had several reissues incorporating various amendments.
Nostredame now composed a sonnet 'Sur la tyrannie, et ruine de
Charles de Cazaux', and Gallaup added to his 1597 edition of the
penitential psalms a 'Prosopopée de feu Monseigneur d'eternelle
memoire Henri d'Engolesme' dedicated to Henry III and a 'Poeme
sur la reduction de Marseille' dedicated to Henry IV.

There thus seems to have been a crisis of conscience resulting
from the clash of three elements—loyalty to Provence, to the
Catholic Ligue, and to the French monarch. The moral confusion
was heightened by popular preachers of opposed parties, and
especially the presence of Gilbert Génébrard, whose public affirma-
tion of the Tridentine decrees and continuing support of the
Ligue embarrassed the Aix humanists who admired his erudition.[17]
Condemned for *lèse-majesté* by the Parlement in 1596 he was
replaced by the equally learned, but Gallican Paul Hurault de
l'Hôpital. The new Archbishop, who politically stood for the
alliance of Church and State and for the dependence of the parle-
ments on the Crown, also actively encouraged the Aix poets,
notably Gallaup and Nostredame.[18] Henry IV's amnesty and
confirmation of the former privileges of Aix introduced an era of
expansion and optimism. The cultural ties between Provence and
the rest of France were reinforced by Peiresc, Malherbe, and in
particular Du Vair who became president of the Parlement of Aix
in 1599.

But the changed mood is symbolized above all in the Provençal
devotion to Marie de Médicis. Nostredame represents her entry
in 1600 into Marseilles, Aix, and Salon almost as an act of salvation.
The municipal celebrations on this occasion were embodied in
a mixture of Christian and pagan mythologies. François Dupérier

---

[17] Cf. Haitze, vol. iii, pp. 134, 387 ff., 450; Nostredame, *Histoire*, p. 963.
[18] He wrote laudatory poems for Gallaup's *Imitation* and Nostredame's
Pièces héroïques.

designed the triumphal arches at Aix, César de Nostredame those at Salon;[19] Malherbe recited his ode;[20] Du Vair and La Ceppède delivered speeches.[21] The marriage of Marie de Médicis to Henry IV, which was believed to have been prophesied by Michel de Nostredame,[22] was emblematically depicted on the triumphal arches as a rainbow after the storm. This symbol, besides being a composite reference to the storms accompanying the queen's voyage and the metaphorical storms of the civil wars, was also, it should be noted, a traditional biblical symbol of the Redemption. Since Provence's cultural and political past was linked with Italy, the marriage and the accompanying ceremonies were also to some extent symbolic of a new Provençal attitude of loyalty to France. The final sentence of César de Nostredame's *Histoire* summarizes a mythic perception of the recent events and of changes in Provençal attitudes. He is commenting on a 'sonnet mystérieux' written to honour the queen,

qui ne degenere point du style de nos antiques Troubadours, et qui fait assez voir, que c'est apres tant de tormentes ciuiles, et de flots de sang, que les rayons de ce Soleil de beauté ont formé cest Arc d'Alliance, presage de toute serenité, et que la venue de ceste Tusque Astree a remis le siecle d'Auguste au monde, apporté la paix en France, et des Dauphins tant desirez à la plus Chrestienne et noble couronne de l'vniuers. Ainsi prindrent fin nos malheurs, ainsi termina ce siecle, et fut ceste histoire accomplie . . .[23]

The turn of the century is thus seen through biblical, solar, and humanist images, as a fulfilment of a cycle: after a period of destruction and deprivation the royal marriage seems to predict a period of peace and prosperity. The extent of the new Provençal attachment to the monarchy was demonstrated in a similar manner in 1622, when Louis XIII entered Aix after defeating the Protestants of Languedoc and proceeded to make a 'voyage de dévotion'

[19] Cf. *Entrée de la Reine*, 1602.

[20] 'A la reine sur sa bien-venuë en France', *Œuvres*, ed. Fromilhague and Lebègue, vol. i, text xiii.

[21] See Nostredame, *Entrée*, ed. Boy, p. 32; La Ceppède's Marseilles speech appears in a collection dated 1604, and is reproduced by Quenot, 'Un discours inconnu'.

[22] An inscription on a triumphal arch at Salon refers to Nostradamus as a prophet 'qui florentes et felices Franciae et Florentiae regios thalamos Sybillino suo carmine decantavit' (*Entrée*, ed. Boy, p. 42).

[23] *Histoire*, p. 1090.

in the province. The event again was the occasion for ritual celebration: Louis de Gallaup's son designed the triumphal arches;
Thomas Billon, a member of the Parlement and an admirer of La
Ceppède, composed anagrams on the King's name; and Malherbe also contributed verse.[24] According to Haitze, Louis declared
that the Aixois received him as a divinity.[25]

This is not to say that all conflicts ceased. While Provence was
not affected by the insurgency that marked seventeenth-century
Languedoc, its traditional fervour left some traces of tension
between Church and State. Underlying differences between the
Parlement and the Archbishop came to a head in 1612 when Du
Vair clashed with Paul Hurault de l'Hôpital over the Gallican *De
ecclesiastica et politica potestate* of Edmond Richer.[26] Nevertheless
it is at this stage that the religious and cultural institutions of Aix
begin to recover and flourish.

It was not until after 1597 that Jean Tholozan, aided by Dupérier, established a press in the town; in 1602 Du Vair succeeded
in bringing about the foundation of the Collège Royal des Bourbons
and of three *régences royales* in the University; the following year
four new faculties were added. The religious life of Provence
advanced towards its own characteristic forms of seventeenth-
century spirituality.[27] With the aim of forestalling any alliance with
the Ligue, Henri d'Angoulême had set a pattern for lay devotion
by becoming the rector of the Aix Penitents of Notre Dame de
Piété.[28] The Capuchins had been introduced during the Ligue
occupation 'pour consoler ceste cité'.[29] After the civil wars the
emphasis on penitence was replaced by preaching and instruction.
The Jesuits were regarded with some suspicion, but Richeome was
admired by Nostredame as a native of Provence,[30] and Pierre
Coton, future confessor of the King, preached in Aix itself in spite

[24] Malherbe, *Œuvres*, vol. I, texts LXXXVI, LXXXVII, LXXXVIII. On
Billon see Haitze, vol. iv, p. 106; he wrote pieces for the *Théorèmes* (I, p. 528,
II, pp. 645 and 649).

[25] Haitze, vol. iv, p. 107.

[26] On this episode see Haitze, vol. iv, pp. 59 ff.

[27] For the religious sensibility of this period in France see for instance,
Bremond, *Histoire littéraire du sentiment religieux en France*; Dagens, *Bérulle et
les origines de la restauration catholique*; Pourrat, *La Spiritualité chrétienne*; for
the devotional movement and its relation to poetry see Cave, *Devotional Poetry
in France*.

[28] On his relationship with the penitential orders see Haitze, vol. iii, pp. 27 f.

[29] Nostredame, *Histoire*, p. 812.

[30] *Histoire*, p. 800.

of Hurault's anxiety.[31] But Provence produced its own devotional school embodied in the Congrégation de la doctrine chrétienne, a catechizing order of secular priests, which was founded in 1593 at Avignon by César de Bus and Jean-Baptiste Romillon, and continued by Romillon at Aix from 1600. In 1612 it was renamed the Congrégation des Prêtres de l'Oratoire, and abandoned independent status in 1619 to join the Oratoire of Bérulle. This development suggests a preference for the Gallican as opposed to the Jesuit influence that accords with the increasingly close links between Provence and the Crown. At the same time the Ursulines were set up by Romillon and Claire de Perussis, who came from a family of *parlementaires*.[32] La Ceppède himself, as was acknowledged by his contemporaries, represented the ties between the lay and religious communities. In 1599 he acquired the estate of Les Aygalades, and became the patron of the Carmelite convent sited there.[33] It is likely also that he had contact with François de Sales who addressed to him a letter expressing admiration for his poetry.[34] While lay devotion was a widespread movement by the beginning of the seventeenth century, in Provence it might be said to be related to a need to harmonize secular interests, especially the royal cause, with the intense and rebellious religious passions of the recent past. It can perhaps be regarded as the means whereby Provence both achieved an identity and atoned for past aberrations.

2. *The Development of Poetry in Aix*

The development of the poets closely connected with Aix between about 1580 and 1630 should be distinguished from other provincial poetic movements, such as the Puys, and more especially the Jeux Floraux of Toulouse.[35] It is true that the Toulouse group of poets had much in common with the group at Aix at this time: it was a Catholic stronghold, was dominated by its Parlement, and produced notable religious poets. Further, La Ceppède himself must

[31] Cf. Hurault's letters to the king, BN, ancien fonds français, 23195, fo. 405. On the Parlement's continuing opposition to the Jesuits cf. Haitze, vol. iv, chs. 65, 69, 72.

[32] On the Congrégation and the Ursulines in Aix cf. Haitze, vol. iv, ch. 1 and 44. François de Perussis contributed a laudatory sonnet to the *Théorèmes* I, p. 526.

[33] Donaldson-Evans, 'Notice biographique', p. 127.

[34] François de Sales, *Œuvres*, ed. Mackey and Navatel, vol. xvi, pp. 286-7.

[35] On Toulouse see Dawson, *Toulouse in the Renaissance*.

have been known there, since two *conseillers* from the town wrote sonnets for the *Théorèmes*.[36] However, the Aix movement can be seen to have had its own characteristic development, which was closely bound up with the historical changes already discussed. This development has three distinguishable phases: from the formation of a court academy around Henri d'Angoulême in about 1580 to its collapse after his assassination in 1586; the period of rebellion under the Ligue, that is, from the ascendancy of de Vins to the return of the royalist Parlement in 1594; and the period from this date onwards under the tutelage of Du Vair and Malherbe. The phases span two generations and are accompanied by changes in themes and styles.

In the first period literary assemblies were held in the medieval *palais des comtes* in Aix, in Henri d'Angoulême's Salon residence, the Château de l'Archevêque, and possibly also in the Hôtel Margalet, the Aix home of Malherbe, who was at this time secretary to the Grand Prieur.[37] César de Nostredame describes Henri, who had been educated by Dorat, as an encyclopedic humanist, and his residence as 'une continuelle et universelle Académie'.[38] Nostredame himself was distinguished as a musician and painter as well as a poet and historian.[39] In view of the political role of Henri d'Angoulême, and his interest in penitential devotion, the Aix academy at this time may have some affinity with the contemporaneous academy of Vincennes of Henry III, which combined syncretic humanism with ritual atonement for France's ills.[40]

Many of the adherents of the circle published no complete poetic work; but they are represented in preliminary verses in a way

[36] G. de Terlon, F. le Conte (see *Théorèmes* I, pp. 520–1). On Terlon cf. Dawson, *Toulouse*, p. 82, n. 99.

[37] On Henri d'Angoulême's court and Malherbe see Fromilhague, *Vie de Malherbe*, and 'Malherbe et le "côté" de Provence' in *Quatrième centenaire de la naissance de Malherbe*; also Aude, 'La Poésie en Provence au temps de Malherbe'; Legré, 'Le Grand Prieur Henri d'Angoulême'; L'Hôte, 'Malherbe et la Provence'.   [38] *Histoire*, p. 841.

[39] On parallels between Nostredame's poetry and painting see Cave, *Devotional Poetry*, pp. 268–76. Nostredame was renowned as a miniaturist: cf. the extant miniatures of Henry IV in Gallaup, *Imitation* (Ing. MS. 17, fo. 3), and of Béatrix de Provence in *Registre de tous les seigneurs, gentilshommes et blasons* (see Anglade, *Vies*, p. 26); and references to miniatures of Henry IV and Marie de Médicis in Nostredame, *Entrée*, pp. 51–2, of the sieur de Craponne in a letter to Peiresc (see Anglade, p. 26), and of portraits given to Hurault de l'Hôpital in *Poésies de L. Gallaup*, Ing., MS. 386, fo. 37ᵛ; and in the same MS. cf. 'Sur les vers le pinceau et le luth du sieur de Nostredame', fo. 41ᵛ.

[40] Cf. Yates, *French Academies*, ch. 8.

that suggests the existence of a network which embraces both Provençal- and French-speaking poets of the region, and which remains coherent through all phases of the movement. The earliest evidence of such a network is in Jacques Perrache's *Triomphe du Berlan* dedicated to Charles de Bourbon, Cardinal of Vendôme, published in 1585. This allegorical moral work was acclaimed in French by César de Nostredame, François Dupérier, Honorat Aymar, Malherbe, and Louis de Gallaup, and in Provençal by Bellaud de La Bellaudière and H. Gantelmy. Much more verse must have been written and circulated around this time, but none was published till the following decade, a delay that may be due to the lack of a permanent press in Aix and Marseilles until the late 1590s. In the preliminary pieces included in La Ceppède's *Théorèmes* of 1613 and 1621 it is essentially the same group of poets that is represented.

The verse written during this early phase was predominantly, though not exclusively, in the tradition of Petrarchan and Plé-iade love-poetry. Henri d'Angoulême wrote occasional and erotic verse;[41] La Bellaudière (who wrote in Provençal), La Roque, Gallaup, and Malherbe exchanged pieces in the same vein.[42] La Ceppède himself refers to his early liking for elaborate love-poetry:

I'en parle [de la poésie profane] comme experimenté; car dés le plus tendre auril de mon âge affriandé de ses chatoüilleuses mignardises, ie la receus comme ma plus delicate delice.[43]

It is highly probable that La Ceppède contributed love-poems of a neo-Platonic nature, for a sonnet by Gallaup is headed 'A. M. le Grand. Prieur. Gouverneur. de. Provence sur l'Idée de la beauté à luy dédié par M. J. de. la. Ceppède. President. du Roy en sa cour des Aydes'.[44] It is evident both from the title and the verse that Gallaup is writing before Henri d'Angoulême's death in June 1586; La Ceppède had become a president of the Cour in the preceding February. It seems likely, therefore, that the poem or

---

[41] *Œuvres poétiques*, BN, ancien fonds français, 378.
[42] Cf. Gallaup, *Poésies*, 'Sur l'Yole du Sieur Du Périer' (fo. 51), 'Pour la Floris du Sr. Malherbe' (fo. 51ᵛ). On Malherbe's role see Fromilhague, *Vie*, pp. 70–91.
[43] *Théorèmes* I, pp. 5–6.
[44] *Poésies*, fos. 39ᵛ–40. Cf. Braunschweig, 'Petites découvertes sur La Ceppède'.

poems entitled *l'Idée de la beauté* reached completion some time in the spring of 1586.[45]

Devout poetry, represented by, for instance, Malherbe's *Larmes de Saint Pierre* and Henri d'Angoulême's sonnet 'A la Madeleine de la Sainte Baume',[46] coexisted alongside profane verse in this initial period; but it is only after the dispersion of the academy in 1586 that penitential themes predominate. The relationship between the two currents in the transition period is particularly well illustrated in Gallaup. It is a love-poem, 'Les Amours d'Apollon et de Cassandre', dated 1590, that he maintains was written as a means of consolation in a time of war.[47] On the other hand, the renunciation of profane poetry, and the means of doing this within the framework of profane styles, is demonstrated in his two almost identical sonnets, one of which (presumably the earlier) refers to 'ma Dame', the other to the Magdalen.[48] It seems that the appropriate moment for the emergence of serious peniten-tial poetry was the period during and immediately after the Ligue revolt in Aix. Thus, although he had probably studied the Psalms in the 1580s, it was not until 1595 that Gallaup completed and circulated his *Imitation et paraphrase de la pénitence royalle*.[49]

This work, dedicated to Henry IV, can be seen as a collective offering of repentance after the confused loyalties of the wars. It was endorsed by the preliminary verse of Paul Hurault de l'Hôpital, and by leading members of Henri d'Angoulême's circle such as François Dupérier, César de Nostredame, and La Ceppède, whose own *Imitation* had been published in Lyons in 1594. This literary act of penitence seems to have been closely associated by the poets with a definitive change from the pagan to the Christian Muse. It is at this time that Gallaup adopts the device, later used also by La Ceppède, of a crown of thorns bearing the motto 'haec mihi

---

[45] He may also have composed a play on an amorous theme. Alluding to Bandello's sixth *novella*, C. de Nostredame notes 'Le President [i.e. La Ceppède] auoit composé et fait iouër ceste histoire en ses plus ieunes ans' (*Histoire*, p. 870). The work probably pre-dates the Aix academy. Cf. Lebègue, 'L'Influence des romanciers sur les dramaturges français'.

[46] BN, ancien fonds français, 482, fo. 63ᵛ.

[47] *Poésies*, fos. 28–33.

[48] *Poésies*, fos. 48ᵛ and 82ᵛ; *Imitation* (1597), p. 26. Cf. Braunschweig, 'Une Source profane de la "Sainte Pécheresse"'.

[49] Ing. MS. 17; printed as *Imitation des pseaumes de la pénitence*, 1596; reissued 1597. There are notes in Latin on the penitential psalms in the earlier MS. 193, fo. 23.

laurus erit'.[50] The possibility of further connections between Gallaup's and La Ceppède's paraphrases is discussed in Chapter II, but it may be noted here that both mark a decisive stage in the literary, as well as in the general historical, development of Aix.

By its nature this moment of atonement was short-lived. It is true that Nostredame's psalms, and his *Larmes*,[51] appeared after the turn of the century, but by then a third phase with new predominant themes and styles was emerging. Two men dominate, and give coherence to this period: Malherbe, who returned to Provence in 1595, and remained there, with the exception of two brief absences, until 1605, and whose house may, as earlier, have been used by the literary circle; and Du Vair, the head of the Provence Parlement, who surrounded himself with the literary and scientific minds of Aix, both at his town house and his country residence known as La Floride.[52] The scientific spirit was represented above all by Peiresc, who shared Du Vair's interest in astronomy, and who was, moreover, La Ceppède's cousin.[53] Malherbe's literary doctrines were at that time already formulated in their essentials, and he himself was accepted in Provence as an authority and a teacher.[54] It is important to distinguish this from the earlier phases of the Aix movement. Peiresc, who was born in 1580, represents a new generation, while the mature Malherbe and Du Vair introduce a rationalist as well as a patriotic element. This renewal and increased stability is reflected in the composition of a variety of extended works, some by authors not previously active in the region. Religious literature is particularly diverse in form and content: the Aix Carthusian Marc-Antoine Durant, for instance, recast the penitential themes in a quasi-epic form;[55] Jean Caze wrote not only the *Méditations sur l'histoire de Job*,

[50] See Gallaup, *Poésies*, fo. 19; cf. La Ceppède, frontispiece to *Théorèmes* I and II.

[51] *Les Perles, ou les Larmes de la saincte Magdeleine*, Toulouse, 1606; the psalm paraphrases appear in *Pièces héroïques*, Toulouse, 1608.

[52] On this period cf. Fromilhague, *Vie*, ch. IV; Lebègue, 'Nouvelles études malherbiennes'; L'Hôte, 'Malherbe et la Provence', pp. 123 ff.

[53] The letters from La Ceppède to Peiresc (Ing. MS. 1878, fos. 413–16), which are the only documentary evidence of their exchanges, concern administrative matters.

[54] On the dating of the maturation of his doctrine at around 1600 see Fromilhague, *Vie*, pp. 151–6.

[55] *La Magdaliade ou Esguillon spirituel pour exciter les ames pecheresses à quitter leurs vanités*, Tours, 1622; an earlier edition, Loches, 1608.

which owes its stoic element to Du Vair,[56] but also an apologetic work, *De la providence de Dieu contre les épicuriens et athéistes*.[57] Apart from Nostredame, however, La Ceppède was the only original member of the circle to publish substantial works after 1600. His *Théorèmes*, the first part of which has its roots, as will be seen, in the preceding period, constitutes the culmination of the diverse aspects of the Aix poetic movement.

By the time of La Ceppède's death in 1623 the distinctive poetry of Aix was merging with the mainstream of French literature as a result of the influence of Malherbe on the new generation. Amongst others from the region, Jean de Gallaup and Scipion Du Périer became his disciples. François Garnier de Montfuron, whose preliminary verse was placed with that of Malherbe and Du Périer in the second part of the *Théorèmes*,[58] was also appreciated as 'un digne disciple de Malherbe' at the court of Louis XIII.[59] His *Recueil de vers* published in Aix in 1632, at Du Périer's request, marks the point at which Aix poetry loses its distinct identity.

However, it is likely that Malherbe's influence was experienced already by the first-generation poets during the early period of the movement. The hypothesis of Malherbian influence on such poets as Louis de Gallaup and La Ceppède might seem improbable at first sight. The Aix poets, regarding themselves as the inheritors of the troubadours, exalted love as a poetic theme, and imitated the Petrarchan manner either directly from Italian models or as mediated by Desportes.[60] They shared with the Pléiade the neo-Platonic myth of poetic inspiration.[61] Moreover, there was a belief in the mysterious cognitive function of obscure verbal allegory;[62] Gallaup's interest in symbolic forms and his belief in the intrinsic

[56] Montpellier, 1608. The 'épître au lecteur' acknowledges the influence of Du Vair's meditations on Job, contained in *Traictez de piété, et sainctes méditations*, Paris, 1607.

[57] Montpellier, 1606. Cf. Du Vair's apologetic *Saincte philosophie*, Rouen, 1603.   [58] p. 648.   [59] See Goujet, vol. xv, p. 295.

[60] On sources cf. Fromilhague, *Vie*, pp. 70 ff.; Brun, *Bellaud de La Bellaudière*, pp. 149 ff., *Poètes provençaux*, pp. 113 ff.

[61] Cf. Nostredame's reference to 'la première fureur de Poésie, de laquelle parle le diuin Platon au dialogue intitulé Io' (*Entrée*, p. 48; cf. also *Histoire*, p. 1090).

[62] Cf. Nostredame's remarks on the 'sonnet mystérieux', mentioned above, and on his own anagrammatic verses described as 'prophétique et quasi miraculeux' (*Entrée*, p. 53). A Provençal precedent would be the prophetic quatrains of Michel de Nostredame, but also the older notion of *trobar clus*, which may have been known to some of the Aix poets; on its compatibility with Renaissance theory cf. Clements, *Critical Theory and Practice of the Pléiade*, p. 90.

symbolism of Hebraic characters are in line with much humanist speculation about language that Malherbe's age was leaving behind.[63]

Nevertheless, there are adequate grounds for thinking that the poets associated with these ideas, including La Ceppède, attempted a compromise with Malherbian style. Tallemant des Réaux recounts that Malherbe criticized the verse of the Grand Prieur;[64] La Bellaudière speaks of 'lou saber Malherbin' admired by the poets in the first phase.[65] Signs of textual collaboration appear in the similarities between certain lines in Nostredame's sonnet on the fall of Marseilles, Gallaup's poem on the same subject, and Malherbe's two odes 'Sur la prise de Marseille',[66] at a point in the evolution of Aix where it was politic that Provençal and French culture should be seen to combine.

From Malherbe's correspondence with Peiresc it is apparent that literary exchanges continued even after Malherbe's departure in 1605. He may have been in part responsible for La Ceppède's nomination as first president of the Cour in 1608; in his letters he frequently expresses admiration for his personal qualities.[67] It seems likely from the correspondence that La Ceppède was sympathetic towards Malherbe and received from him information about both political and literary events at court. La Ceppède's request for the laudatory poems on the *Théorèmes*[68] is not the only evidence of his active interest in Malherbe's work. In a letter of 1607 Malherbe refers to some of his verse that he wishes to be sent expressly to La Ceppède and Dupérier, and in 1614 he promises to send more verse to La Ceppède and Du Vair.[69]

The possibility of some degree of Malherbian influence on the style of the Aix poets can, however, only be substantiated by examining their texts. Fromilhague has shown that certain odes in Nostredame's *Pièces héroïques* resemble Malherbe's thematically and conform to his requirements in rhyme and syntax.[70] But more

---

[63] Cf. his *Poésies*, fo. 16ᵛ. On the sixteenth-century view of Hebrew see Dubois, *Mythe et langage*, pp. 76 ff.

[64] *Historiettes*, ed. Mongrédien, vol. i, p. 163.

[65] See Brun, *Bellaud de La Bellaudière*, p. 121.

[66] Malherbe, *Œuvres*, vol. I, texts XCIII, XCIV. Fromilhague, *Vie*, pp. 146 f.

[67] See Malherbe, *Œuvres*, recueillies par Lalanne, vol. iii, pp. 70–3.

[68] Ibid., vol. iii, pp. 259 f.   [69] Ibid., vol. iii, pp. 23, 392.

[70] *Vie*, pp. 166 f. On Malherbe's principles see Brunot, *La Doctrine de Malherbe*.

surprising is the possibility that Louis de Gallaup corrected his verse in accordance with the new principles. Thus Goujet speaks of Gallaup's inflated and obscure style, but adds,

On y remarque cependant certains traits qui se ressentent de sa fréquentation avec Malherbe; il travaillait beaucoup ses ouvrages, et on s'en aperçoit dans ses poésies.[71]

The neglected variants between his manuscript *Imitation* of 1595 and his printed versions of 1596 and 1597 make these features clear.[72] For instance, provincial or outmoded words are replaced: the verb 'œillader' in psalm 129, and 'oreiller' in psalm 142. In psalm 37 clumsy syntax is transformed in one sentence in order to remove the combination of a mixed subject with a personal verb. Certain obscure or ambiguous metaphors are clarified. And in some cases, as in the following, corrections affect several levels at once. The lines

Celuy deuient sauuage à qui la lote plet,
Il aduient en lieu d'homme & cheual & mulet

are rewritten as

Celuy qui de la lotte a gousté la poison
Priué d'entendement foule aux pieds la raison (psalm 31)

where the two syntactiaclly parallel lines of the first version have become a single complex sentence, and the concrete symbols ('cheual', 'mulet') are rejected for abstract and literal terms. At the same time Gallaup removes unsatisfactory rhyme, and eliminates the archaic synonym of 'devenir'.

It is true that the corrections are not totally consistent. Nevertheless, there would seem to be enough evidence to suggest the possibility of some Malherbian influence. In particular Gallaup pays attention to archaic or provincial elements, and to communicative clarity. If this is the case, the variants imply a significant turning-point, since Gallaup was previously entirely representative of the Provençal revival and the cult of poetic obscurity.

This stylistic clash might be compared with the historical tensions operating on many levels in late sixteenth-century Provence.

---

[71] *Bibliothèque françoise*, vol. xiii, p. 439.
[72] Jeanneret (*Poésie et tradition biblique*, pp. 368 ff.) considers Gallaup's psalms but not their variants.

The whole period of Provençal revival can be seen in terms of the tension in space between the province and the capital, complemented by the transition in time from civil war to national peace. In the religious life these oppositions are represented in Provence, as in the country generally, in the development from a predominantly penitential spirituality to outgoing educative institutions seeking a stable relationship with the State. In the historical consciousness of the region a sense of separate destiny gives way to a ritualized sense of national salvation. In literature there is a confrontation of local styles rooted in sixteenth-century humanism with the new norms exemplified by Malherbe. It is this pattern of contrasts that Gallaup's poetry was beginning in some degree to embody before he died in 1598. It is the same pattern that was inherited by La Ceppède's own *Imitation*, and subsequently by the *Théorèmes*.

II

GENESIS OF THE *IMITATION DES PSEAUMES DE LA PÉNITENCE* (1594–1612)

1. *Circumstances and Sources*

O F La Ceppède's attitude towards the nature and function of the psalms there is little direct evidence. Much can, however, be gleaned from the date and circumstances of the composition of the first edition of the *Imitation*.

The *Imitation des pseaumes de la pénitence de David* was published in Lyons by Jean Tholosan in 1594. Prefaced to it is a dedicatory letter to 'Madame Loyse d'Ancesune, Dame de Sainct Chomond, Caderouse, et Sainct Alexandre'. La Ceppède was connected to the Ancesune family through his wife's mother, Françoise d'Ancesune.[1] The significance of the dedication lies in the fact that Louise d'Ancesune was the founder of the Jesuit seminary at Avignon. La Cèppede refers obliquely to this fact when he expresses his assurance that her 'deuotieuse et religieuse piété, agréera ces deuots et religieux exercices'.[2] It seems from this that La Ceppède regarded his paraphrase as related to (though not necessarily in the same form as) the devotional exercise of the Counter-Reformation.

Whether one concludes that the work was composed entirely or only in part in Avignon and at what date depends on the interpretation of some remarks found in the dedication to the psalms and in the preface to the 'Douze meditations' which are included in the 1594 edition. In the Preface to the meditations La Ceppède states: 'ce trauail spirituel [i.e. the *Imitation*] m'a aleché à l'enterprinse d'vn plus grand œuvre [i.e. the *Théorèmes*]'.[3] The dedication to the psalms hints that this interruption corresponds partly to a suspension of normal life in Aix, due to the civil war. Speaking of the

---

[1] See Donaldson-Evans, 'Notice biographique', pp. 124 f.
[2] *Imitation* (1594), †3ᵛ.
[3] Ibid., p. 39.

Psalmist, and of his own desire to imitate the Psalmist's verbal act of repentance, La Ceppède continues:

A quoy ayant autresfois donné les heures qui me restoyent de la pressée occupation de ma charge, & depuis quelque iournée de nostre affligé loisir: l'Esprit de l'Eternel, . . . a fait esclorre à mon ame ce petit œuure . . .[4]

It is not altogether clear from this whether la Ceppède began his psalm paraphrases or merely his penitential devotions during the 'pressée occupation de [sa] charge'. The preceding sentence to which 'A quoy' refers could mean either. However, the tense of the main verb and the expression 'esclorre à mon ame' seem to place the initial conception of the work in the recent past— presumably that of La Ceppède's 'affligé loisir'. Nevertheless, he seems here to regard his *Imitation* as springing ultimately from penitential exercises begun while he was still in office in Aix. This would tally with what we know of the existence of penitential movements in Aix during the 1580s.

Since La Ceppède appears to be still in the period of 'affligé loisir' at the time of writing, the composition of the *Imitation* can safely be assigned to a period that can be fairly well defined. The Ligue faction gained the upper hand in the Aix Parlement early in 1589 and by August most royalist officials had left the town. But La Ceppède was detained by the Ligue. Until when he was detained is not known; but in his letter to Henry IV dated 19 March 1594 he says he has been in Avignon, unable to rejoin the exiled Parlement for four years.[5] The *Imitation* was, therefore, written during a period stretching from some time in 1590 or 1591 to some time in 1594, when the complete collection was published. But the official *approbation*, dated July 1592, enables us to be more precise. The two Dominican theologians examining the *Imitation* approve the '*Imitation des Pseaumes de la pénitence de Dauid* . . . Comme aussy les Paraphrases du Ps. *Benedic anima mea Dominum*. Et de *l'Himme de la Passion, Vexilla Regis*. Ensemble les trois son-netz suiuantz', but make no mention of the 'Douze meditations' which follow in the final version. It seems then that the psalms, the *Vexilla*, and the three sonnets were executed between some time in 1590 and July 1592, that is, at the climax of the religious wars after the assassination of Henry III, and while France was

---

[4] Ibid. †3–†3ᵛ.   [5] Cf. ch. I above.

still divided between the Protestant Henry of Navarre and the Spanish-aided Ligue. Between July 1592 and publication in 1594, La Ceppède added the sample from the *Théorèmes* and a collection of encomiastic pieces written by ecclesiastics and amateur poets of the region.

Why La Ceppède temporarily abandoned the *Théorèmes* is clear enough. The political situation of the period from 1589 to 1593 centred on a question of succession and legitimacy with which La Ceppède as a magistrate and officer of the Crown was professionally and personally involved. The town of Aix itself had rejected the legitimate monarch; not only was civil order disrupted, but the legal foundation of the State was in danger. The *Imitation* is related to this situation as an expression of instability and sense of guilt. It is true that references to the historical background in the work are sparse, and that to relate the mood or style of literary work to the spirit of an age is always a matter of speculation. However, it does seem possible to argue that in the metaphors of his dedicatory letter, politics, penitence, and poetry come together.

The passage is an apparently inflated discourse on the importance of penitence and the use of the penitential psalms. It is structured throughout on the basis of the commonplace Petrarchan metaphor of ship, shipwreck, and haven. The significance of a metaphor, however, lies in its use in context and in relation with other metaphors. La Ceppède's use of the metaphor in question is characteristically polyvalent, and the way the underlying ideas are related is revealing.

The ship and associated imagery has a long history in the Middle Ages and Antiquity. It has three main uses: (a) the ship is the devout soul in a sea of worldly turmoil; (b) the ship stands for the State; (c) the ship and its voyage stand for the work of art.[6] Using the metaphor in its first sense La Ceppède dwells on the theological aspects of his theme. It is conceivable that the penitential emphasis on sin was not congenial to La Ceppède's humanist background. His words suggest that he regards the recourse to a formal literary act of repentance as an unusual measure bound up with special circumstances:

Combien que la Penitence . . . soit appellée la seconde table apres le naufrage, & qu'il soit beaucoup meilleur de surgir au port du salut

---

[6] In connection with the devotional use of sense (a) cf. Lemaire, *Les Images chez Saint François de Sales*, pp. 39 ff. On sense (c) cf. Curtius, *Europäische Literatur*, pp. 136 ff.

eternel sur la nef entière. . . .: Si est-ce encor beaucoup de bien d'y
pouuoir aborder en quelque façon, et à quelque prix que ce soit.[7]

Apparently La Ceppède is thinking here outside the general
framework of Fall and Redemption. The tenor of the whole
passage seems to imply the identification of the archetypal 'naufrage' with recent personal or national history. The sinner, or
France herself, has as the sole remaining means of salvation an act
of repentance. There remains only 'vn petit ais, apres auoir veu
briser son vaisseau contre les escueils, & fait perte d'vne bonne partie de ses joyaux'. Since the ship-metaphor is ambivalent—that is,
since it associates the storm-tossed State with the troubled soul—
the boundary between moral and physical or political collapse is
blurred. In this perspective social turbulence and insecurity appear
as a punishment: penitence is thus an escape from 'la fureur des
flots bouillonnants de l'ire de Dieu'. The attitude is one common
enough in the Old Testament. The conception of Jehovah as
vengeful and wrathful is preserved in the Judaeo-Christian tradition; it provides in times of stress a myth that explains national
catastrophe in terms of moral decline. As the elaboration of the
image proceeds, the association of sin and national disaster, and
the claims for the role of propitiatory acts in the nation's life,
become clearer:

Puis donques que pour sauuer ce peu qui nous demeure, & nous mettre
à couuert du violent orage, qui nous noircissant nos jours de tant de
longues années, nous menace du naufrage dernier, nous ne pouuons
surgir au haure de la diuine misericorde, que par ceste seconde table
ou raseau de la pénitence: ie desire de disposer mon ame, & auec elle
celle de la France affligée, à s'y venir rendre, pour appendre desormais
à l'antenne de la Croix, les voiles de nos affections.[8]

Allowing for hyperbole, the reference to doomsday suggests at
least that La Ceppède regarded events as drawing to a crisis.
The penitential response to the situation is in accordance with
the attitudes that seem to have been encouraged at the court of
Henry III.[9]

Having called for national atonement, La Ceppède goes on to
relate penitential devotion in general to the composition of psalm

---

[7] *Imitation* (1594), †2.   [8] Ibid. †2^v.
[9] See Yates, *French Academies*, chs. 8 and 10, on this aspect of his religious
policy.

paraphrases in particular. It is at this point that he introduces the third sense of his central metaphor (the ship as literary work), combining it with the first (the ship as the penitent soul):

> . . . comme il est tousiours besoing d'auoir quelqu'vn aux mœurs duquel les nostres se redressent, ie l'ay choisi [i.e. David] pour Nocher en ceste perilleuse nauigation, pour laquelle, attendant d'en haut que le souffle de l'Immortel empoupe ma nasselle: i'ay aduisé de prendre tandis en main les plus legers auirons de ce penitent pilote, et m'exercer cependant à retracer les roides élancements de sa compunction, les pitoyables accents de ses plaintes, et l'ardente deuotion de ses prières, pour obtenir la mercy desirée.[10]

The last sentence suggests that the 'nasselle' here is the literary composition—the paraphrase of the Psalms. The whole passage thus seems to include the notion that poetic inspiration is received while the poet is immersed in penitential exercises. La Ceppède goes on to state this more explicitly in terms of the Christian doctrine of inspiration. Since he has given himself up to the devotions he has described, 'l'Esprit de l'Eternel, qui fauorisant les sainctes intentions se deigne bien seruir des mortels organes, a faict esclorre à mon âme ce petit œuure . . .'.[11]

Personal penitential exercises and literary activity are thus intimately bound up. This is the meaning of the title-page of the work. The heading of the first paraphrase is even clearer: 'Imitation de la pénitence de David'. The term 'imitation' unites the sense of the contemplative *imitatio* of Thomas à Kempis, and the literary *imitatio* of Pléiade poetics. Further, the work itself is intended as an exemplar to be imitated by the nation for its salvation.

In general terms La Ceppède's psalm paraphrases can thus be seen to belong to the wave of penitential poetry that comes into evidence after about 1570. It is a poetry characterized by the cult of the figure of David, by the application of biblical themes and images to contemporary problems, and in some cases by the notion that the harmony of the verse itself is an element in the act of propitiation.[12]

Although La Ceppède refers (*Théorèmes* II, p. 278) to Desportes's psalm paraphrases (approved by Génébrard, and cited by François

---

[10] *Imitation* (1594), †3–†3ᵛ.   [11] Ibid. †3ᵛ.
[12] On penitential poetry cf. Cave, *Devotional Poetry*, ch. 4; Jeanneret, *Poésie et tradition biblique*, pp. 418 ff.

de Sales), there is little evidence to suggest that he was influenced by them in his own paraphrases. The more cogent comparisons are, perhaps paradoxically, with the provincial Louis Gallaup on the one hand, and with Malherbe on the other.

In the case of Gallaup, evidence of his probable connection with La Ceppède's *Imitation*[13] is provided by the existence of the tightly-knit group of Aixois poets, and by the existence of a distinct penitential phase related to the political fortunes of the town.[14] The preliminary sonnets exchanged by the two poets in connection with their paraphrases suggest a common background of ideas on the subject. Both sonnets speak of the opposition between sacred and profane poetry, and of the effects of music or poetry in a time of trouble. La Ceppède's sonnet also alludes to the lead taken by Provence in the conversion of profane poetry.[15] Gallaup's reveals more about the relationship between the two works. In the first place the sestet may refer to some literary rivalry between the two poets:

> Ie vous rends grace, ô Christ, de vostre humble couronne,
> Ie demeure content, et ne serai marri
> Ne ialoux qu'vn plus docte, et de vous plus cheri,
> De superbe laurier ses temples enuironne.[16]

In the second place, this suggests that Gallaup's psalm paraphrases (though he may be thinking not merely of these) were written before those of La Ceppède were finished in 1592, in spite of the fact that Gallaup did not publish them until 1597. It is in fact the case that there exists an early version of Gallaup's psalms contained in a manuscript collection dated 1590.[17] It is also true that there are certain internal parallels between La Ceppède's and Gallaup's versions. This means that there are three possible conclusions to be drawn concerning the direction of the influence (if any) and the date of La Ceppède's work established earlier. First,

---

[13] Braunschweig raises, but does not develop, this question in 'Petites découvertes'.

[14] See ch. I above.

[15] In Gallaup, *Imitation* (1597), pp. 34 f.: in the 1595 MS. version, fo. 31, the first quatrain is lacking.

[16] In La Ceppède, *Imitation* (1594), ††ᵛ. There may be an allusion here to their shared device of the crown of laurels converted to thorns; cf. ch. I above.

[17] In 'Les Secondes pensées de la muse de Loys de Gallaup Sieur de Chasteuil. MDXC', Ing. MS. 386, fos. 57 ff. The psalms are followed by 'Sonnets chrétiens', fos. 82 ff.

La Ceppède's work may have been influenced by the 1590 manuscript version by Gallaup; second, La Ceppède may have influenced Gallaup if he himself began his paraphrases before 1590;
third, La Ceppède may or may not have been influenced by
Gallaup's 1590 manuscript, but may himself have influenced
successive variants of Gallaup's work (1595 and 1597).

The source of the influence obviously depends on determining
the date of La Ceppède's version. As has been seen, this cannot
be done with any great certainty, although it does look as if his
Imitation was in some sense prepared in Aix before his escape
around 1590. The most that can be said is that both La Ceppède
and Gallaup were interested in the penitential psalms some
time before 1590 and that they may have discussed the question of paraphrase in the literary circle at Aix. Given that the
available evidence suggests that Gallaup's version is prior, one is
inclined to conclude that it was he who influenced La Ceppède
(if anybody was influenced), rather than the reverse. As for the
third possibility, it seems that although the variants over the
successive versions of Gallaup's psalms are stylistically significant,
few seem unequivocally connected with La Ceppède's text.

Nevertheless, there are grounds for thinking that La Ceppède
and Gallaup at least share certain features of style and organization.
In the first place, there is some similarity in the way the two poets
use the apparently synonymous terms 'imitation' and 'paraphrase'.
Gallaup's 1590 version is entitled *Imitation des psal. de la pénitence
royale Et Paraphrase. dicelle*, and the 1595 version *Imitation et
paraphrase des pseaumes de la pénitence royalle*. In the former the
fourth of the penitential psalms consists of a verse version on the
left of the page opening, and of a prose version on the right; in
the latter the first and the fourth of the psalms have accompanying prose versions, which are not, however, arranged facing one
another. Since Gallaup elsewhere in the 1590 manuscript heads
the verse translations 'imitation', the choice of this slightly unusual
term may be deliberate; the prose translation would thus be regarded as a 'paraphrase' either of the original or of the 'imitation'.
In 1597 the prose translations are dropped: accordingly, the title
of the work is simply *Imitation des pseaumes de la pénitence royale*.
Now since La Ceppède also uses the term, it has been said that the
fact clearly links him with Gallaup.[18] But though there may well

---

[18] Braunschweig, 'Petites découvertes'.

be some similarity in the parallel use of verse and prose translations, the term 'imitation' in La Ceppède has also the wider pious and literary sense discussed above. Furthermore, La Ceppède uses the term 'paraphrase' to designate his (verse) translations of the non-penitential psalms and of the Latin hymns, and to designate the prose versions (in the 1594 edition at least), the non-literary term 'oraison'.

In the second place, there are certain parallels in Gallaup's and La Ceppède's texts. In the case of the prose 'paraphrase' or 'oraison' there is some inevitable similarity in the vocabulary used, and in the ideas expressed. Independently of this the only other obvious similarity is the shared idea of parallel verse and prose translation; and this idea is abandoned by Gallaup in his 1596 and 1597 editions.

In the case of the verse translations there are varying degrees of resemblance. The rhymes, for example, in the second stanza of Gallaup's and the third stanza of La Ceppède's seventh penitential psalm are the same. There are, of course, numerous lexical similarities. One which is probably significant, since it does not depend on the common biblical text, is the use by both La Ceppède and Gallaup of the term 'Trine-unité' (La Ceppède (1594): 50, strophe 13; Gallaup: 129, 1. 25 (1595 only)). The word is explained by La Ceppède as having a technically different sense from more usual words for the Trinity.[19] Moreover, the term is used by both poets in the doxology with which they conclude each psalm— a practice not common in contemporary paraphrases. There are instances where La Ceppède and Gallaup introduce the same image, where the biblical text does not already have it, but treat it in different ways. Thus Psalm 50: 13 is embellished with fire imagery by both poets. La Ceppède has:

> Ne m'eclipse le iour de tes yeux bien aimés,
> De ton Feu, ton Amour ne me priue iamais. (50, 9)

Gallaup uses a similar image deriving from the realm of love-poetry:

> Arreste sur ma nef ces deux flammes iumelles
> Et cest arc redoré du iour de tes prunelles . . .[20]

---

[19] Cf. *Théorèmes* II, p. 631: 'Vn docte Poëte de nostre temps appele la saincte Trinité vne essance Triple-vne. Il eut mieux dit en bons termes de Theologie, Trine-vne . . .' Du Bartas, e.g. in *Judit*, livre sixiesme, 1. 198, uses 'Triple-Unité'.   [20] *Imitation* (1597), p. 13.

This is clearly not a case of direct influence. But there is a stylistic resemblance in the use of secular literary formulas to expand the original text and make it more familiar, and in the use of light- and fire-imagery.

There are, however, important differences in paraphrase technique which seem to show that in spite of certain accompanying similarities the versions are largely independent of one another. An illustration of this fundamental difference is the respective treatments of Psalm 31: 7–8:

> 7 Tu es refugium meum a tribulatione, quae circumdedit
>   me: exsultatio mea erue me a circumdantibus me.
> 8 Intellectum tibi dabo, et instruam te in via hac,
>   qua gradieris: firmabo super te oculos meos.

In both Gallaup and La Ceppède the first member of verse 7 not unexpectedly calls forth a marine image. La Ceppède, however, unlike Gallaup, explicitly places verse 8 in the mouth of Jehovah:

> Courage (me dis-tu) i'ay ton salut tres-cher,
> Voici, ie te don'ray mon Esprit pour Nocher
> Mon Œil sera ton Ourse, & ma Loy ta Boussole. (strophe 6)

Gallaup's version resembles La Ceppède's in the source of its images only:

> Le Seigneur soit mon Nort, mon Azil, mon recours
> Mon Temple, mon Autel, mon Ancre, et mon secours,
> Son desiré salut mes Ennemys confonde,
> Dans ce bas vniuers ie seray le tableau,
> Ie seray le miroër, ie seray le flambeau:
> Table, Miroër, Flambeau, qui dressera le Monde.[21]

But it differs radically from his in interpreting the Vulgate verse 8 as spoken by the Psalmist. This is a point of interpretation that affects the structure and style of several strophes of the paraphrase. It would surely have been the same in Gallaup and La Ceppède if there had been any close imitation. The two passages also bring out a subsidiary stylistic difference between the two poets. Partly as a result of his particular interpretation Gallaup brings in a string of obscure metaphors or symbols. La Ceppède's version on the other hand is a logically coherent (though commonplace) allegory.

---

[21] *Imitation* (1597), p. 8.

In general any resemblances between La Ceppède's and Gallaup's paraphrase point not to direct borrowing, but to the common background of Aix poetics. With respect to the close paraphrases in the Catholic tradition of Baïf and Desportes, they represent a distinct style. Indeed, stylistic finish, as is clear from Gallaup's variants, and as will be clear also from those of La Ceppède, is an important preoccupation, testifying to a desire to harmonize the genre with secular writing.

However, it can be seen from La Ceppède's *Imitation* that textual and exegetic matters are not ignored. It is certain that in the *Théorèmes* he also uses a liberal range of vernacular Bibles. There is some evidence that he used for the *Imitation* also versions of the Bible other than the Vulgate. The evidence in favour of a Latin text—and probably therefore of the Vulgate—cannot be ignored. One or two Latinisms are traceable to the Vulgate text: ' . . . épuré par vostre grace de dol',[22] where the use of the word 'dol' is prompted by the Vulgate 'dolus' (31: 2); and 'Ie tombe dans le lac de l'Eternelle Nuict' (142, 3), where 'lac' is used in the Vulgate Latin sense of 'lacus', 'the place of the dead'.

The surest guide is given by the numerous readings of the Vulgate which diverge from versions based on the Hebrew text. Two clear-cut examples will make the point. In Psalm 1: 1 the third member in the Vulgate reads: 'et in cathedra pestilentiae non sedit', whereas versions following the Hebrew have, for instance, 'qui ne s'assied point au banc des moqueurs'.[23] La Ceppède speaks of 'sieges pestés'.[24] Again the reading of Psalm 50: 8, 'incerta et occulta sapientiae tuae manifestasti mihi', is peculiar to the Vulgate: versions based on the Hebrew have the verb in the future. La Ceppède follows the Vulgate: 'Tu m'ouuris les cayers de tes plus hauts mysteres' (50, 5).

That La Ceppède relies heavily on the sole text sanctioned by the Catholic Church is hardly surprising. But it seems that he also drew on an unidentifiable translation or translations of the Hebrew. The translation of the original Hebrew 'Jahve' is an indication as to the intermediate translation an author is using. Olivetan's translation of 'Jahve' as 'l'Eternel' was adopted in all Protestant translations after 1535. There are two cases of its use in the *Imitation* of 1594: 'l'Esprit de l'Eternel' and 'de cest Eternel

---

[22] *Imitation* (1594), p. 6. [23] See the Geneva Bible of 1588.
[24] *Imitation* (1612), I. 1.

l'Eternelle Clemence'.[25] The latter was suppressed in the 1612 edition, but the aim may have been to remove the rhetorical repetition and inversion. These cases may not be conclusive. But there is at least one clear piece of evidence that La Ceppède did draw from some translation of the Hebrew text. It is impossible to determine which translation this was. Several Protestant translations would have been available. But so would Catholic versions such as Jerome's Hebrew Psalter; Catholic commentaries on the Psalms would also in some cases give Hebrew variants.[26]

The Vulgate reading of Psalm 31: 4 runs: 'conversus sum in aerumna mea, dum configitur spina'. In his prose version La Ceppède renders the last phrase of this: 'esueillé . . . par les poignantes verges de vostre courroux'.[27] But in the verse paraphrase (which in the 1594 edition is significantly designated the thirty-second according to the Protestant and Hebrew division of the Psalter) he writes

> Mon corps se flétrissoit comme la ieune fleur,
> A qui du Sirien la brulante chaleur
> A dérobé l'humeur nourrice de sa vie (strophe 3)

which corresponds to versions based on the accepted Hebrew text. La Ceppède is here selecting a reading which provides an image that had already become a commonplace in penitential poetry. In general it seems likely that when La Ceppède did select a Hebrew-based variant rather than any other it was at this period less for the sake of textual accuracy than for the sake of poetic decoration.

Not only does La Ceppède tend to decorate the letter of his text, but also to gloss the spirit of it. For the most part the glosses he incorporates are theological commonplaces. Thus the hyssop in Psalm 50 is the blood of Christ, and the paraphrase of Psalm 31, interpreted as referring to the doctrine of grace, opens with the words: 'De tous les dons gratuitz la grace est le Greigneur' (line 1). Interpretations of this kind increase in the 1612 edition. Thus 'the sacrifices of righteousness' at the end of Psalm 50 are interpreted

---

[25] *Imitation* (1594), †3ᵛ and 102, 8. Cf. also 'l'Immortel' used rhetorically in antithesis to 'le perissable', *Imitation* (1594 and 1612) 101, 8.

[26] For instance the *Psalterium sextuplex* of 1530, which included the versions of Jerome, Pagninus, Felix Pratensis, and the Septuagint and Vulgate; or the commented Vulgate edition by Génébrard, *Psalmi Davidis* of 1581.

[27] *Imitation* (1594), p. 6.

in 1594 as the sacrifice of the Crucifixion, but in 1612 not only as the sacrifice of the Crucifixion, but also (in true post-Tridentine fashion) as the sacrifice of the mass (strophe 12). La Ceppède does not comment systematically on his text. The aim seems to be to clarify the most difficult images for the uninstructed. But these aspects of La Ceppède's *Imitation* do suggest the presence of the kind of problem clarified by Laval[28]—that the meanings embodied in the original Psalms can be conveyed to the uninitiated only in discursive exposition, not in literal verse paraphrase. La Ceppède's ornamental paraphrases whether in verse or prose fall between the extremes of literalism and exposition, and do not solve the problem. It is only in the *Théorèmes* that he succeeds in combining textual fidelity and exegetic depth with the poetic fabric.

2. The 1594 and 1612 Editions

La Ceppède also has in common with Gallaup the fact that he extensively revised the verse of his paraphrases. The 1594 edition of the *Imitation* was enlarged in 1612 by six extra pieces; approximately 240 lines of the verse section out of 572 are affected in the 1612 edition by changes of one kind or another. Obviously this is a high proportion and warrants attention. The differences between the two editions throw light not only on the history of La Ceppède's style, but also on that of stylistic cross-currents in general at this period. It is relevant to consider the possibility of Malherbe's influence. As has been seen, his literary views were received by the Aix poets. Moreover, his views had a particular importance for the style of the psalm paraphrase.

In the 1594 edition[29] the seven penitential psalms are followed by a verse paraphrase of Psalm 102, a 'Paraphrase de l'Hymne de la Passion. *Vexilla regis* &c.', two sonnets entitled 'Sur les sainctes reliques, et dévote solitude de l'isle Sainct Honnoré de Lerins', and one 'Sur la dévotieuse retraicte du monastere de Gentilin'. This combination of psalms, Latin hymns, and original devotional

---

[28] Preface to *Paraphrases des Pseaumes* . . . (1610).
[29] The discovery of this edition was announced by V.-L. Saulnier and A. Worthington in 'Du nouveau sur Jean de La Ceppède' in 1955. The transformation of the 'Douze meditations' into certain sonnets in the definitive *Théorèmes* has been studied by Donaldson-Evans in 'L'Édition de 1594 de l'*Imitation*'. The psalm variants have until recently been ignored: cf. Jeanneret's inconclusive survey in *Poésie et tradition biblique*, pp. 381 ff.

pieces was normal in collections of psalm paraphrases from medieval times. Partly as a complement to the penitential section and
partly as a sample, the publisher adds, 'Douze meditations sur le
sacré mystere de nostre redemption', prefaced by an 'Au Lecteur'
by the author.

In spite of its fragmentary external appearance the 1594 collection does possess a thematic unity which is quite distinct from that
which characterizes the 1612 collection. After the predominant
pessimism of the penitential psalms, their prophetic hints of
redemption become a confident hope in Psalm 102 which immediately follows them:

> Sa Iusticiere grace aidera, fauorable,
> (Iusqu'aux derniers nepueux) la race venerable
> Qui suit ton Testament, qui faict ses volontés. (strophe 9)

The *Vexilla regis* paraphrase serves as a transition between the
psalms and the 'Douze meditations' in, for instance, the lines:

> Ainsi l'auoit sonné la Dauidique lyre:
> C'est ores que suiuant ses Prophetiques vers,
> Du Bois le Tout-puissant établit son Empyre. (strophe 4).

Likewise the three sonnets on the theme of rural and monastic
solitude, with their references to redemption through disciplined
devotion, prepare the way for the twelve meditations on the
Crucifixion:

> O saincte Solitude, où nostre humanité
> Sublimée au fourneau de vostre austerité
> Peut d'vn agile saut se guinder sur le Pole.
> (*Reliques* I, ll. 9–11)

The sonnet sequence itself refers constantly to Old Testament
prefigurations of the Crucifixion. The seventh of the twelve, for
instance, is in the theological perspective complementary to the
prophetic sacrifice mentioned at the end of Psalm 50:

> Quitte ton vieil Autel, & retire ta main
> Du sacrifice antique, ores abominable.
> Adore cet Autel, ce Prebstre souuerain
> Qui s'est luy mesme offert pour ton crime damnable. (ll. 5–8)

The meditations on the Crucifixion are thus linked in an obvious
way with the penitential paraphrases.

The second edition is dated 1612 and is bound with the *Théorè-mes*,[30] Part I (dated 1613). The twelve 'meditations' are, of course, omitted: they are incorporated in various parts of the *Théorèmes*. The *Imitation* is filled out with new material on themes reflecting the increased stability and assurance of the royalist peace. The paraphrase of the *Super flumina Babylonis* (Psalm 136) is, it is true, an adaptable partisan psalm of the civil war period which speaks of the suffering of the chosen people. But the tense of La Ceppède's version included in the 1612 collection is retrospective. And the other two new psalms (Psalm 1 and Psalm 14) celebrate the victory of the righteous over the vanquished. The import of Psalm 102 is modified by this intercalated matter: hope of redemption conditional on piety begins to look like the self-satisfaction of hindsight. It is followed as before by the *Vexilla regis* which now introduces not the Crucifixion meditations but a paraphrase of the *Stabat Mater*. Significantly headed 'imitation' rather than 'paraphrase', this piece corresponds to the 'Douze meditations' as a contemplation of the Crucifixion through the figure of the Virgin. To the sonnets on solitude already included in the 1594 edition are now added two more on apparently unrelated themes: one 'Sur l'Evangile du Dimanche des Rameaux', the other entitled 'Rapport des voluptez à la mer'. The Palm Sunday sonnet is, however, connected with the victory theme and the sea-sonnet with the imagery of the preceding pieces and the theme of the passion–reason conflict found in the penitential paraphrases.

Two main points emerge from these considerations. In the first place the slight shift in over-all meaning between the two editions —from a predominantly repentant mood to a predominantly triumphant one—is another indication of the way the genre of biblical paraphrase is often bound up with contemporary events. The second point concerns the unity of the collections and their relationship to the *Théorèmes*. From what has been said it seems clear that La Ceppède regards penitential and redemption poetry as complementary. The inclusion of the 'Douze meditations' in 1594 and the binding of the *Imitation* with the *Théorèmes* in 1613 make this clear. These combinations are also in accordance with the idea of the complementarity of the Old and New Testaments which is so extensively used in the *Théorèmes*.

[30] In the known extant copies. The leaves are signed and paginated in an independent series.

The textual variants of the psalm paraphrases are of considerably greater interest than those of the sonnets of the 'Douze meditations'. When the latter reappear in the *Théorèmes* they are not merely corrected but reconstructed in such a way that for the most part there is little basis for comparison with the earlier versions. They are, however, of some importance for the genesis of the *Théorèmes* and will be re-examined in Chapter III. The variants of the psalm paraphrases are especially revealing because they are tied to a given text with an established meaning and characteristic style. The changes that occur between 1594 and 1612 range from isolated words to whole stanzas. They can be classified in a way that makes it possible to draw some conclusions as to the principles underlying them.[31] The following classification is based on selected examples:

(i) *Language and style.* Malherbe's doctrines, disseminated from the late 1590s onwards, emphasize the rapid changes taking place in linguistic norms in literature.

La Ceppède's peculiar style is usually thought of as the antithesis of the manner encouraged by Malherbe, that is, as provincial and archaic. This is too simple a view of the matter. The variants of the 1612 edition of the *Imitation* point to the fact that La Ceppède was in all probability fully aware of the new stylistic and linguistic standards. Failure to comply with new literary norms is not necessarily to be regarded as an indication of mere archaism or provincialism. Certain characteristics that were unacceptable to the Malherbians may have a special association with poetry in the Christian tradition.

Dialect-words are ruthlessly rejected by Malherbe. Now the role of Provençal in the poetry of the region was considerable at the end of the sixteenth century. La Ceppède himself may have spoken the dialect. The distinction between dialect-words and archaic words is, of course, blurred since words normal in French in one period may be retained in the provinces while they drop out of the standard language. In the case of Provence this conservative tendency would be reinforced by the coexistence of an idiosyncratic and vigorous dialect.

'Ma palle cher' becomes 'ma fraisle chair' (6, 2). If this is not merely a typographical or orthographic correction, then La

---

[31] Jeanneret (*Poésie et tradition biblique*, pp. 381 ff.) gives a brief account.

Ceppède may be changing the meaning to avoid the archaism 'chere'.[32] 'Grandesse' is changed to 'grandeur' (101, 12). A few examples of the former are to be found in the sixteenth century, while the word is common in Old French.[33] In the general rewriting of Psalm 142, 11 the infinitive 'secourre' (in the sense of 'secourir') is removed. The form 'secourre' (from *subcutere*) survived into the seventeenth century only in the sense of 'secouer' (La Ceppède may have been influenced by Provençal usage here in his first version[34]).

But most of the archaisms that are removed are not related to the dialect factor. The adjective 'crimineuse', condemned by Pasquier as outdated,[35] becomes 'mal-heureuse' (142, 2); 'hommageable' is removed (102, 10), as is the noun 'humblesse' (101, 12). But such examples must be weighed against the old words and forms that remain in the 1612 version. Furthermore, there are cases, such as the change of the usual 'brindilles' into 'brindelles' (101, 2), where a common but older form is introduced for the sake of rhyme (with 'mouëlles'). Latinate words becoming archaic are, however, eliminated in some of the revisions: 'ton Estre est perdurable' becomes 'ton Estre n'est passable' (101, 8); 'tarde colere' becomes 'tendre cholere' (102, 4). Some derivatives also disappear: 'la démise' (from 'démis', 'humble') is replaced by 'l'amendement' (101, 8). A common diminutive is removed when 'tendret renouveau' becomes 'tendre fleur' (102, 7), and at the same time an unusual sense of the word 'renouveau'. Some compound derivatives also go in the course of rewriting. 'Char porte-lumière' disappears in 1612 in Psalm 142, strophe 7, and 'contr'oppose' (50, 1) is suppressed as part of a general clarification of the sentence in which it occurs.[36] As for the other areas of the lexicon that came under Malherbe's fire, a cursory glance at the *Imitation* shows that they are an intrinsic part of its poetic style. The few variants affecting these areas ('low' words, technical terms, classical allusions) are probably entirely incidental.

[32] Cf. Provençal 'cara' for 'visage'. The word is used by the Pléiade in the form 'carre' and 'care'; cf. Marty-Lavaux, *La Langue de la Pléiade*, vol. i, p. 187.
[33] The Provençal form remained 'grandesa' or 'grannesa'.
[34] In Provençal 'secouer' had the form 'secodere' (< subcutere), 'secourir' the form 'socorre' (< succurrere).
[35] See Brunot, *Histoire de la langue française*, vol. 3, part I, p. 109.
[36] Cf. Malherbe's condemnation of 'contre-respond' in Desportes. See Brunot, *Doctrine de Malherbe*, p. 293.

On the syntactic level there is, in spite of the many irregularities that remain in the 1612 text, a clear move towards greater cohesion and simplification. It is true that certain corrections introduce minor solecisms. The omission of 'pas' (always necessary according to Malherbe) is one instance. However, what is significant is the large number of cases in which La Ceppède's revisions show a concern to rationalize the relations within sentence-structure.

In the extensively reworked paraphrase of Psalm 102 unsatisfactory grammatical relations in comparative phrases are corrected and the whole of strophe 6 is given a symmetrical structure closer to the parallelisms of the biblical original:

> (1594) Ains tousiours pitoyable enuers l'humaine race
> Qui le craint, il r'enforce, il r'approche sa grace,
> Et recule l'Enfer qui vous guigne de l'œil,
> Il écarte de nous nos offences mortelles,
> Comme la terre est loing des célestes Chandeles,
> Comme l'Aurore est loing du repos du Soleil.

> (1612) Tout autant que le Ciel sur la Terre s'éleue,
> Tout autant tous les iours la posterité d'Eue
> Sent éleuer sur elle, & fondre sa Bonté:
> Qui pardonnante écarte aussi loin tous ses crimes
> Que l'Olympe est distant des infernaux abysmes,
> Que l'Occident est loin du Soleil remonté.

The borderline between the adjectival and verbal functions of the present participle in the sixteenth century is ill defined; the use of the periphrastic present and future tenses adds to the confusion. In the following example La Ceppède resolves two periphrastic forms and a rhetorical periphrasis:

> (1594) Et bien qu'ores sur nous sa dextre soit pesante,
> Elle ne sera pas longuement foudroyante,
> Ce courrou n'ira pas à l'immortalité.

> (1612) Et bien que maintefois sa main prenne la foudre,
> Ce n'est pourtant à fin de nous reduire en poudre,
> Son courroux n'est pas tel, il veut nous conuertir.
>
> (102, 51)

In several cases in the 1594 version La Ceppède seems unconcerned to relate the subject of a subordinate infinitive phrase to the subject of the main verb. For instance, he writes: 'ie sçay bien que

pour guerir *des* maux . . . vous demandez ma conuersion.' 'Guerir'
here may appear intransitive, and to have God ('vous') as its
subject. The ambiguity is solved by correcting 'des' to 'les'.[37]

Co-ordinated nouns and phrases are frequent in the *Imitation*,
as in its model. The 'and' may signify identity or distinction.
Considerations of logicality seem to determine the modification of
'la Terre, & les œuures de tes puissantes mains', where the
conjunction is ambiguous, into 'la terre & les cieux (œuure de vos
puissantes mains)' (101, p. 24 (1594), p. 33 (1612)).

Many of these revisions have a stylistic value: they mark a
movement towards a more up-to-date manner based ideally on
logical clarity and formal elegance. The exceptions are, of course,
numerous. And it should be pointed out that when rigidly balanced
phrases occur in the *Imitation* it is just as likely that they should be
traced to the parallelisms of the biblical text as to a desire on La
Ceppède's part to produce Malherbian clarity of structure.

(ii) *Imagery*. It should be said at the outset that the 1612 version of
the *Imitation* is full of concrete and relatively abstruse imagery
that Malherbe would have run his pen through. But it is curious
to note on close scrutiny that a high proportion of bold images are
suppressed or attenuated. Clearly, many other factors (textual
fidelity, rhyme, etc.) may be in play in those corrections where
such changes are apparent. But the large number of changes
affecting imagery seems sufficient to suggest a distinct trend.[38]

Certain changes in wording may be set aside at the outset, since
they do not materially alter the image as such: 'Flamme amoureuse'
becomes 'Flamme durable' (142, 12), although the slight modification of the erotic element here may be significant; 'elle le tirera du
trouble qui le mine' becomes 'elle le tirera d'emmy ces durs alar-
mes' (142, 9). Such alterations are obviously made for the sake of
the rhyme. This is even more obvious in cases where the image
is rearranged syntactically without major changes in vocabulary:
'pour reparer mes pertes' is replaced by 'par qui seront mes
pertes recouuertes' to rhyme with 'ouuertes' (142, 5).

The clear cases of image suppression or attenuation cannot all
be listed here; but the following will give some idea of their range.

[37] p. 10 (1594), p. 17 (1612). The correction could be typographical.
[38] Approximately 58 images are affected in the revisions, of which around 39
could be said to be replaced by more sober phrases; but there are obvious
difficulties in determining the degree of attenuation or intensification of images.

The revision may reject a proliferation of images unconnected with the biblical text. Thus the line 'Et du cygne imitant le chant presagieux', with its classical allusion, is eliminated in 1612 (101, 5). A series of metaphorical synonyms for angels is simplified:

> (1594) Nos cœurs . . .
> Plaisent à tes seruants, à tes sacrés Heraux.
> Ces diuins Truchementz, ces courriers pitoyables . . .

> (1612) Nos cœurs . . .
> Plaisent à tes seruans, touchez de nos douleurs.
> Tes seruans effroyez de nos maux effroyables . . .
>
> (101, 10)

This literally translates 'placuerunt servis tuis . . .'. But there are interesting cases where the concrete imagery of the biblical text itself is amended. In the 1594 version 'sicut passer solitarius' is rendered faithfully:

> Solitaire ie semble vn passereau sauuage.

But in 1612 this is replaced by the periphrasis:

> Je ressemble à l'oiseau qu'on nomme solitaire. (101, 5)

On the other hand the image of the pelican (strophe 4) and the owl (strophe 5) have an appropriate symbolic richness, and are retained. A classical image is in one case replaced by a biblical one:

> (1594) Ainsi la Mort nous porte au gouffre lethé.

> (1612) Ainsi nos plus beaux iours passent en vn moment.
>
> (102, 8)

A number of similarly conventional images are turned into literal expressions:

> (1594) . . . leur forme perissable
> Suit la faux du vieillard . . .

> (1612) . . . leur forme perissable
> Perira . . .   (101, 16)

This is a literal translation of the 'peribunt' of the text. In the same way 'Soubs le chien-étoilé qui rechaufe les iours' becomes 'au plus extrême chaut' (142, 5); 'ce Canibale' is expanded to 'cette ame déloyale' (*Vexilla*, strophe 5), and 'celestes chandeles' to 'Ciel' and the commonplace 'Olympe' (102, 6).

Metaphors combining physical and mental references are cut out:

> (1594) . . . ie porte à iamais au cœur de ma Memoire
> De ses rares bien-faicts le souuenir empraint.

> (1612) . . . ie porte en la memoire
> De ses rares bien-faits l'immortel souuenir. (102, 1)

A more elaborate but related example is the following:

> Souffre que mes sanglots enfoncent la barrière,
> Qui me deffend l'accez à ta douce Mercy

which is replaced by the literal and less violent

> . . . permets que mon ame opressée
> Pousse iusques à toy les cris de sa douleur. (101, 1)

With the removal of this type of image may be classed that of certain hyperbolic images. 'Ceste Terre beante Soubs le chien-étoilé' (translating 'sicut terra sine acqua') is replaced by a precise realistic description:

> . . . les creuasses menuës
> De cette terre aride, au plus extreme chaut (142, 5)

and 'Fai regorger sur moy l'Ocean de ta Grace' is turned into an abstract and precious metaphor: 'Verse benin sur luy ta douceur nompareille' (101, 1). The line 'Mes yeux estoyent cauez, ma face estoit ternie', is replaced by a commonplace metaphor from the language of love-poetry: 'Ma vie à mille morts languissoit asseruie' (31, 3). This latter tendency is evident whenever metaphors are introduced where they did not exist before or expanded from previously existing metaphors. The 1594 version of Psalm 129 omits to paraphrase 'sustinui te Domine' (129: 4), but the 1612 revision does so by means of a Petrarchan (but also mystical) image: 'Ie dure toutefois au feu de ces tormens' (strophe 2). Fire-imagery is an important part of the thematic network of the second edition. The erotic aspect of such imagery is used by La Ceppède in the 1612 work to transform even biblical images. Speaking of the Holy Spirit he writes in 1594: 'de ton Feu Sainct la Colonne brillante'; but in 1612 he changes this to: 'de ton feu sainct les flammes amoureuses'. In some instances the reverse occurs: images are made more biblical. The close and neutral translation:

> . . . il est temps,
> Que ta misericorde emporte nos miseres

is replaced with an image common in the Bible, but not used at this point in the source text:

> . . . il est temps
> De retirer les fleaux de ta iuste vengence. (101, 9)

There is one striking case of the introduction of a bold non-biblical metaphor, when 'm'exempte à ce coup de ta iuste vengence' becomes:

> Passe sur mes forfaits l'éponge de ta grace. (50, 1)

But on the whole it should be emphasized that the images used in connection with references to grace in the two editions show a general tendency towards simplification and greater theological precision. The example just quoted from the paraphrase of Psalm 50 reintroduces the metaphor of washing-away of sin, which is frequent in the original Psalms, but which La Ceppède in his revisions for one reason or another tended to reduce. In the 1594 version grace is associated with images of washing, forgiving, and forgetting. The 1594 paraphrase of Psalm 50 (strophe 7) has the line: 'Et plonge mes pechés dans l'Oubly de ta Grace', and of Psalm 129 (strophe 2) the line: 'la douce Amnestie abolit nos offences'. There is some ambiguity in the case of both 'Oubly' and 'Amnestie'. But if the ambiguity of 'Amnestie' ('pardon' and 'forgetting') is harmless, that of the former ('forgetting' but also 'oblivion' and even 'oversight') is unfortunate. In 1612 both lines are recast: one in a literal form: 'ma grace estoit preste auant que ie patisse' (129, 2); the other in the form of a common marine metaphor: 'Et mes deuoyemens par ton phare redresse' (50, 7).

Three conclusions may be drawn concerning La Ceppède's correction of imagery. First, some are revised in the interests of simple theological acceptability and textual fidelity. Second, there is some evidence that unelevated and hyperbolic images are removed. And third, some concrete images are attenuated by bringing in common conventional metaphors from secular poetry.

(iii) *Rhetorical devices*. While there is some sign of a movement towards the Malherbian position with regard to metaphor in the variants, the same is not true of the use of rhetorical devices. In 'O père pitoyable, aye pitié de moi . . .' (50, 1) the repetitive figure is removed in 1612. Similarly, '[ta bonté] ruinera tous ceux qui cherchent ma ruine' becomes in 1612 'ruinera mes ennemis par l'effort de leurs armes' (142, 9). And in

> Troublé i'ay ma resource aux doux rais de ta face.
> Tous les iours de mon trouble . . . (1594: 101, 1)

the repetition is suppressed along with the metaphor. But there are several examples of the reverse process.

'Pour l'Amour de ton nom, et Sainct et Venerable' is rewritten in the form: 'En faueur de ton Nom sainctement fauorable' (142, 9). The 1612 version also introduced repetition of the word stem (polyptoton): 'Tes seruans effroyez de nos maux effroyables' in Psalm 101 (strophe 10), and in Psalm 37 (strophe 9): 'ilz forcent le fort de mon courage', where the 1594 edition had 'ils forcent mes remparts . . .'. Repetition of the same word in 'A ce iour, à ce iour d'eternelle memoire' is modified by the addition of a second balancing adjective: 'A ce iour magnifique, à ce iour memorable' (101, 11). The synonymy of repetitive phrases in the following is slightly modified, the rhyme (with 'grâce') is improved, and chiasmus is brought in: 'Ie te crie mercy i'implore ta clémence' becomes 'I'implore tes pardons, ta clemence i'embrasse' (50, 1).

(iv) *Rhyme*. If certain images and rhetorical figures appear to be toned down in the course of the 1612 revision of the *Imitation*, many nevertheless remain as an intrinsic part of the final version. So far then the evidence for possible Malherbian influence in the psalms is not conclusive. But one feature of La Ceppède's style can be assessed with greater accuracy than those features discussed above. Reference has already been made to the role of rhyme changes in the two editions. Rhyme is the most obvious technical aspect of poetic style for any poet of this period. Certain rhymes with a particular cadence enjoyed considerable popularity amongst poets and rhymesters. A case in point is the rhyme 'éternellement', which was favoured by members of the Aix group of poets, including Malherbe and La Ceppède.[39] If there are any traces of Malherbe's influence in La Ceppède's revision of the *Imitation* it is in the rhyme that they may be expected to show up most clearly.[40]

Out of 286 pairs of rhyming words in the complete collection of 1594 nearly half (138) are affected by the revisions of 1612.[41] This is clearly a significant number and justifies a close examination.

In comparing Malherbe's rhyme system with that of La Ceppède some reservations must be made. Malherbe's choice of rhyme-words and his admission of certain non-rich combinations depend on certain strictures: the exclusion of words considered unpoetic; the exclusion in the rhyme of words which in Racan's terms 'avoient quelque convenance'; and words based on a similar root. In La Ceppède the language of Christian poetry largely eliminates the first stricture. The second does not apply either. In his 1612 version La Ceppède appears sometimes deliberately to combine synonymous and antithetical rhyme-words and words reflecting an association of ideas: 'étincelante'—'brillante' (37, 10), 'moment'—'eternelement' (102, 8), 'iournées'—'années' (101, 15), 'obeïssance'—'Puissance' (50, 10), etc. Neither does the third apply. None of the revisions affecting the 1594 rhymes eliminates a rhyme based on a common root; in the 1612 version nine such rhymes are retained from the first version, and seventeen are actually introduced.[42] This tendency is contrary to that observable in Malherbe and in the secular court-poets, but is explicable in terms of the over-all characteristics of La Ceppède's style and language. Synonymous and antithetical rhymes, and rhymes which are semantically related in other ways, may be regarded as an extension of the rhetorical repetition and punning that plays such a fundamental part in La Ceppède's poetry and in that of the Aix school in general.

[39] See Fromilhague, *Vie*, pp. 80 f. La Ceppède uses the rhyme in *Imitation* (1612), 102, 8; for Malherbe, cf. 'Au Roy Henry le Grand', *Œuvres*, vol. i, text VII, l. 210.

[40] On Malherbe's rhymes see Fromilhague, *Malherbe. Technique et création poétique*, pp. 445 ff.

[41] The 1612 version includes an extra *sizain* in the paraphrase of Psalm 50; the rhymes of this *sizain* are excluded from the following assessment.

[42] Some of these are included in Racan's account of Malherbe's condemnation of this type of rhyme: 'ordonné'—'abandonné' (137, 8); 'pardonne'—'abandonne (102, 8); 'offense'—'defense' (101, 6). See Fromilhague, *Technique*, p. 597.

Nevertheless, it is possible to infer the influence of Malherbe on other aspects of La Ceppède's rhymes. In the first place, the vowels of rhyme-words are improved. The rhyme 'mouëlles'—'brindilles' becomes 'moüeles'—'brindeles' (101, 2). The rhyme 'soleil'—'œil' is twice (142, 10 and 102, 6) exchanged for completely homophonous pairs. Combinations indicating a provincial pronunciation are eliminated:[43] 'future'—'meure' (verb) is replaced by 'promise'—'remise' (101, 15), where etymological similarity is preferred to dissonance, and 'épure'—'demeure' by 'pensées'—'élancées' (102, 1).

In the second place, the homophony of the consonants supporting the rhyming vowel is improved. The desire to introduce rich rhyme accounts for by far the greatest number of revisions. Out of a total of 286 rhymes 138 are affected: 115 out of 138 were *non-rich* in 1594; 126 out of 138 become *rich* in 1612. To put it another way, in the 1595 version 166 out of 286 rhymes are non-rich, while in the 1612 version 63 are non-rich, 223 are rich. Moreover, it is possible to correlate different types of rich rhyme positively with Malherbe's own practice, to show that La Ceppède is even more advanced in this respect than even a poet so close in manner to Malherbe as Bertaut.[44] The evidence for the similarity is overwhelming; but difficulties in over-all interpretation remain.

Since La Ceppède has on the face of it little in common with Malherbe, there has been some reluctance to conclude unequivocally that there is any connection. It has been pointed out[45] that La Ceppède's rhyming in the 1612 *Imitation* brings him into line with the Grands Rhétoriqueurs. As an explanation of the revisions this would be a weak hypothesis, for the influence of Rhétoriqueur techniques would also have been potentially operative before the first version. The alternative hypothesis is more plausible, particularly if one also considers the correction of syntax and imagery, and the corrections made by Gallaup on his own paraphrases. Moreover, as has been seen, Malherbe's literary contacts with the Aix circle, and with La Ceppède in particular, are beyond question.

[43] Cf. Malherbe on Desportes's rhyme 'mesures'—'heures': 'rime provençale ou gasconne d'une diphthongue avec une voyelle'. See Fromilhague, *Technique*, p. 564.
[44] These conclusions are based on a detailed comparison; cf. table in Appendix I. Statistics for Malherbe and Bertaut are presented in Fromilhague, *Technique*.
[45] By Jeanneret, *Poésie et tradition biblique*, p. 384.

It is impossible not to take seriously the rather unexpected conclusion that La Ceppède may have sought to accommodate Malherbian doctrine.

The mere fact of the influence is not, however, the most interesting implication of La Ceppède's revision. The fact remains that the text of the final version could hardly be mistaken for a representative of emergent classicism. It remains to ask whether and how the peculiarities of the 1612 edition can be explained. The conjecture is that most if not all can be connected with Christian poetics and style. If this is so, then one can conclude that La Ceppède went perhaps as far as he could in correcting the style and technique of the *Imitation* without destroying its religious character. The variants of the *Imitation* represent one of the many sets of oppositions in La Ceppède's work. They pose a problem which the following chapters serve in part to elucidate: why could La Ceppède go so far and no farther in adopting Malherbian norms? Age and provincialism are only part of the answer.

III

GENESIS OF THE *THÉORÈMES*

THE final version of the first part of the *Théorèmes* was elaborated over a period of some twenty years, and the second part over a period of about ten years. These thirty years constitute a period during which France in general and Provence in particular underwent profound social, political, and cultural changes. While some connection between the *Théorèmes* and their historical situation may be assumed, it is not easy to pin down the composition dates of individual sonnets. Furthermore, the evidence for the stylistic evolution of the *Théorèmes* is less abundant than for that of the *Imitation*. However, much can be deduced, and in one respect at least the secrets of the work's composition are made explicit. The neglected prose annotations provide much evidence for three important aspects of the work: (i) the precise sources adduced by La Ceppède, a full account of which should clarify and modify the by now well-known fact that the *Théorèmes* have some connection with the devotional practices and literature of the period; (ii) La Ceppède's attitude to and treatment of his main source, the Bible; (iii) his intellectual orientation and world-picture within the limits of contemporary Catholic orthodoxy. These aspects are especially important, as will be seen in later chapters, because they throw considerable light on La Ceppède's conception of poetry and on the linguistic structure of his work.

1. *Historical Points of Reference*

Chapter I examined the course of social and political events in Aix-en-Provence from the period of Henri d'Angoulême's literary revival to the final cultural assimilation of the region into the French nation. Under Henry IV, the Regent Marie de Médicis, and Louis XIII the dominant problem was how to reconcile the politics of the national State with the politics of religion. Aix itself exemplifies this with its strengthened royalist Parlement under Du Vair, its educational expansion under the tutelage of the monarch, and its fostering of religious orders. However, tensions remained between the Parlement and the Chapter of Saint-Sauveur. It is relevant to see the search for orthodoxy and national loyalty against the background of sporadic Protestant insurrection in the south and elsewhere during the period of composition of the *Théorèmes*. The militant orthodoxy of the work might also be seen against the rise of 'libertinism'. La Ceppède had contacts in Toulouse, and he would no doubt have known of the scandal caused there by Vanini and of his execution three or four years before the publication of the second part.

It is of course true that the text of the work does not refer in any explicit way to this background. But this does not necessarily mean that there is no connection, and it is indeed arguable that the historical context of the *Théorèmes* is essential for a proper understanding both of the poetry and the piety. The first thing to be noticed is the change in attitude behind the *Imitation* and the *Théorèmes* respectively. The *Imitation* was written in a period of confusion and disturbed conscience; its tone was passive and supplicatory. It was written in retreat from the dangerous situation in Aix, and included three sonnets on monastic seclusion from the troubles of this world. The *Théorèmes*, on the other hand, seem related to the confidence, action, and constructiveness of the post-civil war phase of the Counter-Reformation in France. It is true that both works reflect the wave of devotional practice that swept through French society at the end of the sixteenth century. But they reflect different aspects of the movement which appear to have received different emphasis under different conditions.[1] From a retiring penitential mood La Ceppède seems to shift to a more optimistic mood that is closely bound up with public service. His admirers stress this merging of the devout and the civil life:

> Quand tu fus Conseiller ce mot t'aloit souuent
> Du grand, & vray Conseil, l'Ange ramenteuant.
> Puis tes Comptes reglant, faisant tousiours la guerre
>   Aux abus, tu pensas (sage & iudicieux!)
> A compter pour toy-mesme, affinant sur la terre
> Les Comptes qu'il faut rendre afin d'aller aux Cieux.[2]

---

[1] Cf. Cave, *Devotional Poetry*, p. 55 f.
[2] Preliminary sonnet by G. de Terlon, in *Théorèmes* I, p. 531.

It is the secular devotion of, for instance, François de Sales that is reflected here and in the *Théorèmes* themselves. In his letter to La Ceppède concerning the work the saint emphasizes the concept of poetry as the infusion of piety into a primary secular activity for concrete moral ends in society.[3] At the same time the writers of laudatory sonnets link La Ceppède's devotion and poetry with peace. These few remarks are an indication of the way the poet and his function could be thought of in a devout milieu. The relation between the religious work and its immediate social context is indirect. There is no explicit comment on it; it even turns away, as it was bound to do, to contemplate the divine. But the remarks of La Ceppède's contemporaries make it clear that his work is regarded as originating and terminating in day-to-day religious life. It is, however, possible to go a little further than this. Some passages in the *Théorèmes* can be interpreted as allusions to topical issues. Most of these revolve around the themes of religious and political unity.

La Ceppède selects Augustine's interpretation of the miraculous haul of fish (John 21: 6) as an allegory of ecclesiastical schism (II. ii. 82). But it could conceivably have a contemporary application. There is concern that the clergy should be exemplary. In the sonnets and in the accompanying notes several pieces of advice are offered to the clergy. They are urged to 'compatir à l'infirmité des autres' (I, p. 38), and to exercise charity (II, p. 388).[4] In particular, they should seek unity. Sonnet II. iv. 18, which is said to have special relevance for religious houses, is represented in the 'Sommaire des sonnets' as stating 'que le seul feu de la charité est capable de pouuoir remettre l'vnion entre les Ministres, & officiers de l'Eglise . . . auec vne brieue exhortation aux Prelats Ecclesiastiques seculiers ou reguliers à ceste vnion & concorde'. But there is nothing to suggest that La Ceppède had any particular dispute in mind. Strict control of clerical vocation is recommended: 'Pour mettre en charge vn homme il faut l'examiner' (II. ii. 88). And Chrysostom is adduced as authority 'Pour l'examen des Prelats, & comme ils doiuent s'examiner eux mesmes auant que de s'endosser vn si pesant fardeau que la Prestrise & la prelature' (II. pp. 38 f.). In a sonnet on the distribution of the Holy Spirit they

[3] François de Sales, *Œuvres*, vol. xvi, pp. 286 ff.
[4] Cf. II, 'Table alphabétique': 'Prelats de l'Eglise sans charité monstres effroyables.'

are exhorted to read Scripture (II. iv. 27). This emphasis on the moral and educational requirements for the ministry is, of course, characteristic of the Counter-Reformation. It is a reflection also of religious orders in Aix itself, in particular of Romillon's Congrégation de la doctrine chrétienne.

The question of the source of sovereignty and of the relationship between Church and State may lie behind La Ceppède's discussion of the primacy of St. Peter. He states that Christ 'iette sur sainct Pierre le solide fondement . . . de son Eglise militante . . . & depose entre ses mains la supreme authorité promise sur tout son troupeau, & l'en constitue chef' (II, p. 377). This is not apparently a tendentious statement, but La Ceppède seems aware that he is touching on a sensitive point, for he goes on to say:

Ie ne veux pas m'estendre icy en la dispute des controuerses. Ie sçay bien qu'aucuns ont nié ce primat ou preeminance de sainct Pierre. Mais ie demeure en l'ancienne croyance de l'Eglise . . . (II, p. 377)

Moreover, he is careful to ground his position in authoritative texts. Two of these, Coster's chapter on papal sovereignty in his *Enchiridion controversiarum* (1581) and Bellarmine's *De summo pontifice*,[5] were influential works of Catholic political theory inspired by a desire to minimize the power of monarchs. If what lies behind these references to disputes is indeed the Church–State controversy, it is worth recalling that the Gallican and ultramontane wrangles during the Regency were felt in Aix, especially in 1612 after the clash between the Parlement and the Archbishop over Richer.[6] There is little clear evidence, however, to suggest that La Ceppède favoured one or the other side in this debate. It is true not only that he cites Bellarmine approvingly, but that he often expresses admiration for the disgraced Ligueur Génébrard. But he is probably thinking of Génébrard's erudition and contribution to Aix culture. In the same way he restricts his remarks on episcopacy and papacy to a protestation of theological orthodoxy, disclaiming possible political implications. Although he was doubtless aware of them, he steers a devout middle course.

---

[5] Vol. i (1586) of *Disputationes . . . de controversiis christianae fidei*; enlarged 1610 as *Tractatus de potestate summi pontificis in rebus temporalibus*. It should be borne in mind that Bellarmine attacked the succession of Henry of Navarre in *Responsio ad praecipua capita apologiae . . . pro successione Henrici Navarreni* (1587). On the political theory of this period, see, e.g., Allen, *A History of Political Thought in the Sixteenth Century*, Part 3.

[6] See above, p. 14.

In any case there is no doubt about his loyalty to the Crown. However concerned he may have become in the second part of the *Théorèmes* (i.e. during the period 1613–22) to emphasize a rigidly Catholic position, his civil duty in the earlier, immediately post-war period is stated unequivocally:

> Pour vne fin tres-bonne, il n'est pas conuenable
> De faire vn mauuais coup. Ce coup est vicieux
> Puis qu'il enfreint les loix. Aprens ambicieux
> (Qui t'appeles Zelé) que ton Zele est damnable.
> Il faut Zeler l'Eglise, & l'Estat: Mais pourtant
> Tu ne seras iamais qu'iniuste combatant,
> Si l'adueu de ton Roy tes vœux ne fauorise.
> L'authorité d'armer n'appartient qu'à ton Roy,
> Si son commandement tes armes n'authorise,
> N'atten de tes combats qu'vn sanglant desarroy. (I. i. 67)

This is an allegorical interpretation of Jesus's rebuke of Peter for drawing the sword (Matthew 26: 52). The term 'roy' applies in the allegory both to God and the monarch. Against the contemporary historical background the ambiguity acquires significance.[7] There is no question of the monarch's power deriving from any source other than from God. The king in turn delegates power to the magistracy, though the exact relation between the two is not without difficulties. The episodes involving Pontius Pilate provide ample opportunity for reflection on these matters:

> Tout pouuoir est du Ciel. Le Ciel le donne aux Roys,
> Les Roys aux Magistrats, pour rendre la iustice:
> Dont les iustes decrets, dont le sainct exercice,
> Par l'effort de la peur sont forcez maintefois.
>
> Qui se laisse forcer à l'enfreinte des loix
> Peche: mais beaucoup plus celuy dont la malice
> La forte calomnie, & les forçans abbois
> Font destiner le iuste à l'iniuste supplice . . .
> Iuges, qu'aucun ne soit de ce mot amorcé.
> 'L'excuse de la force est vile, & deceuante.
> 'Qui sçait, & veut mourir ne peut estre forcé. (I. ii. 81)

---

[7] The annotation on line 12 of I. i. 68 emphasizes the political implications: 'tous les Docteurs ont tiré cette conclusion, que parmy les trois qualitez requises pour faire vne guerre iuste, cele du commandement, ou congé du Prince souuerain est la premiere, & la principale . . .' (I, p. 156)

This emphasis on the ideal impartiality of the law has an obvious relevance to the historical context—as is made clear in La Ceppède's warning in another context to magistrates who do not stand firm against rebellion, whether of the populace or of the nobility. Another sonnet on Pilate has the title 'Aduertissement aux Magistrats, qui ont a soustenir l'audace des peuples mutins, ou les menaces des Grands de ne lascher rien de leur accoustumée iustice, pour ne se rendre imitateurs de Pilate' ('Table des sonnets', I. ii. 89).[8] The independence of the individual magistrate is to be strictly maintained, and again (I, p. 234) La Ceppède points out the dangers of allowing 'les Princes, ou les chefs' to influence legal decisions. But by the time of the writing of Part II of the *Théorèmes* La Ceppède has found a formula for the relation between the magistracy and the monarchy which qualifies somewhat the earlier statement:

> Les Roys donnent ainsi leur supreme puissance
> Aux plus hauts Magistrats: les Roys l'ont de naissance
> Les Iuges l'ont des Rois, & les vont hommageant.
>
> (II. ii. 70, ll. 9–11)

The relation between the two spheres of civil power, La Ceppède says, is the same as that between the authority of the priest and that of God: 'les Roys . . . donnent leur puissance supreme à leurs plus hauts Magistrats, retenans neantmoins à eux & à leur personne le droict de souueraineté' ('Sommaire des sonnets', II. ii. 70). Although these statements occur as one element in a comparison, and are in any case rather vague, they nevertheless seem to reflect the gradual acceptance by the Provence Parlement of royal control.

In view of all this it is not surprising to find La Ceppède dedicating his work in 1613 to Marie de Médicis and France in general and in 1622 to Louis XIII. Since her entry into Aix in 1600 Marie de Médicis had been regarded as a patron of the region. In the dedicatory Preface to the *Théorèmes* of 1613 La Ceppède recalls this turning-point in the history of Provence, and reaffirms his loyalty (I, pp. 2 f.). But the purpose of the dedication seems also

---

[8] Such allusions can be explained in terms of the civil war period in Provence; but cf. also La Ceppède's letter to Henry IV, 13 October 1601, reporting on popular disturbances in Arles (BN: MSS., ancien petit fonds français, 23196, fo. 425).

to be to gain a wider circulation for a work, which, while it would attract the devout, lacks the advantage of a celebrated author (I, pp. 1–2). The conventional modesty has a practical purpose, as becomes evident in the *Avant-propos* entitled 'A la France'. The *Imitation* was in many respects a provincial work. In the *Théorèmes* La Ceppède is evidently aiming at a wide national audience. He still has in mind the 'embrasements de nos derniers mal-heurs' (I, p. 8), but he offers a work of consolation rather than of consolation. It is intended both for the devout and for the indifferent, and is 'escrit dedans pour les doctes, & dehors pour les ignorans' (I, p. 8). He believes that the work possesses the power of morally reforming the nation's life at all levels, and lists carefully the members of the moral and social hierarchy together with the virtues that become them—from the king, who will learn 'iuste et douce domination', to 'le seruiteur', who will become imbued with 'affectionnée loyauté', and from the miser to the voluptuary who will find the means to dominate their passions (I, pp. 9–10). Thus Provençal desire to be integrated into the mainstream of the nation's life, and the desire of the devotional movement to penetrate secular life, combine to form the basis of a distinctive conception of poetry.

The circumstances of the dedication of Part II of the *Théorèmes* are an even more striking expression of Provence's new-found devotion to the Crown. References to the power and dignity of the Crown have already been mentioned. Metaphorical and conventional though such images are, the theme of the victorious monarch and the suppression of rebellion has a certain topical appropriateness:

> Le conquerant ialoux d'vne victoire preste,
> Part de son Throsne: Attaque: Et puis victorieux
> Y reuient, s'y r'asseoid, s'y repose, et s'arreste
> Chez soy, pour sur les siens regner imperieux. (II. iii. 30)

Protestant rebellion had simmered since 1617, especially in the southern provinces. Louis XIII marched south in 1621, and his suppression of the rebels culminated in a triumphal entry into Aix. The *Extraict du privilège* states that printing of the second part of the *Théorèmes* was complete on 1 February 1622.[9] The King did

---

[9] The *Approbation* is dated 26 December 1620. Some copies have a frontispiece dated 1621.

not arrive in Aix till November, so there is no question of any influence of these events on La Ceppède's work. Nevertheless, the work is dedicated to the King, and its coincidence with his victorious campaign and acclamation by the Aixois may be indicative of a general mood in the province. The Preface 'Au Roy' is in fact full of allusions to Louis's military successes. Indeed, La Ceppède makes bold to suggest that the King should curb his martial spirit by cultivation of the Muses. To poetry is attributed the exalted task of effecting a union of throne and altar:

Pource donc que c'ét l'Eternel qui donne & qui oste, qui esleue & bouleuerse les Royaumes, les Roys doiuent bien l'aymer & le craindre, & pour cet effet cherir les nourriçons de la saincte Vranie, qui tout doucement leur font embrasser estroictement la Religion . . . (II, ã3)

There is no doubt that the devotional practice of the Counter-Reformation lies behind the circumstances and intentions of much of the *Théorèmes*. But it is also possible to see the move to merge the secular with the pious life reinforced in the background by a parallel desire in Provence to combine traditional Catholic enthusiasm with service and loyalty to the French monarch and nation. The *Théorèmes* is perhaps the crowning literary manifestation of the need in Provence to resolve regional and national, civil and ecclesiastical tensions.

2. *The Composition of the* Théorèmes

The two parts of the *Théorèmes* took an exceptionally long time to produce. Although the evidence is scanty it is possible, especially in the case of Part I, to deduce approximate phases of composition for approximate groups of sonnets. The earliest sign of the *Théorèmes* is the 1594 edition of the *Imitation* which includes 'Douze meditations sur le sacré mystere de nostre rédemption. Prinses de l'Œuure entier des Theoremes de M. I. de la Ceppede'. They appear to have been added as an afterthought to the psalm paraphrases which were probably completed by 1592. Two things in this title are noteworthy. First, the use of the term 'meditations' does not necessarily imply that the whole of the *Théorèmes* is to be thought of as such. Second, it is implied that the *Théorèmes* are already complete at this date. However, this last point is modified by the statement in the Preface 'Au lecteur':

CE trauail spirituel[10] (Ami Lecteur) que tu viens maintenant de lire, m'a aleché à L'entreprinse d'vn plus grand œuure dont (auec l'aide de l'Immortel) i'espere bien tost te faire voir quelque heureux succés. Cependant ie t'en ay voulu donner icy vn echantillon, à fin de pouuoir iuger par l'accueil que tu luy feras, si l'etallement du tout pourra faire du fruit, & donner quelque consolation aux ames Chrestiennes parmy tant, & tant de maux qui les affligent . . . (*Imitation*, p. 39)

From this it looks as if the *Théorèmes* were only approaching completion. And in the *Avant-propos* of the 1613 edition La Ceppède states that the work was 'born' *after* 'les embrasemens de nos derniers malheurs' (p. 8). This suggests that the bulk of the *Théorèmes* as they are now known stems from the post-civil war period, and is to be distinguished from the 'Théorèmes' previously announced in 1594. What then constituted this early version? From La Ceppède's wording it seems possible to assume that the *échantillon* he gives is representative of the whole of his work as it then stood. All but one of the 1594 sonnets have more or less complete correlates in the 1613 version. Nine of these occur in the third of the three books into which it is divided.[11] All these revolve round the theme of the Crucifixion, and it is likely, as Rousset and others have pointed out, that they formed the original core of La Ceppède's intentions.[12] This initial insight may be elaborated.

The preliminary sonnet by G. de Terlon quoted above links the writing of the *Théorèmes* with La Ceppède's magisterial duties, and refers specifically to his offices:

> Or, fus tu Conseiller, & l'vne des retraites
> Des Loix de ton Senat; puis President tu pris
> Tes Comptes, à tout faire heureusement appris:
> Qu'eut cela de conforme au suiet que tu traites?

Terlon's statement is by no means explicit, but, given that La Ceppède was a *conseiller* between 1578 and 1586, it is not unlikely

---

[10] i.e. the psalm paraphrases.

[11] Cf. Donaldson-Evans, 'L'édition de 1594 de l'*Imitation*'; *Poésie et méditation*, Appendix B. The correspondences between the sonnets of the 'Douze méditations' and those of the *Théorèmes* are: 1: I. iii. 20; 2: I. iii. 21; 3: I. i. 51; 4: I. ii. 60; 5 and 6: fragments in I. iii. 22, 23, 24, 28, 29; 7: suppressed; 8: I. iii. 26; 9: fragments in I. ii. 63, I. iii. 23; 10: I. iii. 89; 11 and 12: fragments in I. iii. 86.

[12] Rousset, Préface to *Les Théorèmes*; Donaldson-Evans, *Poésie et méditation*, pp. 185 f. Their conclusions are confined to the statement that I. iii was largely begun and finished before I. i and I. ii.

that he would have begun his work during the 1580s.—However, it is clear from the remark in the *Avant-propos* that a new start was made after the wars. The points at which the old material is assimilated and the new material introduced are difficult to determine. For one thing they are dependent on La Ceppède's methods of composition. Something of these can be glimpsed by comparing the 1954 sonnets with the final version of 1613, and by considering the relation between the verse and the prose annotations in this version.

The sonnets of the 'Douze meditations' are transferred to the *Théorèmes* in a fragmented and radically reworked form. It is clear that they have been adapted from loosely connected individual pieces on a central theme into a structure in which the narrative, interpretative, and logical continuity is much stronger. Beyond this the alterations are so extensive that it is impossible to draw any concrete conclusions as to the finer principles of the revisions, although general aesthetic improvements have been observed.[13] Some shifts in emphasis in the content may, however, also be significant. Sonnets 5 and 6 of the 'Douze meditations' are absorbed into the sequence I. iii. 22–9. The extended use of Old Testament prefiguration in the new sequence may be symptomatic of an intensified interest in the Bible and in 'proofs' of the events of the New Testament. Sonnet 8, which is taken up in I. iii. 26, loses its stress on man's guilt. The antagonist becomes Satan not Adam, the redemptive act of Christ is more prominent, and an ambiguous allusion to war is abandoned. Again, sonnet 11 loses its tone of stoical forbearance in its final form (I. iii. 86): the metaphor of man as a suffering soldier disappears and the emphasis remains on the vicarious victory of the Redemption. But what is most striking about the later sonnets is their increased intellectual rigour and their accumulation of fresh source material.

It is precisely this material, indicated in the prose annotations to the sonnets, that makes it possible to gain further insights into La Ceppède's method. In one sense the notes are posterior to the poems. This is no doubt chronologically true in some cases where references to authorities seem to have been amassed after composition in order to support a point. But the character of the notes varies. While some are brief references to sources, others explain

---

[13] See Donaldson-Evans, 'L'édition de 1594' and *Poésie et méditation*, pp. 185 ff.

obscure expressions and theology, and others can be regarded as full-length essays working out ideas incorporated in the accompanying sonnet. There are two senses in which the verse may be dependent on the notes rather than the reverse. In the first place, the sonnets depend heavily on the paraphrase of biblical, patristic, and scholastic texts quoted or referred to in the notes. And in the second place, they often depend on ideas derived from such texts but worked out in the accompanying prose. Thus one finds the comment: 'Cette proposition est estendue au Sonnet precedent 68. & prouuée en la 4. annotation' (I. iii. 69 n. 3). This suggests the possibility that the sonnets, or some of them, evolved from a discursive prose draft of the argument. In terms of classical rhetoric the notes represent *invention*, the phase of composition concerned with seeking out material and argument. This procedure is particularly obvious in the case of I. i. 37 where the sonnet embodies conclusions which would have been impossible without the prior contribution to the problem of the miraculous nature of Christ's sweating blood given in a long annotation. The sonnet itself is prosaic. It is noticeable that the rhythm and rhetoric of theological prose seem to be characteristics of the later poems—that is to say, of those poems written for the second part of the *Théorèmes* after La Ceppède had absorbed the increasing volume of contemporary religious publications.

It is reasonable to suppose that many of the sonnets are dependent on the notes, and on the sources given in them. The publication dates of works cited in the notes may therefore be used as rough guides to the phases of composition. Any conclusions will, of course, only establish approximate dates, since there is rarely any evidence as to the edition used by La Ceppède or as to when he acquired it.[14] Furthermore, one has to remember that in view of the constant revision different parts of a given sonnet may

---

[14] In order to establish with any plausibility the earliest date *after* which a given sonnet is likely to have been composed, it is therefore necessary to assume first editions were used. Clearly, this is not an infallible guide, because there is no means of determining the date (other than publication date) *before* which a given piece must have been composed. By 'first edition' is meant the earliest known edition. The following bibliographical works have been used: Dagens, *Bibliographie chronologique de la littérature de spiritualité*; Augustin Backer, Aloys Backer, and C. Sommervogel, *Bibliothèque de la Compagnie de Jésus*, vols. i–x; Hurter, *Nomenclator literarius theologiae catholicae*, vols. ii and iii; Wadding, *Scriptores ordinis Minorum*; also *The Catholic Encyclopedia*, ed. Herbermann *et al.*; *Dictionnaire de théologie catholique*, ed. Vacant *et al.*

belong to different periods. It has already been established that the central section (sonnets 20, 21, 22–32, 89) of I. iii was conceived some time between 1578–89. It remains to ask whether any chronological order can be fixed for the composition of the rest of the work.

The most interesting guides to dating are the references to the following:

Franciscus Suarez, *Commentarii ac disputationes in tertiam partem divi Thomae* (vol. i, Alcala, 1590, Lyon, 1592; vol. ii, Alcala, 1592, Lyon, 1594; vol. iii, Salamanca, 1595) and *Disputationes metaphysicae* (Salamanca, 1597, Paris, 1605).[15] Maldonatus, *Commentarii in quattuor Evangelistas* (Pont-à-Mousson, vol. i, 1596; vol. ii, 1597).[16]

An earlier work by Cornelius Jansenius (Bishop of Ghent) entitled *Commentarius in concordiam et totam historiam evangelicam* (Louvain, 1572)[17] is also a relevant guide, since there are few references to it in Book iii, which for the reasons given above can be regarded as the earliest of the three. These are the only significantly datable works that La Ceppède refers to with any frequency.[18] Maldonatus and Jansenius are particularly useful because they cover the whole of the biblical material utilized in the first part, so that reference to them is probably not dependent on special context.

In I. iii there are only four references to Suarez's *Commentarii*: in sonnets 2, 96, 97, 100. Since these come right at the beginning and right at the end of the book, they tend to support the suggestion that the early core of the work was the Crucifixion. There are only two references to Jansenius's commentary, both in I. iii. 40. The count in the other two books is much higher. The same sonnet contains also the sole reference in Book iii to Maldonatus's commentary. It is a straightforward narrative sonnet on the reviling of Christ of a type that is not represented in the 'Douze meditations', and could well be relatively late.[19]

---

[15] See Backer and Sommervogel, vol. vii, cols. 1661 ff.

[16] Later editions published at Lyon, 1598, 1601, 1607, etc. See Backer and Sommervogel, vol. v, cols. 403 ff.

[17] An extension of the *Concordia evangelica*, 1549. See *Encyclopédie catholique*, article 'Jansen, Cornelius, the Elder', and Hurter, vol. iii, cols. 67 ff.

[18] There is unfortunately nothing to indicate the editions used of the earlier writers who constitute the bulk of La Ceppède's sources.

[19] It is also relevant to mention here La Ceppède's use of Franciscus Toletus, *In Sacrosanctum Joannis Evangelium commentarii*, Rome, 1588, Lyon, 1589. See Backer and Sommervogel, vol. viii, cols. 69 f. The discrepancy in distribu-

In Book ii the only sonnet foreshadowed in the early sample concerns the scourging of Jesus.[20] It is conceivable that part at least of this episode, which contains much description of an emotive and meditative character, belongs to the early stage of composition. Moreover, the early sonnet in question opens thus:

> Pilate en fin voyant, qu'il ne peut contenter,
> Sans mefaire au Sauueur, cete race Gorgonne (*Imitation*, p. 42)

where the time adverb and the demonstrative may suggest an already established narrative context in a sequence of sonnets. If the section on the scourging in the *Théorèmes* (I. ii. 60–74) belongs to the period of the 'Douze meditations', the remainder of the book consisting of accounts of Peter's denials and Christ's trials could well be a later extension. In contrast with the scourge sequence these sections are a complicated intertwining of two narratives combined with the somewhat abstract argumentation of the trial scenes. The view that they were composed relatively late tends to be supported by the two references to Maldonatus, which occur in two key sonnets: I. ii. 20 in which Jesus replies to Caiphas, and I. ii. 23 in which the high priest condemns the prisoner. Thirteen sonnets now refer to Jansenius, and all of these occur in the first half of the book,[21] that is, in the section concerned with the trial of Jesus by the Jews.

In Book i a single sonnet is again derived from the series of 1594.[22] It concerns the capture of Jesus and like the sonnet on the scourging employs a demonstrative at the beginning which could indicate a context of accompanying sonnets not included in the sample. This does not necessarily mean that the whole of Book i was conceived at the same time as the other two. It is possible, for instance, that the original sequence began with Jesus's capture and concentrated thereafter on the physical events of the scourging and the Passion. And there is reasonable ground for thinking that most of the rest of Book i was composed later. The tone of the book is markedly different from that of the other two: it consists

---

tion over the three books is not as marked as in the cases already mentioned. But the references within Book iii are concentrated towards the end, thus: 12, 33, 68, 77, 94, 95, 99.

[20] 'Douze meditations' 4: *Théorèmes* I. ii. 60.

[21] I. ii. 6, 9, 10, 12, 13, 17, 20, 21, 23, 28, 31, 35, 44.

[22] 'Douze meditations', 3: *Théorèmes* I. i. 51.

of a sequential narrative, but, more importantly, it introduces rational argument on a wider and more detailed scale. While Book ii shows some signs of a preoccupation with the status of law—a preoccupation which may well reflect the disorders of the 1590s—Book i shows an interest in medicine and natural philosophy. La Ceppède's interest in these subjects was evidently fairly strong. He refers to contacts in the medical faculty both in Montpellier and in Aix.[23] Interests of this kind no doubt stem from the period after the turn of the century when academic life and scientific activity began to expand in Aix under royal patronage. For the first time works published after 1600 appear amongst the references. Olivier de Serre's work on agriculture[24] published in 1600 is cited in I. i. 16. The Portuguese Franciscan apologist Jacobus Suarez is used for the first time in two sonnets: I. i. 37 (p. 100) and I. i. 67.[25] The fact that Saurez was *prédicateur ordinaire* to Henry IV and a favourite of Marie de Médicis helps to explain La Ceppède's use of his work. The *Disputationes metaphysicae* (1597) by the Jesuit Franciscus Suarez also makes a first appearance: in I. i. 2 and I. i. 37 (p. 109). References to his commentary on the *Summa* of Aquinas have risen to eleven as against four in Book iii and none in Book ii: I. i. 2, 9, 14, 20, 22, 37, 45, 46, 66, 67, 97. Maldonatus's commentary on the Gospels is mentioned eleven times as against twice in Book ii and once in Book iii: I. i. 3, 18, 37, 45, 46, 47, 49, 50, 52, 61, 82. Of these 45 to 52 concern the actual capture of Jesus and relate to the single sonnet (51) foreshadowed in the 'Douze meditations'. This is simply evidence that La Ceppède elaborated over a period of years a theme conceived at an early stage. The general trend of the pattern of references still points to a relatively late date for the composition of Book i, and to a relatively early one for Book iii. This tends to be confirmed by the references to Génébrard, who is referred to not at all in Book iii and not as frequently in Book ii as in Book i and Part II. Génébrard was banished by the Aix Parlement in 1596, and it would obviously

---

[23] He refers also to a case of fever observed in 1596: I. i. 37, n. 4 (I, p. 106).

[24] Olivier de Serres, seigneur du Pradel, *Le Théatre d'agriculture et mesnage des champs*, Paris, 1600; La Ceppède refers to the list of antidotes given in Book viii, ch. 5, for the purposes of an extended image of Christ as physician.

[25] La Ceppède seems to be using the *Trésor quadragésimal, enrichi de plusieurs relevées et admirables considérations tant de l'Escripture saincte que de la doctrine des SS. Peres pour les sermons de tous les jours de caresme*, Paris, 1607. See Dagens, *Bibliographie*, p. 183; and Wadding, *Scriptores*, p. 126.

be some time before the royalist La Ceppède could refer to him in tones of respect.

To sum up, the overwhelming impression is that although composition is to some extent continuous between approximately 1578 (at the earliest) and approximately 1612, the date of the *privilège*, the order of composition is Book iii, Book ii, Book i. Book iii does not seem to have been substantially expanded after the mid-1590s. The original material (i.e. the material from which the 1594 sample was drawn) may have included, as well as the Crucifixion, the arrest of Jesus and his suffering at the hands of Pilate. The themes of the arrest and scourging subsequently found their way into Books i and ii respectively when the whole work was elaborated. From the available evidence it seems that some, and perhaps most, of Book ii was composed after 1596–7. Book i (apart from the brief arrest sequence) appears to have been developed around the turn of the century, along with some very restricted sections of the rest of Part I, the latest determinable *terminus post quem* being 1607 for one at least of the sonnets.

The clues to the writing of the second part of the *Théorèmes* are even fewer and less fruitful. The relatively late sources of the first part, such as Franciscus Suarez and Maldonatus, become increasingly common, the Suarez references being spread more evenly since the Gospel commentaries of Maldonatus are irrelevant where Acts and the Creed form the basis of the poetry. The *Commentaria in concordiam et historiam evangelicam* by the Jesuit Sebastian Barradas appeared from 1599 to 1611 and had many reprints. The latter part of the work (vols. ii–iv, 1604–11) is used extensively throughout.[26] Jean de Lorin's *In Acta Apostolorum commentaria* (Lyon, 1605)[27] are employed mainly in Books iii and iv for the Ascension and Pentecost narratives. There are also a number of single references to works published around the beginning of the century: Del Rio's *Disquisitiones magicae* (Louvain, 1599–1600) is referred to in II. ii. 56;[28] Ribadeneyra's *Flos sanctorum* (Madrid, 1599–1601) in II. iii. 18; Salmeron's commentaries on the Gospels

---

[26] See II. i. 27, 29, 30; ii. 64, 84, 88–93, 95, 97, 99; iii. 7, 9–11, 12, 14–17, 30, 32; iv. 2, 4, 6, 18–21, 29, 30. On Barradas see Backer and Sommervogel, vol. i, col. 911.

[27] See Backer and Sommervogel, vol. v, cols. 1 ff.

[28] See Backer and Sommervogel, vol. ii, cols, 1898 ff. Del Rio is cited in a note on the return of spirits as an authority for the view that they serve to 'affermir vne belle ame chancelante en la foy de l'immortalité' (II, p. 277).

and Acts (Madrid, 1598–1601) in II. iii. 7; and Ghisleri's commentary on the Song of Solomon (Rome, 1609, Paris, 1618) in II. iv. 4, 6, 15, 16, 18, 22.[29] It is perhaps significant that these relatively late references are concentrated in Books iii and iv. Although their publication dates fall before 1613, they do not appear in Part I. In general there is no case for thinking that La Ceppède may have begun or intended to begin the second part before this date. As for the order of composition there is in the case of the second part of the *Théorèmes* no objection to the assumption that the bulk of the sonnets were written consecutively following the narrative line. Book iv has some late references, in addition to those mentioned, which would support such a view. The *Commentaria in pentateuchum Moysis* of Cornelius a Lapide (Cornelis Cornelissen van den Steyn), which is mentioned in sonnets 15, 17, 18, 19, 21, 24, 25, appeared in Paris as late as 1617.[30] There is a single reference (II. iv. 10) to a medical work of 1621.[31] At what date the second part of the *Théorèmes* was begun is difficult to determine. The most that can be said is that it was undertaken after 1613, that the narrative was composed consecutively, and that La Ceppède was constantly gathering new theological and exegetic material right up till printing in 1621–2.

Some conclusions may be drawn from this outline of the phases of composition. Firstly, Part I of the *Théorèmes* is a radical transformation and extension of whatever work constituted the 'Théorèmes' alluded to in the *Imitation* of 1594. Secondly, there is a progression in choice of sources, from the predominantly meditative and penitential mood of I. iii to theological, exegetic, philosophical, and even medical interests. Presumably this transition reflects the resumption of intellectual activity in Aix after the wars. Although Part II may not have been originally planned, its intellectual outlook has much in common with the later Books (i and ii) of Part I. Finally, the evidence suggests that the *Théorèmes* should not be regarded as largely complete by 1594 and held back because of unfavourable circumstances, but as continuously evolving over

---

[29] See Backer and Sommervogel, vol. vi, cols. 1737 ff. for Ribadeneyra, vol. vii, cols. 479 ff. for Salmeron; and Hurter, vol. iii, cols. 1067 ff. for Ghisleri.

[30] On Cornelius a Lapide see Backer and Sommervogel, vol. iv, cols. 1511 ff., and vol. ix, col. 573.

[31] Sieur du Laurens, *L'Histoire anatomique*, cited concerning the relation between the tongue and the rational faculty. Date as given by Wickersheimer, *La Médicine et les médecins*.

a period. Thus, if the literary style of the *Théorèmes* is archaic, it is not necessarily due simply to a delay in publication. On the contrary, the style must have developed in the same way and within the same limitations as that of the *Imitation*.

3. *Sources: the Bible and the Exegetic Tradition*

It is an obvious fact that La Ceppède's debt to the Bible is very large. Two aspects of this have usually been emphasized. In the first place, the use of the tradition of typological interpretation has attracted attention, and in the second, this has been seen in the context of the devotional exercise based on a biblical theme.[32] But further investigation is required in order to establish the precise nature of La Ceppède's debt to the Bible, and to the exegetic, theological, and devotional traditions. He exploits to the full the sanction given by the Council of Trent to biblical scholarship within the limits of traditional interpretation and the patristic consensus. It is true that La Ceppède's primary text is still the old Vulgate in the earlier parts of the *Théorèmes*, and in the later parts the Clementine Vulgate of 1592 ('la commune version que nous auons maintenant', II, p. 435). But it seems that he was constantly at pains to compare it with other available versions. It is not always possible to identify the version used, and in some cases where he is unusually negligent in giving precise references the motive could be a desire for caution in what is intended as an exemplary work of orthodoxy. It is unlikely that La Ceppède knew Hebrew, since he appears to rely heavily on popular indexes of Hebrew names and on Génébrard's explanations of Hebraisms,[33] but it is clear from the annotations that he was intensely interested in the language. He seems to share the almost mystical literalism of the humanist editors and translators of the Bible based on a belief in the intrinsic symbolic properties of the words and characters of the original biblical languages.[34]

The Septuagint is often cited for comparison (e.g. I, pp. 414, 490, 500, 605), and Aquila's second-century Greek translation of the New Testament is referred to (I, p. 490). The immediate

---

[32] Cf. Cave, *Devotional Poetry*, pp. 216 ff.; Donaldson-Evans, *Poésie et méditation*, pp. 62–88, 144–81.

[33] e.g. the commentaries in *Psalmi Davidis*.

[34] Cf. e.g. the Preface to the Complutensian Polyglot of 1514–17, cited by Hall, *Cambridge History of the Bible*, vol. ii, p. 51.

source for the latter is no doubt Jerome, who supplies much information on Hebrew texts, particularly in the case of the Psalms (cf. II, p. 501). It is primarily to the Fathers that La Ceppède turns when confronted with a textual problem:

La lecture des paroles duquel [i.e. of John 21: 22] a esté par les anciens si fort diuersifiée qu'à peine peut on les coucher auec certitude. Les aucuns ont leu en ce lieu, *sic eum volo manere, etc. Ie veux qu'il demeure ainsi.* Comme sainct Augustin au dernier traicté sur sainct Iean, & au sermon 149. du temps, Eusebe Emiss. en l'homilie de sainct Iean Euangeliste, sainct Ambroise au liure 7, sur sainct Luc, & sur le Pseaume 45. & sur le Pseaume 118. sainct Bernard au sermon *de Natal. Innoc* . . . (II, pp. 401–2)

This extract illustrates the almost obsessive caution with which La Ceppède proceeds when setting up the model on which his poems are based. But he does not stop at patristic orthodoxy. He prefers the conclusions arrived at by a variety of modern scholars:

La troisieme lecture est *si eum volo. Si ie veux qu'il demeure, iusqu'à ce que ie vienne.* Laquelle nous suiuons auec nos Bibles modernes, Latines et Françaises imprimées ez années 1581. & 1574.[35] et auec la verification qui en a esté faite sur les exemplaires Syriaques, et Grecs, mesmes sur celuy qui est conserué au Vatican, comme atteste Maldon. sur ces versets . . . (II, p. 402)

The concern for philological justification is evident, although it is by no means clear which recent editions La Ceppède had in mind. It is conceivable that as a Catholic humanist he would be familiar also with the Royal Antwerp polyglot Bible of 1569–72.[36]

La Ceppède is specific about one at least of his Latin texts. Discussing variant readings of Proverbs 30: 18–19, he points out that 'il est certain que bien qu'en la vieille traduction on lise *Viam viri in adolescentula*, toutesfois en la nouuele translation sur l'Hebrieu, on lit *Vestigium viri in Virgine*, version receuë, qui coupe toute difficulté. De cette verité fait foy la Bible imprimée par

---

[35] Logically this should mean a Latin Bible of 1581 and a French Bible of 1574. According to Darlow and Moule, *Historical Catalogue*, and van Eys, *Bibliographie*, there is no original French edition for either date. Buf cf. the revised edition of the Louvain translation, Lyon, Jean Pillehotte, 1581.

[36] Cf. his reference to 'la Bible Royale', II, p. 137; he mentions also the *Isagoge ad sacras litteras* (Lyon, 1526) of Sanctes Pagninus, one of its main contributors (but not his translation of the Bible of 1527–8), and the exegetic work of its chief editor, Arias Montanus.

Robert Estienne en l'an 1557' (I, p. 491).[37] Even at the date at which the *Théorèmes* were composed it is probably significant that La Ceppède is sufficiently concerned about textual accuracy to have recourse to a Bible which was condemned by the Sorbonne on publication. Whenever he has occasion to refer to a Latin version of the original Old or New Testament (I, p. 122; II, pp. 143, 304), it seems to be to this Bible that La Ceppède turns. It is clear also that he consulted a Greek version of the New Testament, though again which one is not revealed (see for instance II, p. 71).

In addition, the Bible is often quoted in French in the annotations to the sonnets. Most of these quotations are not attributed to any particular source, and La Ceppède is clearly offering his own paraphrase. However, some of the notes (e.g. I, p. 205; II, pp. 70, 71, 278, 293, 403) speak of 'vne des traductions Françoises' or 'la traduction Françoise que nous auons de la Bible', without divulging the version in question. Doctrinally significant passages are, of course, avoided, and there is no point in attempting to determine which vernacular Bible La Ceppède is using. In one instance only is there a clue that the absence of clear references masks the use of Protestant Bibles. Paraphrasing 1 Corinthians 15: 51, 'selon l'edition Grecque, et l'vne des Françoises', La Ceppède offers: *'nous ne dormirons* (C'ét à dire ne mourrons pas tous) *mais nous serons tous transmuez'* (II, p. 71). In the Catholic Louvain version the first verb is positive ('nous resusciterons') while the second is negative ('nous ne serons point transmuez'). But the Geneva version (1588), though it does not, of course, correspond verbatim to La Ceppède's paraphrase, is very close to it indeed. On the same occasion he quotes 1 Thessalonians 3: 15–17 in French. The Louvain version reads 'nous qui viuons et restons' in this passage, whereas La Ceppède, like the Protestant version, puts the verbs in the future. If La Ceppède did indeed make use of Protestant Bibles, and did feel justified in doing so on scholarly grounds, he also seems to have felt it still necessary (around 1620) to be discreet. What is important for his poetry is the close attention to verbal detail, and the immersion in vernacular as well as Latin, Greek, and perhaps Hebrew texts of the Bible. By comparison with the

---

[37] 3 vols., Geneva. This last and largest edition of Estienne's Latin Bible comprised a revision of Pagninus's Old Testament based on the Hebrew, the Apocrypha of Claudius Baduellis based on the Greek text of the Complutensian Polyglot, and the Latin version of the Greek New Testament of Théodore de Bèze.

Imitation (and possibly also with the early draft of the *Théorèmes*) the biblical basis is detailed and complex.

It would be unhelpful and misleading to attempt to trace in detail the specific influences on a work which explicitly acknowledges the absorption of around 250 writers. It is, however, revealing to classify them roughly, and to consider the way they are used in relation to the scriptural material which is the only fundamental model for the substance of the *Théorèmes*. All authors quoted fall naturally into a characteristic dichotomy: profane and sacred. The first group includes the ancient poets, philosophers, and medical authorities. 'Ce grand Socrate' (II, p. 441) is venerated; so is Plato, with reservations (II, pp. 32-3); but neither is as well represented as Aristotle, 'ce Prince des Philosophes'.[38] Borrowings are made from a wide range of Roman writers, including poets and satirists, but with the emphasis on philosophical writers like Cicero and Seneca, who is described as writing 'divinely' (II, p. 553), on historians (Livy, Caesar, Pliny the Elder, Tacitus, Suetonius), and technical writers (Columella ,Vitruvius, Solinus). Among the poets the allegorical Ovid and the prophetic Virgil are prominent. They are supplemented by Virgil's commentators, in particular the prophetic interpretations by the first-century poetess known as Proba Falconia.[39] The Sibylline oracles are frequently referred to as prophecies of the Christian mysteries. In drawing on these sources interpreted in the light of Christian doctrine La Ceppède is following the early tradition represented by, for instance, Lactantius, whom he acknowledges on precisely this point.[40]

In this group may also be included Renaissance humanists like G. Pico della Mirandola, Cardan, and Piccolomini, and mythographers familiar to the Pléiade, such as Valeriano, Verdier, and Natale Conti. Such sources reflect an interest in syncretic symbolism that appears frequently in the sonnets themselves. The medical writers adduced in the *Théorèmes* include obscurer sources as well as Galen, Hippocrates, and the celebrated French physician Fernel. It need hardly be said that all these sources are exploited for purely Christian ends—for proof of doctrine by reference to

[38] La Ceppède draws on the *Metaphysics, Physics, Meteorology, Histories of Animals, Rhetoric, De anima, De caelo.*

[39] Proba Falconia's verse, together with the Sibylline oracles (also freely used by La Ceppède), appears in, e.g., Bigne, *Sacra bibliotheca sanctorum patrum* (Paris, 1575-9), on which see below.

[40] e.g. I, p. 238.

historical fact, prophecy, and philosophical argument, and for exegesis of the sacred text. This willingness to draw upon the ancient world and on contemporary secular thought is a symptom of La Ceppède's humanism—a devout humanism with a rational strain.

The religious writings naturally form the largest group. The vast majority are exegetic rather than devotional or theological works. They may be subdivided into four historical phases or currents: first, the exegesis of the early Church Fathers; second, that of the contemplative orders from the seventh century through a period of eclipse by scholasticism to revival in the fifteenth and sixteenth centuries; third, scholastic biblical commentary and theology from the twelfth century; and fourth, overlapping with the latter, the comprehensive Catholic exegetes of the Counter-Reformation. This represents the whole of the Catholic tradition in biblical exposition. The next step is to determine where La Ceppède's debt is heaviest, and in what ways the various parts of the tradition affect his conception of the Bible and ultimately of poetry.[41]

The early Church Fathers developed the principle of the unity of the Old and New Testaments that was to dominate biblical scholarship throughout the Middle Ages. Their position was based on the assumption that the Bible was a metaphorical system enveloping divine oracles discernible by the inspired exegete. This led to the elaboration of the theory of the fourfold sense of Scripture summarized in the scholastic adage:

> Littera gesta docet; quid credas allegoria;
> Moralia quid agas; quo tendas anagogia.

La Ceppède could hardly have failed to assimilate this principle, and he is careful to base it on impeccable patristic authority. The early development of the tradition is represented in his use of Lactantius, Clement of Rome, Ignatius of Antioch, Justin Martyr, Irenaeus, Hippolytus, Clement of Alexandria, Epiphanius, Leo, and others up to John of Damascus. The abstract Platonist current of abundant allegorical interpretation is reflected in his extensive use of Origen, and of Origen's followers Ambrose and Hilary.

---

[41] On the history of exegesis see, e.g., *Cambridge History of the Bible*; Smalley, *Study of the Bible*; Lubac, *Exégèse médiévale*; Daniélou, *Sacramentum Futuri*; also Berger, *La Bible au seizième siècle*.

However, his outstanding debt is to the three great doctors of the fourth and fifth centuries, Jerome, Augustine, and John Chrysostom. The three have in common the desire to regulate biblical exegesis and to give due weight to both the literal and the spiritual sense. Thus La Ceppède gives Jerome's rules in justification of certain typologies (e.g. I, pp. 130, 458; II, p. 547), his resolutions of textual inconsistencies (e.g. I, pp. 338, 357), and his accounts of biblical geography (I, p. 503; II, p. 479). Chrysostom provides interpretation of the Gospel narrative and christological speculation of a non-allegorical nature based on the letter of the text (e.g. I, pp. 94, 136), and explanation and judgement on the behaviour of participants (e.g. I, pp. 211, 267). Augustine's influence on the *Théorèmes* is difficult to summarize or define.[42] It is to Augustine, for example, that La Ceppède turns not only for allegory and typology (e.g. I, pp. 411, 500), but also for information on Jewish institutions (e.g. I, p. 274), and for solutions to problems of inconsistency (e.g. I, pp. 207, 418). More typically perhaps he draws on Augustine in order to back up pious expansion of the Gospel text (e.g. I, pp. 41, 407) and moral reflection on it (e.g. II, pp. 54, 375). But he goes right to the core of Augustinian theology when he writes on faith and intellect in the commentary on the doubts of Thomas (II. iii, 'vœu pour la fin de ce liure'). The purpose of his poetry is to inculcate faith (II. iii, 'vœu'). As the authority for the primacy of faith over reason La Ceppède adduces (II, p. 534) Augustine's 'intellectus enim merces est fidei. Ergo noli quaerere intellegere ut credas, sed crede ut intellegas'.[43] Whether he was fully aware of the implications of such a principle is unclear. Certainly it coexists beside, and does not necessarily contradict, the intellectualist element and the admiration of pagan philosophers, evident elsewhere in the *Théorèmes*.

The borrowing from the Fathers was facilitated by sixteenth-century publishing ventures. Many editions and reprints in this field became available during the second half of the century.[44] Two such compilations used by La Ceppède as intermediate sources are worth specific mention. Bigne's *Sacra bibliotheca sanctorum patrum* appeared in Paris in 1575-9 and provided early writings

---

[42] Cf. attempts by McCall Probes, 'La Ceppède's *Théorèmes* and Augustinian Sources' and 'La Ceppède's Discriminatory Use of St. Augustine'.

[43] *In Joannis Evangelium Tractatus*, 29 (Migne, *Patrologia Latina*, vol. 35, col. 1630).

[44] See Dagens, *Bibliographie*.

on Scripture, doctrine, and morals combined with sacred Latin poetry, the Greek text of the so-called *Apostolic Constitutions*, pieced together by the pseudo-Clement from alleged apostolic sources, was published in 1563 by the Jesuit Torres (Turrianus), and the Latin translation by J. C. Bovio appeared in the same year. An important event, as the work had been completely unknown in the West throughout the Middle Ages. La Ceppède's use of both these publications illustrates his concern to ground his verse in the most authentic documents made available by recent scholarship.

The mystical and neo-Platonic side of Augustine is continued in the exegetes of the theologians of the monastic centuries and can be said to culminate in the fifteenth-century mystics and the devotional writers of the Reformation and Counter-Reformation. This is the group referred to by La Ceppède as 'les contemplatifs'. Until the sixteenth century at least typological and allegorical interpretations are still basic. On them, however, is built a technique of commentary and expansion which emphasizes moral and reflective application of Scripture for spiritual rather than for intellectual benefit. Gregory the Great, Bernard of Clairvaux, and Bonaventure are La Ceppède's authoritative sources for this tradition. Bonaventure's works are cited relatively little, be it on predominantly meditative points (e.g. the *Stimulus divini amoris* in I. p. 171, the *Meditationes vitae Christi* in II, p. 162), or on factual and theological matters (e.g. the commentary on Luke in II, p. 225). On the other hand, Gregory's *Homilies* on the Gospels (e.g. I, p. 25: II, p. 20) and the *Moralia in Job* (e.g. II, pp. 570–1), in which moral allegory and devotional response are stressed, are used extensively. La Ceppède admires Bernard's rich rhetoric, his 'belles paroles' (II, p. 99). In one instance (II. ii, 'vœu') his subjective interpretation[45] is explicitly preferred to the more abstract one of Gregory. Exactly the same motives are behind the borrowings from the works of the Carthusian mystics—the *De vita Christi* of Ludolphus (e.g. I, p. 369), and the Scriptural Commentaries of Dionysius (e.g. I, p. 168). There are single references to Tauler's and Gerson's meditative works on the Passion (I, pp. 435 and 80 respectively), to the sermons of the Dominican preacher Vincent Ferrier (II, p. 307), and to Erasmus's *Adagia* (I, p. 31).

---

[45] *In ascensione Domini*, sermo 1 (Migne, vol. 183, col. 301).

In comparison with Augustine, Gregory, and Bernard the acknowledged instances of the use of sixteenth-century devotional writers (as opposed to the prominent theologians and exegetes) are surprisingly few. The single reference (I, p. 25) to Luis Vives is from his commentary on the *Civitas Dei*, but the quotation concerns the notion of fate and has no meditative purpose. Guevara's *Livre du Mont de Calvaire* (translated by Belleforest, 1589) is cited for a number of manifestly meditative purposes, but mainly in Book iii of Part I. La Ceppède is aware that Guevara is imitating his contemplative predecessor, Bernard. This may account for the general predominance of earlier meditative writings over the later. Diego de Estella's *Enarrationes in Evangelium secundum Lucam* (1580) is quoted not only for meditative comment (e.g. I, p. 424) but also for his testimony on narrative consistency in the Gospels (e.g. I, p. 240) and on typologies (e.g. II, p. 431), for such historical pieces of information as the birthplace of Pontius Pilate (I, p. 284), and for his contribution to the purely theological problem of the nature of Christ's sweating of blood (I, p. 87). Vincenzo Bruno's *Méditations sur les mystères de la Passion et Résurrection* (translated Philibert du Sault, 1596) is drawn on for broad allegorical interpretations (e.g. II, pp. 341, 358, 370) and philological remarks (e.g. I, p. 409). The sermons for Lent by Jacques Suarez provide similar material.[46] La Ceppède relates Crespet's *Triomphe de Jésus et voyage de l'âme* (1586) to Bernard (I, p. 338), and in conjunction with the earlier contemplatives his work furnishes much of the emotive and graphic description of the third book of Part I of the *Théorèmes*. Panigarola's *Cent sermons sur la Passion* (translated Chappuys, 1586), another important devotional work, is mentioned once only (I, p. 100). The most important of the sixteenth-century devotional works employed is Luis de Granada's *Libro de la oracion y meditacion* (1554)[47] and *Predications* (translated N. Colin, 1582). It is possible that Granada's meditative techniques influenced La Ceppède; but the fact remains that the only explicit references tend to adduce his work in order to support points of literal or allegorical interpretations (e.g. I, pp. 294, 390).

There is thus little doubt that La Ceppède knew and used a wide

---

[46] The *Trésor quadragésimal*.
[47] Translated by Belleforest with the title *Le Vray chemin et adresse pour acquerir et parvenir à la grace de Dieu . . .* , Paris, 1579.

range of devotional treatises.[48] But there is little to suggest the specific influence of systematic meditation. In the first place, there is no direct evidence that La Ceppède used Loyola's *Spiritual Exercises*. The Ignatius referred to is Ignatius of Antioch—a significant difference which underlines his preference for early authorities.[49] Secondly, his use of the meditative works explicitly referred to does not always reflect what are usually thought of as their chief characteristics. Thirdly, the references to the modern devotional treatises tend to be found mainly in Book iii of Part I, that is, in the section most susceptible of meditative treatment, and in the section probably composed during the civil war period and La Ceppède's retreat from active life. No doubt he absorbed the attitudes and some of the rhetoric of the devotional tradition; but the weight of the evidence makes it necessary to place this fact in the context of other influences absorbed over the long period of composition.

As the *Théorèmes* progressed they became increasingly intellectual. Although meditative technique included 'analysis', this was usually in a form and context that made it distinguishable from theology proper. While the rational speculations of the Church Fathers were combined with prayer and contemplation, the scholastic theology was felt by the devotional movement to be uncongenial. Yet, La Ceppède owes a good deal to the scholarly and philosophical current of biblical exegesis. The medieval schools tended to treat the Bible primarily as a source of knowledge on intellectual and moral matters, and to dwell on the literal level with the aid of Jerome's and Augustine's historical explanations.[50] One current of this tradition is represented in La Ceppède's references by Isidore of Seville, Alcuin, Rabanus Maurus, and, in particular Bede. But it is to the scholasticism of the twelfth century and

---

[48] In a few cases in I. iii the general style of a passage in the sonnets is attributed to meditative sources. Thus: 'Toute la conception de ce Sonnet est des contemplatifs, de Ludolphe, au chapitre 48. de la 2. partie, de Gueuarre au 1. liure du Mont de Caluaire chapitre 32. de Crespet Iournée, 28' (I, p. 380). Cf. also I, p. 385.

[49] See Cave, *Devotional Poetry*, p. 91, for the assumption that the reference is to Loyola; cf. also Lawrence, 'La Ceppède's *Théorèmes* and Ignatian Meditation'. La Ceppède refers expressly to 'Ignace Archeuesque d'Antioche & Disciple de S. Iean' (I, p. 440) and to his epistles to Christians at Tralles, Smyrna, and Tarsus (published in Bigne), and the letter allegedly written to the Virgin. See, e.g., I, pp. 52–3, 356; II, pp. 290, 517.

[50] Cf. *Cambridge History of the Bible*, vol. ii. ch. 6.

after, or perhaps more precisely to Thomism, that La Ceppède's debt is most significant. Thomas Aquinas's *Catena aurea* was important as a vehicle for the biblical commentaries of Greek and Byzantine Fathers. Along with the *Sacra bibliotheca sanctorum patrum* and the *Glossa ordinaria*, it is perhaps La Ceppède's chief source for these writings. Quotations from the *Catena* primarily concern matters of fact in the Gospel narrative (e.g. I, pp. 191, 221, 264, 456, 457; II, p. 221), and theological and ethical questions (e.g. I, pp. 321, 481). This does not mean that La Ceppède is interested only in Aquinas as compiler, for both parts of the *Théorèmes* (with, however, a significantly reduced number of references in I. iii) draw heavily from the *Summa theologiae* for overtly theological and philosophical themes such as destiny and providence (I, pp. 26, 65), the hypostatic union (I, p. 61; II, p. 463), the refutation of aspects of Manichaean heresy (II, p. 204), and so on.

It is not simply a case of the inevitable veneration of the most prominent doctor of the Middle Ages. La Ceppède's references follow the Thomist tradition into the sixteenth-century Spanish and Italian revival of scholasticism. He refers to Cajetan's commentary on the works of Aquinas as well as to his biblical exegesis, and to the work of Dominic Soto and Dominic Bañez. Considerably more extensive is his borrowing from Franciscus Suarez's *Disputationes metaphysicae* and his commentaries on Aquinas's *Summa*.[51]

This tradition to some extent overlaps with the fourth group of religious writing used by La Ceppède, namely the biblical commentary proper of the neo-scholastic Counter-Reformation. The references to this body of material are extraordinarily comprehensive. It seems highly probable that this has a direct relevance to the conception and composition of the *Théorèmes* as a whole. There is much variety between individual exegetes, but certain common characteristics stand out. Most of them appear to conceive their work as a riposte to Protestant biblical scholarship, and there is a corresponding tendency to dwell on the literal level in the light of positive theology. This by no means implies that the Fathers and Scholastics are abandoned. Indeed the aim is to combine textual scholarship with tradition, and the result is an encyclopedic exploitation of all previous trends with an emphasis on dogmatics. The vast commentaries of this period were, moreover, intended

---

[51] Cf. above, pp. 60, 62.

not only as original works of scholarship but also as compendiums for the use of pulpit orators and missioners. They were clearly reference works for La Ceppède, and perhaps for other religious poets.

A rapid survey will give some idea of the extent of La Ceppède's borrowing from this rich area. He refers to Sixtus of Siena's commentaries published in Bigne's *Bibliotheca* (II, pp. 64, 428, 566), and it is possible that he knew his encyclopedic work on exegetic method, the *Bibliotheca sancta* (1566), which was immensely influential throughout the rest of the century. Sixtus's position is fairly typical of that adopted in Catholic exegesis at this time and has some obvious affinities with the procedures of the *Théorèmes*. He accepts a twofold literal sense (proper or metaphorical), and a spiritual or mystical sense divisible into many varieties. Translations and exegesis are closely related—an important fact since the *Théorèmes* are in the first place biblical paraphrases. Sixtus's proposed methods draw on all previous traditions. The interpreter's task involves the drawing-up of concordances and the establishment of shades of meaning, the construction of a continuous narrative using, if necessary, profane historians, the systematic rendering of the two basic sense levels, and finally disputations on points arising from the text and carried through in the scholastic manner.[52]

Spanish biblical studies are also fully represented. There are brief references, as has been seen, to Salmeron's sixteen-volume commentary on the New Testament, to Ribera's commentaries (1587) on the Prophets ('sensum eorundem Prophetarum historicum, et moralem, persaepe etiam allegoricum complectentes'), and to Pineda's commentaries on Job (1597–1601). Pereyra's commentaries are mentioned far more often. His commentaries and disputations on Genesis (1591–9) furnish allegorical and typological interpretations (e.g. II, pp. 125, 128, 364), authority for the preference of literal over miraculous meaning (I, p. 100), biblical history (e.g. I, pp. 122, 128), and some theological and philosophical speculation on the nature of stars (II, p. 581), the creation of light (II, pp. 629–30), and other topics. His work attacking astrology is also used.[53] The *Commentaria in concordiam et historiam evangelicam* (1599–1611) by the Portuguese Jesuit Barradas provide

[52] Cf. *Cambridge History of the Bible*, vol. iii. pp. 206 ff.
[53] *Adversus fallaces et superstitiosas artes* . . . , Ingolstadt, 1591.

La Ceppède with much of the theological and historical ground-work for the second part of the *Théorèmes*, especially in the sections dealing with the resurrection of the body (e.g. pp. 74, 75, 79, 87, 306), with Peter (e.g. pp. 381, 382, 386), the Ascension (e.g. p. 458), and Pentecost (e.g. pp. 589, 595, 630–1). Toletus's commentary on John is used widely throughout both parts of the *Théorèmes* for textual variants (e.g. I, p. 500), for philological interpretations (e.g. I, pp. 282, 323, 324), the historical facts of the Gospel narrative (e.g. I, p. 508; II, p. 284), and technical points of theology (e.g. I, p. 481; II, p. 534). Maldonatus, who took the chair of theology at the Collège de Clermont in 1564, was perhaps the most prominent theologian–exegete in France in the second half of the sixteenth century. His emphasis on scriptural and patristic authority was combined with discreet use of dialectics. He is frequently acknowledged by devotional poets.[54] However, La Ceppède's borrowings are from the *Commentarii in quattuor evangelistas* (1596–7), which provides yet another source for pa-tristic readings. At the same time it is used, as one would expect, for textual and historical details of the Gospels (e.g. I, pp. 29, 122; II, p. 435) and for the theological implications of their narratives (e.g. I, pp. 101, 103, 105, 106). The work of Cornelius Jansen (Bishop of Ghent) directed itself to an exact execution of the Tridentine decrees. His *Commentarius in concordiam et totam historiam evangelicam* (1572) insisted on the importance of the literal as opposed to the mystical interpretation of the Bible, and on the importance of the original texts for a full understanding of the Vulgate. La Ceppède constantly adduces Jansen's opinion on, for instance, the literal truth of the agony and bloody sweat (I, p. 100), Pilate's motivation (I, p. 209), Hebraisms in the Vulgate (I, p. 217), and the need for divine aid in revealing the hidden meanings of Scripture (II, pp. 431–2), as well as on such theological subleties as the nature of the risen Christ's digestion (II, p. 302). To a lesser extent La Ceppède uses Cornelius a Lapide, whose voluminous commentaries on the whole Bible (excluding the Psalms and Job)[55] perhaps epitomize this era of Catholic Bible study. Encyclopedic in their sources, these commentaries aim to expound not only the literal but also the allegorical and typological levels. Like other contemporary works they are intended to serve

---

[54] Cf. Cave, *Devotional Poetry*, pp. 10, 74.
[55] Various *Commentaria* published from 1614.

both the historical and scientific study of the Bible and the purposes of pious meditation and pulpit exposition. Finally, mention should be made of La Ceppède's compatriot Jean de Lorin, whose commentary on Acts affords patristic material and theological opinion (II, p. 595), and of Thomas Beaulxamis, who was preacher at the court of Charles IX and Henry III, and who wrote detailed dogmatic and historical works on the Eucharist, Passion, and Resurrection.[56]

What is immediately striking about La Ceppède's exegetic sources is the comprehensive way in which they reflect different parts of the tradition. There is some evolution in choice of sources. While the Fathers seem to exert an influence at all times, there is a concentration of references to sixteenth-century meditative works in Book iii of Part I. In Books i and ii and in all the books of Part II the transition seems to be on the one hand to the work of the scholastic and neo-scholastic tradition, and on the other to the expanding corpus of Catholic Scriptural commentary. This does not mean that the *Théorèmes* are not infused with the devotional spirit. But there is a distinction between the meditative exercise as a genre of religious literature and the devotional attitudes that colour the whole of contemporary religious life. The assumption that the real basis of the *Théorèmes* is the Bible and methods of biblical analysis goes far towards explaining its scale and diversity, the rich structure of its language, and the underlying notion of poetry. It also helps to throw light on La Ceppède's intellectual orientation.

It will be instructive to consider the ways in which La Ceppède is conscious of the modes of biblical interpretation, and the types of sonnet these produce. The *Théorèmes* as a whole can be looked at in terms of four different methods of approach contained by the tradition: (i) the literal and historical approach; (ii) the *quaestio* or disquisition in the scholastic manner on a different point of interpretation; (iii) the 'morality', or moral application of a passage; (iv) the 'figurative' levels of interpretation. At all these levels questions of theology may come into play.

There is no doubt that La Ceppède thought of his work in terms of biblical exegesis. In II. ii. 44 he accepts the tradition that

---

[56] Also known as Beauxalmis, Bellamicus, Pulcher amicus. Cf. his *Commentaria in evangelicam historiam sive concordia ex antiquis Ecclesiae Patribus congesta*, Paris, 1570; *In sacrosanctam coenae mysteriam, passionem et resurrectionem . . . homeliae et tabulae . . .* , Paris, 1570.

Jesus revealed to his disciples hidden Scriptural proofs of his Messiahship. In the accompanying note there is a more explicit explanation of the difficulty of Scripture:

Et mesmes les plus grands Docteurs de la Loy n'ont pas entendu les Escritures. Aussi ne sont elles pas si faciles & triuiales qu'il ne soit pas besoin d'vn grand & clair esprit pour les interpreter. Et n'a point voulu le Seigneur les rendre plus claires, afin qu'on ne les prophanat, & pour nous rendre plus studieux & curieux à les entendre. (II, p. 243)

This is a characteristic Counter-Reformation statement. There is a warning against adherence to the literal or 'carnal' sense of Scripture that benighted the Jews (II, p. 358) and the disciples before Jesus's revelation (II, p. 439). Special grace is necessary for correct interpretation:

... Si le Christ ne délie l'Esprit, il ne peut rien dans les cayers Sacrez. (II. iii. 2, ll. 13–14)

The accompanying annotation cites the passage from Jansenius on which these words are based.[57]

When La Ceppède's use of the literal and historical mode of interpretation is examined, complications begin to appear. He condemns exclusive concentration on the letter of the text. On the one hand he uses such authors as Philo and Josephus[58] to give historical substance to his biblical narrative. On the other his interest in the letter of the text takes the form of philological and rhetorical analysis aimed at revealing concealed truth. The attempt to reconcile the literal with the metaphorical leads to some ambiguities. The problem of the border-line between literal and spiritual levels of meaning had been recognized and debated by scholastic writers.[59] Many of the digressions in the notes to the *Théorèmes* have this difficulty in the background, as for instance in the note on II. i. 50, lines 12–13 which derive from Psalm 21:

---

[57] Pleraque enim, imò omnia penè quae de Christo sunt in scripturis tecte & sub vmbris dicta sunt, sicque se habent vt & in alios aliquatenus tum dicta videantur . . .: proinde nisi is mentem hominis aperiat, qui habet clauem Dauid, qui claudit & nemo aperit, aperit & nemo claudit, propter velamen scripturarum & tenebras mentis humanae, nequaquam intelligere valet quae de Christo sunt, scripturas. (*Concordia*, ch. 150, cited by La Ceppède, II, pp. 431–2.)

[58] Bourgoing's translation (1558) rather than Génébrard's (1578).

[59] Cf. Smalley, *Study of the Bible*, pp. 234 ff.

Tout ce pseau. entier est interpreté purement de Iesus-Christ, en tout sens: non seulement prophetique & mysterieux: mais encore litteral suiuant vne vieille glose des Hebrieux de plus de 2000 ans. au raport de Maistre Genebrard lequel est aussi de cet auis. (II, p. 142)

La Ceppède further adduces Nicholas of Lyra, and the title of the psalm in the Greek and Hebrew versions. The sense in which the term 'litteral' is used is ambiguous. The crux of the problem of the distinction between literal and spiritual levels in scholastic thinking was whether the distinction applied to the text itself or to the method of interpretation. In the case of the Psalms there was the additional problem of the identity of the first person. The interpretation of Génébrard followed by La Ceppède is that 'le Psalmiste a proprement appellé Iésus-Christ vn Cerf, ou biche' (II. p. 143). The interpretation is not really literal at all, except in the sense of its being historical. That is to say, it is claimed that the Psalmist's historical intention was to use a poetic metaphor deliberately apropos of Christ. This kind of confusion has consequences for the language and style of the *Théorèmes*.

Theological subtleties often depend on which level of interpretation is adopted. Thus the problems raised by the notion of Christ's sitting at the right hand of God (Hebrews 1: 13) are considered in terms of alternative literal and metaphorical interpretations (I. ii. 36, n. 1). The note is formally divided into three 'questions' or 'points'. In the first question, the meaning of the difficult phrase is said to be 'L'honneur. et la gloire de la Diuinité'. To the question whether Christ has the position as God or as man La Ceppède considers applying the scholastic concept of 'communication des idiomes' whereby human attributes are transferable to God, but prefers a literal interpretation. He is clearly avoiding metaphor here in order not to dilute dogma: 'Or c'est vn article de nostre foy que l'humanité glorieuse du fils de Dieu est montée au Ciel, non en sens metaphorique, mais réellement' (I, p. 259). The final 'question', the reconciliation of divergent texts, is resolved by the explicit rejection of solutions not based on a literal interpretation. In this case La Ceppède's answer rests on his arguing the synonymy of 'stare' and 'sedere' in biblical style. What is important is the principle of preference for the literal, whether by this is meant textual or historical.

This principle has even wider implications, as can be seen if a close examination is made of the most highly developed of the annotations—the long essay on the sweating of blood. The problem of the level of interpretation is stated at the outset:

> Cette rouge humeur . . . a remply d'estonnement vn grand nombre d'esprits, à tant que les aucuns l'ont tout à fait mescrue . . . Les autres l'ont prinse pour simple comparaison, comme Euthymius . . . Les autres en font vne hiperbole comme Theophil. sur ce passage: les autres l'allegorisent & la tournent au sens mystique (sans toutesfois nier le littéral) comme Beda . . . (I, pp. 85–6)

La Ceppède, however, sets out to prove that 'Iesus-Christ a sué le vray sang, comme la lettre de l'Euangile le marque expressement' (I, p. 86). His proof rests on both ecclesiastical and non-ecclesiastical writing, and on his own logic.[60] The most interesting part of the piece deals with the question whether the phenomenon is natural or miraculous. La Ceppède proceeds dialectically, first citing the case for both points of view. The arguments in favour of a miracle are upheld by Aquinas and the medical opinion of Rhodiginus, J.-B. Silvatique, and 'le subtil Hierosme Cardan', in general by the Fathers and Doctors of the Church, and the contemplatives Estella and Panigarola. Nevertheless, they are rejected in favour of the contrary view which is 'plus probable & plus veritable, & par raison & par authoritez' (I, p. 101). The prime reason for taking this line is revealing not only for his attitude towards Scriptural exegesis, but also for his general intellectual orientation:

> La premiere raison est, qu'en toute bonne discipline il ne faut jamais recourir aux causes extraordinaires, quand les ordinaires suffisent; & de mesme en traitant & interpretant les saintes lettres, il ne faut jamais recourir aux miracles ny à l'absolue puissance de Dieu, sans necessité, c'est à dire, qu'au cas du defaut des causes & raisons natureles. (I, p. 101)

Then La Ceppède argues syllogistically that sweating blood is a natural phenomenon, that its occasional occurrence implies possibility (a principle he derives from Averroes through Jean-Baptiste Silvatique), and therefore that it is to be believed that it was natural rather than miraculous. Much evidence is adduced from authority and from experience to prove the major premiss. Contemporary medical opinion,[61] personal communications,

---

[60] He feels free to exercise his own exegetic skill freely, since Trent issued no decree on this subject (see I, p. 111).

[61] e.g. Rondelet (*Docteur régent* at Montpellier), Louis Duret, Fernel, Merindol (professor of medicine at Aix), Thomas Feyens.

manuscript archives, and biography are all drawn into the argument.[62] But after this proof, which is firmly grounded in contemporary medical science, La Ceppède offers a second, entirely metaphysical argument, though it too has humanist implications in a somewhat wider sense. The divine intention behind the revelation of the bloody sweat was 'pour nous assurer de la verité de la nature humaine de Iesus-Christ, & pour nous exprimer l'extreme violence de ses douleurs, cause de son agonie, & tres-asseuré tesmoignage de son amour' (I, p. 104). The blood cannot be miraculous, or it would not be due to psychological conflict and agony—in which case 'nous perdons cette preuue de sa reelle humanité'. And for La Ceppède Christ's humanity, sacrifice, and love are prime doctrines which he constantly stresses in his work. To clinch his case, however, he returns to proofs of a medical nature. The argument in favour of a miracle is finally refuted with the aid of a recent case history (1596) communicated by the professor of medicine at Aix, Merindol, and references to Fernel's *Physiologia* and the *De viribus imaginationis* of Thomas Feyens.[63] The most interesting of these refutations depends on the argument that miracles are the effect of the imaginative powers—a theory with a medically and theologically orthodox pedigree from Hippocrates and Galen, Jerome and Aquinas, to Feyens and Pereyra.[64] La Ceppède's concern to establish a literal interpretation leads him to conclusions which are, in this instance, and within orthodox limits, rational and sceptical:

C'est la force de cette imagination qui dans vne nuict blanchit entierement le poil d'vn condamné en l'auril de ses ans; qui fit mourir deux autres condamnés, ores que le bourreau ne les touchast, l'vn qu'avec vne houssine, & l'autre qu'auec vn linge mouillé; & qui a produit mille autres teles merueilles (que l'ignorance a creu miracles) marquées en diuers endroits par les bons autheurs ... (I, pp. 109–10)

La Ceppède's views on this issue are reminiscent of Montaigne's in 'De la force de l'imagination'.

La Ceppède's conclusion combines rational exegesis and devotion. The bloody sweat is not literally miraculous; but it is thereby

---

[62] Includes 'vn vieux manuscrit dans la Bibliothèque de l'Obseruance d'Aix sans le nom de l'autheur)', and Marinus Barletius, *Historia de vita et gestis Scanderbegi, Epirotarum principis*, Rome, 1520.
[63] I, pp. 106 ff.   [64] See Busson, *Le Rationalisme*, pp. 251 ff.

the more marvellous, since it betokens Christ's love and suffering for humanity. This attempt to reconcile faith and reason is somewhat analogous to the reconciliation of the literal and spiritual levels of the Psalm mentioned above. In general, the tendency to seek natural rather than supernatural explanations represents a phase of Catholic exegesis coloured by sixteenth-century humanism.

Somewhere between the literal and spiritual senses lay the moral sense, the exposition of which was developed with ingenious applications in the private and political spheres in the scholastic period. It might simply be a matter of pointing the 'moral' in the manner of a sermon. Thus La Ceppède points out 'le sens Moral de l'absence de sainct Thomas de la congrégation de ses condisciples (II. ii. 72, n. 4). The spices of the Magdalen receive an allegorical meditative treatment in order to extract the moral sense (I, p. 511). And the type of moral application of Scripture to topical events has already been seen above in connection with the sonnets which use the Pilate episode as the basis for reflection on the duties of magistrates, and the need for clerical training.

But the frame of reference of La Ceppède's ethical digressions is the much broader one of the Aristotelian and Thomist theory of the passions.[65] While he adheres strictly to patristic and scholastic authority on the psychology of Christ (e.g. I, pp. 47, 84), there are, in his moral psychology of man, modifications of the traditional schema that have a humanist character. In the first place, La Ceppède's tendency is to emphasize the category of the virtuous passions and their compatibility with reason (in, for instance, I, pp. 89 ff., where he argues for the virtuousness of anger). But more importantly, he develops the notion of ethical moderation in sonnet II. ii, 'vœu', and its commentary. The sonnet is a mystical exposition of the notion of the struggle between love of God and love of the world. The accompanying note, however, explaining this distinction, is worked out in an entirely different tone and has somewhat different implications. The starting-point is the statement from the *Nicomachean Ethics* that 'tous les hommes par l'instinct naturel cherchent & suiuent la delectation: c'ét à dire la volupté' (II, p. 147). La Ceppède's elaboration of this tends in two directions, and his sources are correspondingly diverse. As well as relying on Aristotle, La Ceppède draws on Plato, Damascene, and

[65] See Levi, *French Moralists*.

Josse Clichtowe. The discernible types of 'volupté' are cross-classified in the traditional manner. According to one set of criteria there are firstly pleasures of the soul alone, including 'sçauoir' and 'contemplation', and secondly pleasures of the body and soul together, covering bodily pleasure, 'quoique le corps en iouysse conioinctement auec l'esprit' (II. p. 147). According to a second criterion there are on the one hand natural and necessary pleasures, for example, 'l'vsage des viandes', and on the other, natural but unnecessary pleasures, such as 'l'appariage de l'homme & de la femme'. By a third criterion there are true and false pleasures. This distinction leads to a double ethical norm. The 'fausses voluptés' are, of course, condemned (pp. 148–9). But the permitted pleasures are first of all 'celles de l'ame, qui consistent en la speculation de la verité, & aux offices de la vertu' (p. 148). This was to be expected, but no more is said of it. The second type is dealt with much more fully in terms of an ideal of the ethical mean:

Et encor celles du corps & de l'ame ensemble, moderées si iustement par la raison que leur vsage n'aporte point d'amertume, ny d'excés, ny de repentance, & ne nous asseruit, ny empesche point de bien faire. (p. 148)

If this position has certain affinities with Montaigne, the formulation of more cautious rules about how the created world may be legitimately enjoyed suggests François de Sales:

Il nous est bien permis de nous plaire modestement en la beauté des choses creées: Mais il ne faut pas tellement flatter le goust, ny en aualler si auidement les douceurs que nostre affection se tourne en furie . . . Le plaisir que nous auons au goust des viandes & du vin dont nous sommes nourris, est permis: Mais il faut bien prendre garde que la friandise ne nous iette au desordre de Vitellius . . . Le repos et la delicatesse du corps n'ont simplement rien de mauuais: Mais il faut bien nous garder de nous lascher à la faineantise . . . L'amour des femmes (auquel comme par excellence entre toutes les delices, tout chacun a donné le nom de volupté) est naturel, et peut estre innocent. Mais s'il outre-passe les loix de Dieu, & l'honnesteté, & se déborde aux excés, il deuient brutal, & se tourne en rage, & frenezie. (pp. 148–51)

Thus concessions to human nature are made only to be retracted or qualified. A precarious moderation is sought that will resolve the contradiction between the extremes.

The contrast is apparent also in the fact that La Ceppède not only expounds this ethic of relative moderation (with its own inner tensions), but also a more exacting one requiring concentrated contemplation and abstraction from the world:

. . . le cœur de l'homme rempli de l'amour charnel des hommes, des femmes, ou de soy-mesme, & des autres desirs passionnez du monde, ne peut sans premier en estre vuidé receuoir, & donner place à l'amour de l'Eternel. (II, p. 408)

The tension between these two standpoints—the relative indulgence towards human nature versus its rejection—is not resolved in any formal manner. It illustrates a dichotomy that is constant on many levels throughout La Ceppède's poetry.

As an extension of these oppositions one might consider on the exegetic level the coexistence of literal (textual and historical) interpretation with the figurative or 'spiritual'. In spite of the fact that La Ceppède shows a humanist concern with the literal, it is worth considering to what extent the metaphorical mode comes into his use of the Bible, and also whether such a method of interpretation has any wider implications. The spiritual level of biblical interpretation can be reduced to two types: the allegorical, which is a metaphorical mode playing down the literal sense; and the typological, which, though it may sometimes involve allegory, depends primarily on accepting one literal historical fact as somehow analogous to an equally literal historical fact separated from it in time.[66]

La Ceppède himself briefly summarizes the orthodox theory of types or figures.[67] The hidden sense of Scripture is assumed to have been resolved in the life of Christ:

> Il nous a dechiffré tous les Tableaux secrets,
> La verité succede à l'ombre des Figures:
> La vieille Loy fait place à ses nouueaux Decrets. (I. iii. 79)

[66] Anagogical and tropological senses are also distinguished. The difference concerns the content of the figurative meaning, which is eschatological and devotional, respectively. They may be regarded as forms of allegorical interpretation in the broad sense that the figurative content is deduced from a literal term regarded as a mere container. This means they are theoretically distinct from typology, as stated.

[67] Typology enjoyed a prime position in exegesis thanks to its origin in the Pauline epistles (Romans 5: 14; 1 Corinthians 10: 6, 11; Galatians 4: 21–31; Hebrews 9: 24). For a contemporary discussion of the meanings of the term 'figure', which La Ceppède uses exclusively for 'type', see Richeome, *Œuvres*, vol. ii, pp. 109 ff. On this cf. also Auerbach, *Scenes from the Drama of European Literature*, and ch. V below.

The word 'secrets' is explained with the aid of Leo the Great and Cornelius Musso in a way that provides a definition of figures:

C'est à dire les figures, qui nous auoient representé le Christ sous diuers noms, diuerses personnes, & diuers mystères, tout cela est consommé, & changé en la verité de la chose figurée . . . (I, p. 476)

He attempts also to set up a principle of correspondence between what he calls 'le figurant' and 'le figuré'. The problem arises precisely from La Ceppède's concern with historical accuracy. The question is whether the sale of Joseph and that of Jesus can be related if the currencies were not equivalent or the prices different. He concludes:

[il n'est pas] precisement necessaire que la figure soit conforme en tout & du tout à la chose figurée (comme disent les Peres) . . . . Il suffit . . . que la figure soit accomplie en toutes ses autres circonstances principales . . . (I, p. 130)

This exegetic principle enables him to derive parallels fairly freely from both Old Testament and pagan sources, and to incorporate them in his poetry. The boundary between the typological and the allegorical is fluid, since the connection between two real events may depend not merely on the matching of similar features, but on the metaphorical interpretation of one of the events. In such cases, when objects are interpreted in a metaphorical manner, they are no longer 'figures', but 'hieroglyphs' or 'symbols'.[68] Thus, of the casting of lots for Christ's robe, it is said that 'Cet Acte de l'Eglise est le Hieroglyphique' (I. iii. 36). Although the episode prophesies a future occurrence, it does so symbolically and not through any real resemblance.

It should, however, be noted that symbolic interpretations are in general given only after the literal and historical level has been fully established. In the case of I. iii. 36 the elaborate interpretation of the spiritual sense comes after a straightforward narrative of the incident in which the soldiers cast lots. That such a procedure is deliberate is suggested by La Ceppède's remarks on his treatment

---

[68] On the Renaissance theory of hieroglyphs cf. Wind, *Pagan Mysteries*, pp. 12, 17, 207 ff.; and ch. V below. It should be noted that La Ceppède refers to Valeriano's *Hieroglyphica* (II, p. 145).

of Mark 16: 17–18 in II. ii. 100. The different levels of interpretation are clearly indicated:

Nous auons en la precédente Meditation (qui clot ce liure) couché les miracles promis aux croyants selon le sens literal. Nous les allegorisons en ce *Vœu*, & leur donnons vn sens moral selon les intentions de nostre deuoir . . . (II, p. 422)

Once the literal sense has been expounded, the prophecy that the disciples shall cast out devils may be allegorized in two senses. In his annotation La Ceppède goes on to consider the application of the allegory to the Church, but significantly prefers Bernard's application to the individual soul. At this point exegesis and personal devotion seem to coincide. Yet the process whereby this is arrived at depends not on systematic spiritual exercises. Rather, the frame of reference seems to be the exegetic conception of the layers of potential meaning inherent in the biblical text.

In La Ceppède's method of Scriptural interpretation, then, concern with the textual substance and its historical reference on the one hand coexists with the conception of typological and allegorical meaning on the other. It has also been seen that in expounding the letter of the text and its implications he is prepared, for devotional ends, to introduce the resources of humanist scholarship, and natural as well as moral philosophy. His preference is for natural rather than supernatural explanations. But alongside this view of the world is another, which has much in common with the allegorical interpretation of texts, and which is fundamental to the structure of the *Théorèmes*. Renaissance neo-Platonism encouraged a view of the world as a system of signs, which like the sacred text concealed meanings referring to the divine. Thus, in contrast to his statements on nature and miracles discussed above, La Ceppède can also write:

> De miracles diuers l'eternele intendance
> A lambrissé les murs de ce grand vniuers. (I. i. 63)

The analogies and correspondences discerned by exegetes in Scripture are also discerned in the physical world.[69] It is a view of the world that can be distinguished from the quasi-empirical

---

[69] Cf. the exposition of microcosm and macrocosm, II, pp. 356 f.; on such concepts Lenoble, *Histoire de l'idée de nature*; Foucault, *Les Mots et les choses*, chs. 2–4.

view implied in La Ceppède's use of Aristotelian science, medical
authority, and deductive logic in his exposition of Christ's agony.
But in the case of the higher mysteries contained in the text, for
instance the Resurrection, La Ceppède takes care to point out the
inappropriateness of human science:

La Resurrection de Christ, & apres luy de tous les mortels, est vn
article de foy: mais elle est purement hors & pardessus toutes les
forces, sciences, arts & Philosophies humaines, & partant bien loing
par de là tous les plus hauts secrets de la Physique, & de la medecine.
(II. p. 140)

Nevertheless, he does not entirely abandon the attempt to present
the Resurrection in terms of natural phenomena, and to do so
he has recourse to symbolic correspondence and the notion of
the hieroglyph. Thus in II. i. 47 the seasonal cycle constitutes
an 'argument pour preuuer la Resurrection par les euenemens
ordinaires de la nature' (II, p. 135). But since the Resurrection
is beyond natural philosophy its proper 'hieroglyphique' must be
a 'merueille' or 'prodige'. In sonnet II. i. 49 La Ceppède cites
Photinus and Averroes for the phenomenon of the liquid drawn
up by the sun from a golden vessel buried in the earth, which he
relates to the raising of Christ. He comments:

> Quel Esculape eut onc vn secret si parfaict?
> Quel Docteur nous aprend comme cela se fait?
> Comme souffre cecy la loy philosophique?
>   Il n'est point, ô mon Christ, de si profond sçauoir
> Qui sçache déchifrer ce grand hierogliphique.

In the context of the whole sonnet the term 'hiéroglyphique' here
refers not only to the Resurrection but also to the prodigy of
nature. Interpretation of the world and interpretation of Scripture
thus come together.

It will have become apparent that La Ceppède's exegetic framework reflects the atmosphere of devout humanism. The central
exegetic problem is the reconciliation of the literal with the spiritual sense. It is in the discourses arising from this preoccupation
that the similar problems are introduced of the reconciliation of
reason with faith, of natural law with supernatural event, of human
nature with ascetic contemplation. The desire to mediate generally
between the human and the divine leads to an emphasis on the
personal moral application of allegory. There are also implications

for the poetry. In the first place, the philological concern with the biblical text in its Hebrew, Greek, and Latin forms inevitably influences the style of the *Théorèmes* as a whole. Secondly, the various modes of discourse that constitute the work, that is the narrative, logical, emotive, and symbolic modes, suggest corresponding modes of biblical intrepretation. Moreover, the poems themselves are regarded by their author as texts for further exposition. Thus on the line 'Ils entombent celuy, qui n'a point de Tombeau' (I. iii. 99) La Ceppède remarks that 'Ce trait a deux sens, l'vn literal . . . l'autre spirituel . . .' Biblical exegesis sanctions ambiguity, and the use of imagery as vehicles of religious truth; it implies a view of language, of poetic style, and perhaps of the world, which is in marked contrast to that represented by Malherbe.

IV

LA CEPPÈDE AND CHRISTIAN POETICS

1. *The Converted Muse*

THE doctrine of divine fury, the associated myth of the
Muses, and the belief in the divine origin of poetry are
characteristic of Pléiade poetics; but they are, *mutatis
mutandis*, equally central to the theory of specifically religious
poetry in the sixteenth century. Plato's writing on poetic fury was
given detailed interpretation by Italian neo-Platonists. But the
theory of inspiration was already developed in a subtle manner in
Christian theology. Three types of inspiration are distinguishable:
plenary (as in Moses' illumination on Sinai); mantic or prophetic;
and mystical illumination granted to certain saints and contemplatives.[1] These types are related to literary inspiration by medieval
and Renaissance thinkers in two principal ways: by the analogy
between the roles of the prophet and the poet, and the development
of the doctrine of poetic inspiration as a specialized grace. The Old
Testament texts used in considerations of this kind lead to the
idea that prophets (and poets if the parallel is made) not only
possess exclusive means of deciphering God's will, but are also
appointed for moral reform.

These themes appear in various guises both in the classical
humanist and the Christian movements during the Renaissance.
The poet as initiate and moral leader is present in Horace:
Orpheus is represented as a sacerdotal interpreter of the gods
who brings ordered society to primitive man.[2] In his *Art poétique
françoys* Sebillet gives the christianized poetic genealogy including
Orpheus, but beginning now with Moses, 'premier divin Pöete',
passing through David, Solomon, the Prophets, the Greek and
Latin oracles, and concluding with Christian liturgical verse.[3]

---

[1] Cf. Baker, 'Certain Religious Elements in the English Doctrine of the
Inspired Poet'; Campbell, 'The Christian Muse'.

[2] Horace, *Ars poetica*, ll. 391 ff. Discussed by Castor, *Pléiade Poetics*,
pp. 26–7.

[3] Sebillet, *Art poétique*, ed. Gaiffe, p. 11 ff.

Vauquelin de Fresnaye and Du Bartas give essentially the same line of descent.[4] The role of the prophet as leader and orderer of society, whose prototype is Moses, converges with the Renaissance humanist conception of the poet as instructor of monarchs and of poetry as musical law and order corresponding to the harmony of the cosmos. It is a commonplace in sixteenth-century defences of poetry that verse was the ancient medium for the presentation of civil and moral laws.[5] But it is probably David who is the most influential Old Testament figure in the sixteenth-century French view of the religious poet. To him can be attached the beliefs about the poet's various functions: he is a lyric poet, prophet of obscure truths, leader, and teacher. These ideas about the poet's mission and responsibilities in society contained in the composite David-symbol are a basic aspect of Christian poetics, and may lie behind the cultivation of the psalm paraphrase.

But the most striking syncretic development in this area concerns the symbolic representation of the means and source of inspiration. In Christian theology poetic inspiration comes to be regarded as a specialized grace. The Christian account merges with the classical idea of divine madness at a fairly early stage. Prudentius invokes the same divine inspiration as was received by Moses.[6] Isidore of Seville's attempt in his *Etymologiae* to link the ancients' doctrine of divine fury with Christian inspiration would be widely known of the Middle Ages and to the Renaissance. Following Varro, he terms poets *vates* ('a vi mentis appellatos') as well as priests and prophets, and by a false etymology links *vates* with madness, *vesania*.[7] Prophets and poets, according to Isidore, are receptive of a range of visionary states from the Mosaic inspiration to intuition, all of which are gifts bestowed by the Holy Spirit.[8] According to Aquinas,[9] the prophet, seer, or *vates* not only has knowledge of future earthly events, but has access to celestial mysteries. Rapture (carefully opposed to vicious madness) is a degree of prophecy; through images prophets declare for the

---

[4] Vauquelin de la Fresnaye, *Art poétique*, ed. Pellissier, Book 3, ll. 799 ff.; Du Bartas, *L'Uranie* (*Works*, ed. Holmes, vol. ii), ll. 21 ff., 125 ff.

[5] Cf. Sebillet, *Art poétique*, pp. 9–10; Le Fèvre de La Boderie, *Encyclie*, pp. 56–7; Vauquelin, *Art poétique*, Book 3, ll. 825–6.

[6] *Hamartigenia*, ll. 339–45 (Migne, vol. 59, col. 1036).

[7] *Etymologiae*, 8, 7 (Migne, vol. 82, col. 308).

[8] *Etymologiae*, 8, 118 (Migne, vol. 82, cols. 309–10).

[9] *Summa theologiae*, IIaIIae, 171–8.

instruction of others things they know themselves through being taught by God; inspiration by the Holy Spirit is thus essential, and no previous natural disposition is required (IIaIIae, 172, 3).

The prophet's vision is not immediate, but reflected in images in his mind as in a mirror. Like Ficino, Aquinas is here drawing on the pseudo-Dionysius for an idea that was to become central in Renaissance neo-Platonic accounts of the soul's ascent, and which supports belief in the 'spiritual' use of concrete images. In this life truth is naturally and necessarily not manifest 'sine velaminibus phantasmatum' (IIaIIae, 174, 2). Prophecy, however, is not only the production but also the interpretation of obscure speech, especially that of Scripture (IIaIIae, 176, ad 4). Inspiration will thus come into play in Christian poetry not only when a poet seeks aid in composition, but also when a poet such as La Ceppède adopts Scripture as a model and subject, and desires divine aid in interpreting it.

In the sixteenth century neo-Platonist and Pléiade theories frequently link poetic inspiration with divine grace. Richard Le Blanc's Preface to his translation of the *Io* does so explicitly; Ronsard in the *Abbregé de l'art poëtique françois* associates poetic inspiration with 'saincte grace'.[10] In the devotional institutions founded at Vincennes by Henry III the *furor* is accepted as a religious concept.[11] The form of the mythological apparatus of the Muses, as presented, for instance, in Pontus de Tyard's *Solitaire premier*, is evidently compatible with these interpretations. Nevertheless, the religious poets found it necessary to reformulate the allegory in terms of another neo-Platonic myth—Urania, the Muse and mediator, whose attributes were particularly susceptible of christianization.

In Plato Urania is associated both with celestial love and with the knowledge of the harmonies of the cosmos. This foreshadows the later dual development of Urania amongst Renaissance neo-Platonists, in which Urania is on the one hand an initiator into both scientific and divine mysteries, and on the other is the Muse of divine love, Aphrodite Urania, whose counterpart is terrestrial

[10] *Abbregé* (*Œuvres*, ed. Laumonier, vol. xiv), p. 4. For Le Blanc see Lefranc, *Grands Écrivains*, pp. 125 f.

[11] Cf. Yates, *French Academies*, p. 152. On the Pléiade notion of inspiration see also Castor, *Pléiade Poetics*, pp. 24 ff.; Joukovsky-Micha, *Poésie et mythologie*, pp. 124 ff.; Cave (ed.), *Ronsard*, pp. 140 ff., 184 ff.

love.[12] Marguerite de Navarre, in the *Triomphe de l'Agneau*, speaks of 'la sacrée Uranie', whose activity has to do solely with religious verities.[13] In Peletier du Mans, with his sources in Martianus Capella, Pontano, and the Grands Rhétoriqueurs,[14] Urania is integrated into a schema in which she acts as a converter of earthly love not merely into virtue but into intellectual knowledge intuited in the cosmic harmony of her song.[15] Further, Peletier associates astrological scrutiny with religious contemplation, envisaging it as an apologetic weapon. Urania was linked in the Renaissance with ecstatic contemplation; the mystical rapture is termed 'voluptas urania' by Ficino.[16]

These elements evolve in Le Fèvre de La Boderie's *Encyclie* into an Aristotelian–Platonic synthesis of encyclopedic proportions. Urania is now invoked as the Muse of all divine mysteries, and is placed close to the Godhead, as an 'image du Père' present at the creation.[17] She is the mediator between postulant and divine ideas, and meditation is effected by meditation on the heavens inspired by the harmony of her song. It is her function, too, to exhort the 'secretaire' to visionary love, associated by Le Fèvre with the prophetic inspiration of Moses and St. John. Further, these connections with order, creation, and prophetic leadership give her the role of moral and religious reformer in a France ridden with sectarian strife.[18]

But it is the Protestant Du Bartas who makes Urania the bearer of a militant Christian poetic programme.[19] The iconographical delineation of Urania added to the text in the 1579 and 1585

[12] Plato, *Symposium*, 187D, *Timaeus*, 90D; Ficino, *In convivium*, 2, 7 (*Divini Platonis opera*, vol. ii, pp. 206 ff.). On Urania in religious poetics cf. Baker, 'Certain Religious Elements'; Campbell, 'The Christian Muse'; Reichenberger, 'L'Uranie'.

[13] *Triomphe de l'Agneau*, ll. 131 ff., in *Marguerites de la Marguerite des Princesses*.

[14] See Schmidt, *Poésie scientifique*, pp. 23 ff.; on other medieval antecedents and analogues in Baïf and Ronsard cf. Joukovsky-Micha, *Poésie et mythologie*, pp. 24 ff., 39.

[15] *Amour des amours*, ed. van Bever, p. 71; cf. Rousset, 'Les recueils de sonnets', pp. 206 ff.

[16] Cf. Schmidt, *Poésie scientifique*, p. 20; Wind, *Pagan Mysteries*, p. 150.

[17] *Encyclie*, p. 123.

[18] Ibid., 'cercle settieme', p. 120. The 'advertissement' and the dedicatory 'chant' make explicit the desire to resolve conflict through the effects of poetry.

[19] Du Bartas was accepted in Catholic circles, and was admired by Henri d'Angoulême.

editions of *L'Uranie*[20] fixes the elements in the tradition seen hitherto. She is introduced as a 'sainte beauté, that is, as Venus Urania, and her discourse consists of the ninefold cosmic harmony; as a muse of the heavens her head is covered with a crown representing the motions of the spheres, and her body is decked with a blue mantle studded with symbols of heavenly bodies. Her prime function is the elevation of souls to contemplation of the heavens, and the inspiration of poets, so that they in turn may inspire others. The opening of the poem uses the image of the prostitution of poetry—an image also used by La Ceppède—in an attack on the degrading dependency of court-poets, and argues that the poet, inspired in the same way as the prophets, should be a moral leader of the people. Thus Du Bartas relates the power of poetry, the poet's social responsibility, and his prophetic insight into the divine will. Reformulating the Pléiade view of their social role, he tells poets that if they converted their verse, 'les grands commetroient en vos mains leurs affaires'.[21] Urania becomes a symbol for a poetic theory, a moral regeneration, and a religious mission— a function which La Ceppède transposes into more specifically Catholic terms.

The 'Avant-propos' of the *Théorèmes* constitutes La Ceppède's fullest statement of his view of poetry. He begins with the familiar account of the divine origin of poetry, stressing the notion of celestial beauty as opposed to mutable earthly beauty. He offers historical evidence for the belief in poetry's divinity. The French humanist historians, who have 'foüillé curieusement dans les monumens de l'antiquité', know that poetry takes first place amongst sacred and immortal beauties. The fact is further demonstrated iconographically in 'le fabuleux crayon des vieilles peintures parlantes', which depict the goddess Poetry as the daughter of Jupiter and Mnemosyne, as honoured by names all expressing her perfections, as ascending Olympus, and as the companion of Apollo.[22] This allegorical figure of Poetry, who subsumes the nine Muses, corresponds to the supreme Muse Urania.

In further defence of poetry La Ceppède invokes 'l'irreprochable tesmoignage de ceux, qu'on estime auoir diuinement philosophé' as the pagan authority for the sacredness of the poetic spirit

[20] In *Works*, ed. Holmes, vol. ii. pp. 172–4.
[21] ll. 118–21.
[22] I, p. 4.

(I, pp. 4–5). But poetry has been the favoured instrument also of the Hebrew and Christian God:

... & l'Eternel (pour passer des ombres à la lumiere) nous fit iadis bien voir clairement combien il agreoit cette belle, luy faisant ores prononcer les arrests de sa volonté; ores entonner ses louanges; ores rechanter ses bienfaits; ores croniquer la vie & les gestes de son bien-aymé. (I, p. 5)

Most of the allusions here are those traditionally introduced by Christian defences of poetry. La Ceppède indicates in a marginal note the Old Testament examples of poetry in Moses, David, Deborah, and Judith. But his continuation of the history of divine poetry departs from the usual account. He does not mention explicitly the writers of the Gospels; and he does not refer, as Sebillet had done, to liturgical poetry. The poetic chronicle of Christ's life to which he alludes (on the authority of St. Jerome) is revealed in a further marginal note to be the Virgilian imitation of the Gospels by Juvencus.[23] La Ceppède apparently believes that post-apostolic accounts of this kind are also directly inspired by God. In the extended allegory that follows (I, pp. 5–6) he treats the degradation of Poetry in the same manner as Du Bartas's Urania had treated her 'sœurs macquereles'. The accusations made are the stock charges brought against poetry by Christian critics: poetry has associated itself with false gods, lying, and idolatry, with lasciviousness and meretriciousness. Furthermore, the insidious effects of poetry have perverted the impressionable. He was, therefore, about to banish poetry entirely.[24]

But the Platonic banishment is replaced by the idea of conversion, already well established, but given biblical authority here by La Ceppède. According to his interpretation of the story of Hosea and Gomer (Hosea 1: 2–4), and of Deuteronomy 21: 10–13, it is possible to convert the prostituted foreign Muse (I, p. 6). It is presumably the Italianate love-poetry of the Court that La Ceppède has in mind here.[25] The call for Christian poetry often expresses itself in terms of national need at this period. The dedication 'Au Roy' of the second Part of the *Théorèmes* echoes these themes. Adopting the illuminated reformatory attitudes of the Old Testament prophets, the poet advises Louis XIII to temper his warlike

---

[23] *Evangelicae historiae libri IV*.
[24] Cf. Du Bartas, *L'Uranie* (*Works*, vol. ii. pp. 177–8).
[25] Desportes himself makes frequent use in his sonnets of the anti-Petrarchan theme of conversion.

ardour with cultivation of the sacred Muses, the 'nourriçons de la saincte Vranie', and warns against the 'Muses prophanes & débauchées (dont vostre France formilloit au dernier siecle)'. By implication the troubles of late sixteenth-century France are associated with poetic corruption, and the converted Muse with a national and moral revival. The conversion itself is presented as a transition from earthly to celestial love—a transition in which the earthly affections are irresistibly transformed into supernatural rapture by contemplating the Passion:

comme eut-elle [la Poésie] plus longuement sçeu cherir ces amours charnels & voluptueux, voyant que par le banissement de ceux-là elle pouuoit auoir facilement pour obiet de la vraye & parfaicte amitié celuy, qui . . . a noyé sa chere vie dans ce vaste Ocean de son amour eternele? (I, pp. 7–8)

The notions of love and pleasure as poetic themes are not rejected, but transposed to a theological plane. The allegory specifies further the characteristics of and effects produced by a work (in this case the *Théorèmes*) created under the converted Muse. In the first place, since such a work is depicted as 'portant en sa main le liure du Prophete enuelopé des mysteres, escrit dedans pour les doctes, & dehors pour les ignorans',[26] it is concerned with inspired communication of hidden truths to the world. In the second place, just as the conversion of the Muse is presented in terms of the extremes of human and divine love, so the effects of the converted poetry are presented in terms of the antitheses of 'les plus iustes & pitoyables lamentations' on the one hand, and 'les plus ioyeuses & plus agreables chansons' on the other. The former are designed to bring home the degradation of humanity in sin, the latter its exaltation through the Incarnation and Redemption. (I, p. 8)

The figure of converted poetry in the 'Avant-propos' matches that of the sixteenth-century Urania in essential respects: she is associated with divine love, mediates between the divine and the human, is the guardian of mysteries, and is linked with the idea of harmony, be it civil or celestial. However, it is in the poetry that Urania appears in association with inspiration—an association that seems to lead to certain modifications in the tradition as it has

---

[26] Allusion to Ezekiel 2: 9–10; in the continuation the prophet digests the book, the words of which he is to address to wayward Israel: cf. Du Bellay's metaphor of literary imitation, *Deffence*, ed. Chamard, pp. 42–3.

been described so far. La Ceppède accepts implicitly the doctrine of special inspiration for literary composition based on Scriptural interpretation. In his dedicatory epistle to the *Imitation* he assumes in himself the operation of the Holy Spirit. He is 'secrettement inspiré to turn to the Psalms:

L'Esprit de l'Eternel, qui fauorisant les saintes intentions, se daigne bien seruir des mortels organes, a fait éclorre à mon Ame ce petit Œuure, (*Imitation* (1612), p. 5)

Similarly, in Part II of the *Théorèmes* (p. 422) La Ceppède explains that he has interpreted his Scriptural text partly by including 'ce que le S. Esprit nous a suggeré'.

One significant feature of La Ceppède's petitions for inspiration, which occur at the beginning or end of certain books of the *Théorèmes*, is that they are repeatedly associated with the idea of purification. The invocation opening Part I of the *Théorèmes* centres on purgation by fire. In the same way as Le Fèvre de La Boderie,[27] La Ceppéde seeks to be cleansed by the seraphic flame that touched the lips of Isaiah. Although poetry is a spiritual exercise for its writer, by means of which he aims at his own as well as others' moral elevation,[28] the poet cannot in the first place compose until he has been purged. Since his spiritual exercise is also bound up with the deciphering of mysteries, the vatic poet must transcend his sensual being, in order to rise above the 'carnal' or literal sense of Scripture.[29] Thus, with an allusion to the interpretation of Old Testament prefiguration, he prays:

> Espure donc cet air de mes poulmons batu,
> Et m'aprens à chanter ce Propiciatoire. (I. i. 1)

The Holy Spirit may be invoked directly (as in II. iv. 1) or in some other form, such as the pillar of fire in I. ii. 1. But the invocation of inspiration most frequently centres around the complex figure of Urania, whose precise role in Catholic thought La Ceppède clarifies.

In the sonnet I. iii. 1 La Ceppède seeks divine aid to meditate on the Passion. He makes two petitions, one for grace, the other

---

[27] Cf. *Encyclie*, pp. 150–1.
[28] Cf. *Théorèmes* I, 'vœu pour la fin de cet œuvre', ll. 9–10.
[29] Cf. II, pp. 439–40 for the literal as carnal.

for the skill to represent Christ's anguish. It is a question of a new Muse:

> Quelle nouuele Muse à mes nombreuses loix
> Inspirera la grace, & me dourra l'adresse
> De retracer icy ton extreme detresse?

The answer modifies in some respects the sixteenth-century doctrine of divine inspiration under Urania. In the first place, it is Christ himself who will be the 'new Muse' inspiring grace. In the second, Urania is naturally called in to fulfil the second function, but in the process her representation as found in Le Fèvre and Du Bartas is transformed. In the accompanying annotation Urania is explained as a pagan prefiguration of the Virgin Mary. On Urania's dominant attribute La Ceppède cites Ausonius: 'Uranie caeli motus scrutatur & Astra.'[30] Plato (*Republic*, 529) is summarized as believing 'que l'Vranie esleue nos esprits au Ciel, & les y conduit'. This is the usual neo-Platonic allegorical representation of the astral Muse. But

la vraye Vranie à qui veritablement appartient cet office de nous esleuer de la terre au Ciel, de nous apprendre les mysteres celestes, est cette Vierge saincte, remplie du S. Esprit, qui est icy à cet effet à bon droit inuoquée, au lieu des prophanes ordinaires inuocations des Poetes. Et d'autant plus à propos qu'elle fut tousiours presente aux derniers tormens, & à la mort de son Fils . . . (I, p. 352)

Urania's existing functions of raising the mind to contemplation and of meditating mysteries are thus retained. But since Urania is now identified with the Virgin, they acquire a specific association with the Passion and Resurrection. It is further possible that La Ceppède's use in the sonnet of the phrase 'nombreuses loix' is linked with Urania's role as the representative of harmony and order.[31] In any case, the Virgin's association with the stars in, for example, medieval Latin hymns, would facilitate her identification with Urania.

At the same time the status held by Urania in Le Fèvre and Du Bartas is reduced. In the 'vœu' at the end of Part I it is Christ

---

[30] See 'Nomina musarum', *Ausonius* [Works], with an English trans. by H. G. E. White (Loeb Classical Library), vol. ii, p. 280.

[31] In his annotation he cites Ronsard for the expression; it arose, he explains, either because laws were once expressed in verse, or (as he prefers) 'pource que les nombres donnent la loy aux vers' (I, p. 351).

as the 'Prince du Pole' who is the source of celestial inspiration. It is to the Holy Spirit that the composite Muse figure is implicitly subordinate in II. i. 1:

> Clair Esprit, dont ma Muse a cy-deuant apris
> Ses douleurs . . .

and more explicitly in the annotation to II. ii. 1: 'La Vierge est . . . inuoquée en ce Sonnet pour obtenir en nostre faueur le S. Esprit' (II, p. 156). The role of Urania is made theologically more precise by the merging with the intercessory role of the Virgin. La Ceppède's version of the myth is thus distinct from that of Le Fèvre in which Urania plays a vast philosophical role which is theologically undefined. It is from Du Bartas's Urania, Muse of poetic and religious conversion, that La Ceppède's Urania evolves. The identification with the Virgin represents the absorption of the unifying symbol of religious poetry into the orthodox Catholic framework of devotion.[32]

2. *Poetic Language*

Up to the Renaissance the term 'imitation' is pejorative under the influence of Plato's assertion that art was an imitation at two removes from ideal reality, and was, moreover, connected with false pagan theology and false pagan ethics. The implication contained in the *Republic* that poets are liars was continued in the Latin writers, and the Church Fathers had special cause to exaggerate the accusation. The usual defence was based on the theory of metaphorical interpretation, which had the sanction of the Judaeo-Christian tradition of biblical exposition, and could be extended to pagan literature. At the Renaissance the recovery of Aristotle's *Poetics* offered poetic theorists new solutions to the problem of imitation of nature in terms of the concept of verisimilitude, although the debates on truth and verisimilitude tended only to create further problems for Christian poetics, since Christian poetry is concerned exclusively with the true.[33] Aristotle was not,

---

[32] One of the emblematic figures in the frontispiece to the *Théorèmes* summarizes this Catholic Urania linked with devotion, the Passion, Scripture, and law. She has a star-covered gown and a halo of light; she bears a flaming heart in one hand and the Mosaic tablets in the other; behind her is a cross and at her feet a lamb; facing her is a figure of Justice.

[33] On the Pléiade's handling of Aristotelian theory cf. Castor, *Pléiade Poetics*, ch. 5, 11. Amongst religious poets Frénicle, for instance, in his Preface to the

however, the only Renaissance answer to the charge of false imitation. Late sixteenth- and early seventeenth-century Christian poetics tends to retain the medieval doctrine of metaphorical interpretation that applies both to the natural world and to literature. The neo-Platonists, discarding Socrates' accusation in the *Republic*, regarded artistic imitation of nature, at however many removes from the ideal, as a step in the ascent of the soul to divine truth. But it is in particular the patristic, scholastic, and devotional position with regard to the relationship of literary expression to truth and reality that needs to be considered in the case of La Ceppède.

Discussing Christian eloquence in the fourth book of the *De doctrina christiana*, Augustine's recommendations are determined by the criterion of representation of truth, rather than that of effective persuasion, and are justified by reference to Scriptural usage.[34] He indicates how eloquence may serve wisdom, by analysing the style of St. Paul, and by drawing attention to the spiritual benefit to be drawn from the tropes of the prophet Amos.[35] In the *Contra mendacium* Augustine explicitly defends devices such as parables, metaphors, fables, antiphrasis against the charge of mendacity, on the grounds that they are used in Scripture and hide profound truths.[36] Further, the reading of metaphorical passages effects a transition from the corporeal to the spiritual, and causes the reader to be inflamed with divine love. This is a significant passage in view of some of the mystical beliefs held about metaphor by some of the Christian poets (including La Ceppède) of the late sixteenth century:

Credo quod ipsa anima quandiu rebus adhuc terrenis implicatur, pigrius inflammatur: si vero feratur ad similitudines corporales, et inde referatur ad spiritualia, quae illis similitudinibus figurantur, ipso quasi transitu vegetatur, et tanquam in facula ignis agitatus accenditur, et ardentiore dilectione rapitur ad quietem.[37]

Jésus crucifié (1636) rejected the relevance of the concept of verisimilitude: cf. Varga, 'La poésie religieuse au xvème siècle', p. 264.

[34] On Augustine and literature cf. Svoboda, *L'Esthétique de saint Augustin*; Saintsbury, *A History of Criticism*, vol. i, pp. 377 ff.; Baldwin, *Medieval Rhetoric*, ch. 2; Curtius, *Europäische Literatur*, pp. 81 ff.; Colish, *Mirror of Language*, ch. 1.

[35] *De doctrina christiana*, 4, 7 (Migne, vol. 34, cols. 93–8).

[36] Migne, vol. 40, cols. 532 ff.; cf. Svoboda, *Esthétique*, pp. 166 ff.

[37] *Epistolae*, 2, 55, 21 (Migne, vol. 33, col. 214).

Augustine's anti-sophistical treatment of rhetoric rests on an epistemological and moral basis: the redeemed language must reflect divine ideas, however inadequately, and must at the same time bring about a transformation in its receiver.

Although Aquinas's aesthetics is coloured by the intellectualist and empiricist bias of Aristotelianism, neo-Platonic elements are not obscured.[38] Moreover, central to all discussions of theological signification up to the Renaissance are the various comparable notions of exemplarism and analogy. For Augustine the world of creatures reflects divine ideas. Bonaventure in particular, for whom the world is a *vestigium* or *umbra Dei*, or more significantly a *liber scriptus forinsecus*, develops a hierarchy of resemblances between the creatures and God by which the soul may rise to the *liber scriptus intrinsecus*, to contemplation of God.[39] But Aquinas's doctrine of analogical predication of divine attributes also depends on the notion of the likeness of the world of creatures to God; furthermore, he does not reject the Augustinian and neo-Platonic doctrine of exemplarism.[40] Now if language represents the world, which in turn is composed of *signa Dei*, there is a potential defence of imagery, including poetic imagery.

As far as poetry itself is concerned Aquinas classifies it, with Aristotle, as a subdivision of philosophy alongside dialectic and rhetoric, but appears to regard it as an inferior mode of demonstration employing weak proofs by example and comparison.[41] However, the status of poetry is implicitly raised by virtue of its similarities with Scriptural expression. Precisely these similarities are dealt with in the *Summa theologiae*,[42] in reply to the objection that it is not fitting for Scripture to 'set forth in metaphors divine and spiritual things under the similitude of corporeal things', for these are the devices of poetry, the lowest of the arts. If the premiss

---

[38] On Aquinas see, e.g., Kovach, *Die Ästhetik des Thomas von Aquin*; Patterson, *Three Centuries of French Poetic Theory*, pp. 903 ff.; Maritain, *Art et scolastique*.

[39] See in particular the *Itinerarium mentis in Deum*, which was influential in the sixteenth-century devotional movement.

[40] Cf. Copleston, *A History of Philosophy*, vol. ii, Part 2, pp. 74 f., 78 ff.; Colish, *Mirror of Language*, pp. 208 ff.

[41] Curtius (*Europäische Literatur*, pp. 228–9), emphasizes this point. But it does not necessarily mean that Aquinas's classic statements on Scriptural and natural symbolization are not relevant to later poets deliberately imitating that mode.

[42] Ia, 1, 9.

is accepted, the only course is to vindicate metaphor, irrespective of its association with poetry. Metaphor thus takes on a positive cognitive role in Aquinas's epistemological framework.[43] The corollary of this line of argument is that low imagery is more suitable for the expression of divine truth than noble imagery, for the lower the image, the more necessary is spiritual interpretation. With the pseudo-Dionysius, Aquinas argues that the splendour of divine revelation is not travestied by veiling in metaphor, and there is a necessary ascent from perception of the concrete to cognition of the intelligible. Metaphorical expression and interpretation has metaphysical justification, since it is only by this means that language penetrates beyond perceptible reality. This vital role of metaphor rests, of course, on assumptions about reality which became increasingly problematic in the period in question. The Thomist synthesis of reason and faith, of the sensible and the suprasensible worlds, is dissolved with the advent of mechanistic science. In the seventeenth century literary expression itself is drawn into the sphere of reason and clear and distinct reference. It becomes increasingly difficult to maintain that transcendental meanings inhere in natural symbols and their literary counterparts. There are two possible consequences for metaphor: either it is discredited in its serious form and reduced to elegant ornament, or it is confined to theological spheres where a particular view of the world and of symbolization survives.

One such sphere is that of devotional literature, rooted as it is in the revival of patristic and scholastic writing, in the neo-Platonistic background of sixteenth-century humanism, and in the desire to integrate the sacred with the profane, the transcendental with the immanent. The notion of contemplative knowledge of the divine through natural signs was propagated in, for instance, the *Theologia naturalis* of Raymond of Sabunde, and Bellarmine's *De ascensione mentis in Deum per scalas rerum creatarum*. Richeome in his *Tableaux sacrés* distinguishes three kinds of figurative representation: pictorial imitation, verbal description, and, recalling the neo-Platonic interest in hieroglyphs, 'figures de signification' (also called 'allegorie, peinture et exposition mystique'), which conceal theological verities, and induce divine love in the beholder. He relates this scheme to the fourfold interpretation of Scripture. Further, in simultaneously criticizing profane poets he implicitly

---

[43] Ia, 1, 9, ad 1.

recommends the use of such 'figures' to the converted poet.[44] François de Sales, speaking of sermon rhetoric,[45] justifies the use of natural imagery and other 'similitudes' in terms similar to those of the medieval tradition. Again, 'similitudes' are recommended not only because they have Scriptural authority, but also because they illuminate the understanding and move the will.[46]

In the sixteenth century most speculation about language (especially poetic language) in relation to reality has a similar exegetic and theological basis. The doctrine of the Word in St. John's Gospel, alluded to by François de Sales in the passage quoted above, was fundamental: both the Creation and the Incarnation were associated with the conception of a natural and necessary correspondence between words and the world. There is a pervasive concern with the adequation of words to things: to interpret verbal signs is then to interpret the world, and thus to approach the divine. Associated with this quest were the beliefs that Hebrew was the primal universal language intrinsically related to the objects it designated, that it had been lost after Babel, but that its redemption was prefigured in the Pentecostal gift of tongues.[47] Pléiade theory tends to undermine the priority given to Hebrew in its defence of the vernacular, and to weaken both the neo-Platonic and the Aristotelian conceptions of the relationship between poetic language and reality.[48] The Pléiade poets were, however, familiar with the idea of levels of Scriptural and literary interpretation, and retained a version of the neo-Platonic conception of the *poeta theologus*, the guardian of mysteries which he veiled in poetic obscurity.[49] Such views tended to encourage the idea that words contained inherent mystical meaning, and to authorize the utilization of various kinds of imagery and allegory

[44] *Œuvres*, vol. ii, pp. 109 ff. On the visual aspect cf. Cave, *Devotional Poetry*, pp. 278 ff.

[45] Letter to André Frémyot, 5 October 1604 (*Œuvres*, vol. xii, pp. 299 ff., esp. 307).

[46] Ibid., p. 313. It is arguable that in practice S. François's nature imagery is primarily emotive; cf. Lenoble, *Histoire de l'idée de nature*, p. 332; Lemaire, *Étude des images de Saint François de Sales*, pp. 128 ff.

[47] Cf. Dubois, *Mythe et langage*, pp. 17–83.

[48] Cf. Castor, *Pléiade Poetics*, pp. 60 f., on Ronsard's lack of a metaphysical framework.

[49] Cf. Ronsard, *Œuvres*, ed. Laumonier, vol. 14, p. 4. On Dorat's teaching of allegorical interpretation cf. Nolhac, *Ronsard et l'humanisme*, pp. 69 ff.; also Cave (ed.), *Ronsard*, pp. 181 ff. ard Demerson, *La Mythologie classique*, pp. 28–42.

in poetry.[50] However, it is the religious poets marginally associated with the Pléiade who realize these conceptions in the biblical and theological terms indicated above. It is they, with their secure metaphysical framework, who are able to realize the Pléiade dream of a 'theologie allegoricque'.

In his occasional theoretical remarks, as well as in practice, La Ceppède bears this out. Thus he describes his work as the offspring of the divine Muse bearing the prophetic book written within and without, and more explicitly as the 'porteur & gardien de ces diuines Tables, dans les seuls caractères desquels l'ignorant trouue, la parfaicte science: le sçauant, l'immortel profit du sçauoir'.[51] The background to this would seem to be current neo-Platonic ideas about symbolization. The imagery of inner and outer for sacred mystery and uninitiated profanity may be related to the view that pagan poets conveyed divine truths to (and simultaneously protected them from) the common people. But it should be borne in mind that devout humanistic poetics is concerned with communication, and outer and inner are not necessarily opposed. The outer symbol conveys intuitively what can be revealed as inner truth by explication—a notion closely bound up with that of exegetic commentary which has already been seen to be fundamental in La Ceppède.

The same concepts apply to nature, to Bonaventure's *liber scriptus forinsecus*, as apply to Scripture: La Ceppède uses the term 'hiéroglyphiques' with respect to both. In fact he concerns himself quite explicitly with the relationship between levels in the hierarchy of being, especially in so far as such correspondences concern poetry. He is concerned, for instance, with the theology of the Incarnation and Creation, with the relationship between the divine and human persons in Christ, and by extension with the relationship between man, the universe, and God. Thus he states on the one hand that man is created in the image of God to the extent that the resemblance is 'internal' or spiritual, but also in so far as it is 'external' and symbolic:

cette image est aucunement au corps, en signe, ou signification, & en argument.[52]

---

[50] Le Fèvre, e.g., expresses a naturalistic and mystical view of verbal signification: 'Sous le voile du mot l'essence se repose' (*Encyclie*, p. 71).

[51] 'Avant-propos' pp. 8–9.

[52] I, p. 307. He is careful to deny Origen's attribution of the creation of man exclusively to the Word.

On the other hand, he explains at length that the microcosm (man) is an 'abrégé du monde',

> pource que l'homme contient en soy par certaine analogie tout ce qui est en l'vniuers de toutes les creatures.[53]

The creatures, and poetic images based on them, in turn reflect the transcendental world:

> Nous vsons licitement des noms & des comparaisons des choses propha-nes visibles, pource que nous sommes portez à la cognoissance des inuisibles . . .[54] Ces suppositions qui par les choses basses peuuent porter l'esprit à mediter les choses plus éleuées sont practiquées en mille lieux de l'Escriture. Mesmes aux Prophetes, aux Pseaumes, & en l'Apocalypse, & parmi les Peres contemplatifs qui en ont vsé en l'Orai-son soluë. A plus haute raison donques nous est-il loisible d'en vser en poësie.[55]

La Ceppède links this principle with the view that pagan mythology can be interpreted as concealed theology, but emphasizes that mythological personages and events are purely prefigurations fulfilled and superseded. He defends thus his use of 'Genie' as a synonym for Christ:

> Il n'est pas de mesme illicite d'appeler les mesmes tres-sainctes diuines Personnes des noms qui bien qu'vsurpez par les Payens, ont neantmoins de la conuenance par les qualitez qu'on leur attribuoit, auec les attributs du vray Dieu que nous adorons en differentant par quelque Epithete ou suite de paroles le vray du faux. Ainsi le Poete dit parlant de Dieu, *qui vray Neptune tient le moite frain des eaux.*[56]

It is plain from these passages that particular conceptions of the world, poetic imagery, and pagan antiquity are interrelated. It is clear also that they are continuous with patristic, scholastic, and devotional tradition described above. Further, they are compatible with, although regarded as a conversion of, the Pléiade poetics.

La Ceppède also expresses the sixteenth-century belief in the priority of Hebrew.[57] The first language consisted of the synonyms

---

[53] II, pp. 356 f.   [54] II, p. 499.   [55] II, p. 501.

[56] II, p. 499, quoting Du Bartas, *Première Semaine* (*Works*, ed. Holmes, vol. ii, p. 195). Cf. also I, p. 24: 'Le nom d'Alcide conuient à nostre Sauueur . . . & cet epithete, *non feint*, garantit ce vers du fabuleux mensonge: n'estant point illicite de parler ainsi en Poesie & de Chrestienner les fables. Ainsi lisons-nous en meint autheur Chrestien, le vray Iupiter, le vray Apollon, le vray Neptune.' On the standardization of this device cf. Sayce, *French Biblical Epic*, pp. 167 f.

[57] In II. iv. 23-5.

used by Adam to name the creatures: it was therefore universal and faithfully mirrored the world.[58] Unity and clarity were lost after the fall of Babel, although they were conserved in the language of the tribe of Heber, that is in Hebrew.[59] With Pereyra and Lorinus La Ceppède relates Babel directly to Pentecost. In the gift of tongues, what was obscure is revealed to all, and 'Toute langue à sa source est comme revnie'; but the true unity will only be realized hereafter.[60] The relevance of these ideas lies in their close association with the themes of expository and communicative inspiration in poetic activity. Religious poetry thus comes to be associated with a characteristic network of ideas: the poet stands ambiguously between obscurity and clarity, embodying truths in symbolic form, but also interpreting what is concealed; this communicative and cognitive function is possible because language (at least ideally) reflects the world, and the world reflects God; and the power to see through poetry a clarity and universality transcending the material world is granted in divine inspiration. That this should have consequences for the general style of his poetry seems to be well understood by La Ceppède:

Ie confesse que ie l'enuoye vn peu malproprement habillé; non pour le regard de l'estoffe (car ie l'ay toute choisie dans les plus loyales boutiques des plus riches & plus fideles marchands de l'Eglise) mais quant à la façon des habits, elle ne sera peut-estre pas trouuée du tout bien à la Françoise; toutesfois ie me promets que ton naturel debonnaire excusera facilement ce defaut, & le rendra tres-excusable parmy les ames non envieuses: consideré que ce fort drap d'or ne se manie pas aisement à tous les plis qu'on veut, & que nostre ramage natal ne peut facilement estre oublié tout à fait. (I, p. 10)

The defensive tone indicates that La Ceppède is aware that his literary manner is likely to have critics. These critics are not identified, but it is not improbable, in view of the evidence discussed above in chapters I and II, that La Ceppède has Malherbe and his disciples in mind. The passage may also explain the limited extent of Malherbe's influence on La Ceppède's poetry. It contains three explanations of his adherence to an archaic style. One is that

---

[58] Cf. Dubois, *Mythe et langage*, pp. 46 ff.

[59] II, p. 612. This concern with linguistic diversity and civil unity might be seen against the political and linguistic background of sixteenth-century Provence. Cf. ch. I above.

[60] II. iv. 23. On Pereyra and language cf. Dubois, pp. 25, 28.

his writing is influenced by regional linguistic habits ('ramage natal'). It is true that provincial eccentricity often explains the persistence of Pléiade habits into the seventeenth century. But it is not the main explanation stressed by La Ceppède; nor is it the explanation hinted at by Malherbe in his preliminary sonnet. In particular La Ceppède defends his manner on the grounds that his material ('l'estoffe') is drawn from biblical and orthodox theological authority. Furthermore, there is an implicit argument that such material of necessity involves a certain type of linguistic attitude and stylistic procedure. The image of clothing upon which the passage is built gives some indication of the religious poet's position with regard to French classical poetics. Quintilian's metaphor of language as the dress of thought becomes commonplace in seventeenth-century discussions of decorum. Since it is possible to speak critically of the matching of a suitable style to subject-matter, the separability of linguistic sign and its meaning is implied. La Ceppède's opening words appear to fall in with this line of thinking, but the continuation clearly identifies meaning and sign, thought and language, by means of the double meaning of 'estoffe'. The subject-matter itself constitutes the 'fort drap d'or'; it is not just adorned by it. Hence, if garment and content, language and thought are one and the same thing, language is a source of knowledge, and, especially in biblical contexts, should be treated as sacred. It is not surprising that the garment image plays a part in the image network of the *Théorèmes*. The 'fort drap d'or', associated as it is with copiousness and complexity of meaning, is in effect a justification of a poetic style no longer fashionable at the time when La Ceppède came to publish his work.

V

IMAGES AND THEMES

MOST of the studies that have been made hitherto of La Ceppède's imagery[1] tend to omit one essential aspect: the interrelation between images. Obviously the primary themes ('tenors') are interrelated in the sense that persons and objects are linked in the narrative relations of the Passion sequence, and in the sense that moral and theological themes are linked in the system of Christian doctrine. But the relationships between the 'vehicle' components of the images are none the less important. In fact, they are more than mere 'vehicles', since they constitute a network of secondary themes, which has its own meaning structure and its own religious significance. This network of secondary themes is not, of course, absolutely homogeneous. There is a primary distinction between the typological analogies (Scriptural or mythological), which have a temporal dimension, and those images deriving from natural phenomena and human society, which do not—although this does not in practice mean that the categories are not related.

A. THE HISTORICAL DIMENSION

1. *Kingship, War, and Law*

It has been said[2] that La Ceppède's poetry is contemplative and therefore independent of the contemporary world, that unusually for the period it does not refer to the political events of the late sixteenth and early seventeenth centuries. However, the evidence is that the Aix poets were involved in the disorders of their province and that La Ceppède intended his poetry to participate in and

---

[1] Cf. de Mourgues, *Metaphysical, Baroque and Précieux Poetry*, pp. 50 ff.; Rousset, Preface to *Théorèmes*, an emotive concretization; Donaldson-Evans, *Poésie et méditation*, pp. 124 ff., on the cognitive and persuasive function of the imagery; also Laurence, 'Nature Imagery', 'The Renaissance Theory of Poetry' Castan, 'The Realm of the Imaginary'.

[2] Donaldson-Evans, *Poésie et méditation*, p. 120.

influence the life of the nation. In the poetry one would expect the biographical and historical background to be reflected in the recurrent images of warfare, jurisprudence, kingship, and state-craft. It is true that these images were embedded in the tradition on which La Ceppède was drawing, and thus in themselves have no specific historical reference. However, a generalized tendency of the time (particularly clear in the visual arts) to anachronistic representation of biblical narrative means that the details of such images often appear in contemporary guise. This practice makes it plausible to assume that personal experience may sometimes be introduced.

(i) *The Imitation*. In the case of the *Imitation* the biblical text provides images of God as a wrathful warrior–monarch and severe judge, and of man as torn by internal conflict, as criminal, debtor, and prisoner. There are, however, grounds for speculating that La Ceppède's peculiar handling of these given images has links with his personal situation around the time when he wrote the psalm paraphrases.[3]

Isolated images of divine justice, such as 'la main de ta iustice' (37, 1), 'poids de ta iustice' (142, 2), are clearly purely biblical in origin. But the elaboration of such images frequently diverges significantly from the model. The prose paraphrase of Psalm 50 is a particularly clear example of the way images of these kinds are developed so as to suggest some connection with a legal, and to some extent political, background. As a lawyer La Ceppède would be familiar with legal procedure and rhetoric.[4] The penitential meditation is based on an ambiguous structure of self-accusation and self-defence before God the judge—a structure which is analogous to that of the legal trial. The opening words of the prose prayer or oration based on Psalm 50 introduce the dominant metaphor of the passage with a play on the theological and juridical senses of *grace*:

Grace, mon Prince, grace à ce criminel miserable; c'est à ce coup qu'il est besoin d'étaler, non pas seulement vos equitez pitoyables, mais vos absolues & souueraines misericordes. (p. 23)

Having announced his aim to seek unconditional reprieve, the

---

[3] See above, pp. 24 ff.
[4] On the rhetoric see ch. VII, sect. 2, below.

pleader goes on to clarify the nature of the sin or crime in terms of
financial images:[5]

Helas! je vous en supplie & resupplie tres-humblement, par ces in-
nombrables pitiez à tant d'autres pecheurs, & à moy mesme si souuent
départies qu'il vous plaise rayer sur vostre liure l'obligation de mes
nouuelles debtes. (p. 23)

This use of legal and financial metaphors might constitute no
more than a biographical curiosity, were it not for the fact that
La Ceppède introduces increasingly explicit references to the religious wars.

Military imagery in the Psalms is used in connection with three
themes: Jehovah's vindictive attitude towards the sinner; the
anonymous 'enemies' who oppress the sinner; and the sinner's
conflict with himself. The moral conflict between the passions and
reason is traditionally described in terms of civil war:

Comblez mon ame de liesse par le rétablissement de la paix, que la
guerre ciuile de mes sens luy auoit dérobé. (p. 24)

Can it be further argued that this kind of imagery in the *Imitation*
owes something to the historical circumstances of the work? Such
a suggestion is perhaps supported by some details in the prose
paraphrase of Psalm 50, which concludes with an explicit linking
of the sinner's internal torments with those of France in general
and of his birthplace[6] in particular:

Je . . . vous supplie, Seigneur, tres-affectueusement qu'il vous plaise
faire (ainsi qu'à moy) misericorde à cet Estat affligé & à la desolée ville
de ma naissance, sur qui (aussi bien que sur moy) mes iniquitez ont
armé vostre bras de foudre, rendez leur s'il vous plait le jour de vostre
faueur, que mes demerites leur ont éclipsé. (p. 25)

This last phrase seems to set it beyond doubt that the speaker here
regards his own personal sin as a contributory factor in, if not the
cause of, the civil upheavals in France. A further link in the network of image themes is La Ceppède's use of the Hebraic conception of Jehovah as a warrior–monarch. The case the penitent

---

[5] Cf. also *Imitation*, p. 39, paraphrasing 142: 2: 'Mais quitez-moy tout à fait,
sans entrer au particulier examen de mes comptes, car le reliqua en sera si
grand . . .'
[6] Marseilles.

is pleading in the *Imitation* is for unconditional pardon, which is expressed metaphorically as disarmament, as the return of peace:

DEsarme ta fureur, attiedy ton courroux . . . (6, 1)

Ia desia ce bon Dieu me tend ses bras ouuerts,
Mes sanglots de ses mains ont fait tomber les armes. (6, 5)

It is to God as king, to 'vostre Maiesté', 'mon Prince', 'mon souuerain' that such pleas are addressed (50, p. 23). Although regal imagery of this kind is biblical in origin, it may nevertheless be that it should be interpreted on one level with reference to the surrounding legal and military image, and even with reference to La Ceppède's problematic situation in contemporary Provence.

If it is assumed that the influence of tradition and sources on the imagery is a necessary but not sufficient cause, then the picture that emerges from studying the secondary themes in terms of the personal and historical background is this: not merely a devout soul turning for consolation to the Psalms in time of war, but a provincial public servant who feels himself to be responsible in some measure to his monarch for the collapse of civil order, and who seeks pardon and absolution for his supposed shortcomings. In Aix and Marseilles with their Ligueur revolt such personal feelings of guilt would have a political dimension.[7] If there is any expression of particular guilt in the *Imitation* its explanation in these terms rather than in the sexual terms suggested by Ruchon[8] seems better justified by the available evidence.

(ii) *The 'Théorèmes'*. The warrior–king imagery that was prominent in the *Imitation* continues in the *Théorèmes* with somewhat different emphasis. Christian tradition represents Jesus as the Messianic king, conquering the forces of evil, entering the kingdom in triumph, and leading the Church militant to continue the fight. It is not surprising to find Christ designated as 'ce Roy tant redoutable, Par qui Cesar vn iour doit estre détroné' (I. ii. 84), or as 'le Roy de la Gloire' (II. i. 5), 'tout puissant Monarque' (I. i. 28), 'Sire' (II. iii. 24), 'mon Prince' (I. ii. 1; II. ii. 68), 'ta Maiesté' (I. i. 27). In meditative literature earthly kingship is frequently

---

[7] Cf. above, pp. 11 ff.
[8] *Essai*, pp. 13 f., on the basis of 'Mes reins couuoient les feux de la folle Cypris' (37, 3).

offered as an image for the divine majesty.[9] But in medieval and
Renaissance belief not only were the Old Testament kings arche-
types of Christ, but Christ himself was along with them the prototype of all anointed Christian monarchs.[10] Regal imagery may,
therefore, be reciprocal. The Christ of the *Théorèmes* is a king who
is a heroic warrior and a firm ruler. It is possible that the ramifications of this and associated imagery reflect something of the
resurgence of a strong monarchy after the wars of religion.[11]

Some of the minor themes of the Passion narrative such as the
infidelity of the Jewish people to the Messiah are brought out in
the first part of the *Théorèmes* by means of the imagery. On this
level the king is surrounded by a treacherous court and vassals.
There is an allusion (I. i. 80) to the bellicose nature of the nobility,
which is contrasted with the timidity of the disciples at Jesus's
arrest; Judas's betrayal is referred to as an assassination plot (I. i.
8); the Jews are spoken of as 'assassins' (I. i. 90), as 'Ces rudes
Courtisans, que la furie élance' (I. ii. 66), but most frequently as
'mutins' (e.g. I. i. 49, 51, 57; I. ii. 19). The 'reuoltes de l'homme
au Paradis' (I. ii. 64; cf. also I. iii. 70, I. i. 33) have a fundamental
theological meaning; but the clearest images of subversion and
revolt are not always related to the theme of the Fall. Sonnet
I. ii. 9 mentions the clandestine activities of the sowers of seditious
doctrine, with which it contrasts the openness of Christ's teachings.
In I. i. 12 the capture of Christ is represented as an inversion of the
natural order by the use of images alluding to the subversion of
royal and (by the ambiguity inherent in the term 'Pontife', which
ostensibly refers to Christ) papal authority:

> De la main d'vn bon Roy voir le Sceptre arracher
> Par ses mauuais subiets, qu'vn rancueur desespere:
> Voir sur vn haut gibet le Pontife percher
> Pour son mauuais Clergé, par ces fils de vipere.

Thus on the plane of secondary themes of images in Part I of
the *Théorèmes* the divine king is in armed conflict with rebellious

---

[9] Cf., for instance, Loyola's meditation 'Del Rey'; also Calderari's *Trofeo
della Croce*, referred to in I. iii. 25, n. 4; on regal images in de Sales cf. Lemaire,
Les Images, pp. 407 ff.

[10] On this and related themes cf. Kantorowicz, *The King's Two Bodies*.

[11] That is to say, images abstracted from contemporary life are applied to the
text; on the converse process whereby a moral or political lesson is extracted
from the text cf. above, pp. 109 ff.

subjects. As in the *Imitation* La Ceppède exploits the biblical and traditional Christian imagery of the God of battles. But certain details that occur in connection with such well-established military and regal metaphors are not biblical in origin, and may derive from the author's direct experience of the war ethos of his own times. The cult of military glory, for instance, provides La Ceppède with a metaphor for moral excellence. Peter is described in I. i. 73 as 'ce preux combattant'. But it is Christ himself who is the central ideal of heroic chivalry: his Crucifixion is referred to as 'De ce grand, de ce fort, le duel espouuentable', and as 'Les exploits valeureux qu'il a fait en mourant' (II. i. 41). The duel metaphor is obliquely represented in the frequently occurring term 'cartel':[12]

> Ce genereux guerrier a fourni sa carriere,
> Et fait le contenu de son iuste cartel. (I. iii. 79)

And the devout soul is similarly described as capable 'de brauer l'infernal par cent, et cent cartels De deffy confiant' (II. ii. 47). This framework is also used in order to emphasize human weakness by comparing certain actions and spiritual states with cowardice in battle (e.g. I. i. 10; I. iii, 'voeu'; I. i. 41; II. ii. 79). But this is scarcely the major function of military metaphors in the *Théorèmes*.[13] It is rather the imagery of chivalry and heroism that is predominant:

> LE Soldat, qui vaillant se resout au combat
> N'vse point de surprinse, assigne la iournée
> Ne veut point de second, ains à l'heure assignée
> Seul va droit à son homme, & l'attaque, & le bat. (I. i. 83)

With these virtues Christ is the ideal military leader, the 'brave et bon Capitaine', the 'courageux Colonel' whose 'Régiment' is made up of the apostles. It is in Part I that details of contemporary warfare seem to colour the images most obviously. The apostles are compared to over-confident recruits who forget their 'rodomontades' when obliged to 'choquer les ennemis, boire les mousquetades', who are bold only 'Lors que contre leur Chef nul rouet ne desbande' (I. i. 10). The violence of Christ's capture evokes a

---

[12] Used here metaphorically in sense of 'défi' to describe Christ's prophecies about himself.
[13] Cf. Donaldson-Evans, *Poésie et méditation*, pp. 128 f.

comparison with the pillagers of a besieged fortress (I. ii. 24). The journey to Calvary is described as a military procession marching out of the walled city (I. ii. 100).

The emphasis in Part II is on the celebration of victory and the consolidation of peace. Much of this too is provided by the tradition. The harrowing of hell is a battle between Christ and Satan for those souls deserving redemption; the Resurrection is a victory over death (II. i. *passim*); the Church militant is the fulfilment of the Hebrew army whose symbolic banners it bears (II. ii. 23). Christ is now a victorious hero who suppresses rebellion (II. ii. 36). The entry of Christ into hell is furthermore compared with the kind of royal triumphal entries that were experienced several times in Provence during the period of composition of the *Théorèmes*:

> LES chetifs habitants d'vne horrible maison,
> Aprenans que leur Roy doit faire son entrée
> En la ville où elle est, perdent leur marisson,
> Croians de voir leur grace aussi-tost impetrée.
> Mais si de tant d'Amour ce Prince a l'ame outrée
> Qu'il leur vienne en personne ouurir céte prison,
> Leur poictrine est si fort de ioye penetrée,
> Qu'ils iugent leur bon-heur hors de comparaison. (II. i. 8)

This foreshadows the ultimate triumphal entry into heaven which is similarly described in military and regal terms in II. iii. 25 and 26, and which culminates in the coronation of Christ in II. iii. 29. Into the hands of Christ the king are placed by the Father 'Le repos pacifique, & le gouuernement' (II. iii. 30). The Incarnation and Ascension are compared with a cycle of war, victory, and pacification accomplished by a strong monarch. This alternation is supported rhythmically in II. iii. 30 (quoted above, p. 55). There is nothing here to suggest that La Ceppède has in mind any particular monarch or event; but the image has a historical appropriateness. It is again the strength, actual or desired, of the contemporary monarchy that seems to be reflected in an image like 'le secret priuilege Du pouuoir absolu de vostre Majesté' (II. i. 13).

Metaphors of order and law under the Crown occur throughout both parts of the *Théorèmes*—metaphors which can fairly be assumed to have some connection with the author's legal and administrative career. For La Ceppède the physical universe is

directly organized by God, by his 'eternele intendance' (I. i. 63),
and by the angels who are described as

> Des gendarmes aislez la volante milice
> Du Monarque Eternel qui l'vniuers police. (II. iii. 14)

The bestowal of apostolic authority is described in legal terms.
Christ is again acting in his royal capacity:

> Les ayant déleguez il veut rendre authentique
> Leur déspesche. Il y met le seau . . . (II. ii. 67)

The trial of Jesus in Part I creates the opportunity for allusions
to legal institutions. Pilate is accused by the Jews 'd'élargir vn
delit de leze Maiesté' (I. ii. 82); the trial is described as 'cette aigre
Tournelle' (I. ii. 36), the criminal court of the Parlement of Paris;
but at the Crucifixion, an established prefiguration of the Last
Judgement, the legal authority of the monarch provides a metaphor
which represents Christ as 'seant en son lict de iustice' (I. iii. 57).
While such legalistic mataphors do not appear to be distributed in
any historically significant way over the two parts of the *Théorèmes*,
certain images from other areas in Part II seem to reflect a return
to peace and prosperity. Sonnet II. ii. 54 ends in a prayer for peace
and II. i. 16 speaks of the return of peace after the winter storms.
Towards the end of Part II La Ceppède refers to mercantile
prosperity in an image expressing the notion of the Holy Spirit as
a fertilizing wind:

> Et par nostre air émeu l'alme Diuinité
> Le commerce establit: fait qu'auec aduantage,
> L'vn chez l'autre trafique, & forme vn heritage
> Du negoce étranger sans nulle iniquité. (II. iv. 5)

Connected with this theme, but on a more general level, is the
predominance in Part II of images of vegetation and fertility,
which fit into a wider network discussed below.

The present class of images can be regarded not merely as
biblical in origin and having a very general devotional significance,
but also as related through the details of their presentation to
contemporary society and possibly to contemporary events. They
thus imply a particular conception of history, which subordinates
the world to a transcendental temporality. It is a view which
follows from the spiritual interpretation of natural phenomena,

which is encouraged by the exegetic reconciliation of the Old and New Testaments, and which corresponds to the devotional effort to relate the historical present with divine eternity.

2. The Typological Cycle

Of the exegetic methods employed by La Ceppède the most prominent is the typological. Unlike the other methods, typology relates two elements from the same order of things, from sacred history, although both in turn are a manifestation and a demonstration of that which transcends time.[14] Both terms in the typological comparison are regarded as historically real, but are distinguished according to the temporal phases that characterize a conception of history prevalent from Augustine to Bossuet. The period under Mosaic Law (and to this may be added pagan antiquity) foreshadows the redemption through Christ, who in turn foreshadows the eschatological fulfilment. While there is an element of cyclical repetition in this tripartite scheme, each cycle reveals what was obscure in the preceding one. The Old Testament and pagan mythologies contain obscurities that are to be deciphered in terms of the New. Since creation, too, is a book whose spiritual sense is open to interpretation, typology and natural imagery frequently overlap.

(i) *Biblical types.* In the *Imitation* the technique of paraphrase does not lend itself to the highlighting of prospective allusions which could be uncovered in commentary. Some Christian applications of the Psalms, however, could scarcely be ignored. Psalm 50, for instance, would be associated with the liturgy of the mass. Thus La Ceppède in his paraphrase evokes 'le iuste sacrifice du Verbe incarné', the 'Sacrifice immortel . . . mille fois, & mille offert sur son Autel' (50, 12). The central typological figure of the penitential psalms is David (assumed to be the 'I' who speaks in them). In the first place, David is the type of Christ; his suffering and penitence are types of the Crucifixion and Redemption. Actual references to Christ are few, but the inclusion of the 'Douze

---

[14] On typology cf., e.g., Daniélou, *Sacramentum Futuri*; Lubac, *Exégèse médiévale*, Part I, ch. 5; Charity, *Events and their Afterlife*; on types in La Ceppède and contemporary poets cf. Evans, 'Figural Art'; Cave, *Devotional Poetry*, pp. 223 ff.; on theological uses of typology in France cf. Dagens, *Bérulle*, pp. 322 ff.; Mesnard, 'Théorie des figuratifs'.

meditations' suggests a typological parallel between the two parts.[15] In the second place, David, the anointed one, is the archetypal king, and although there is no clear suggestion of an identification with the French kings, the work does spring, as has been seen, from a historical situation in which such an identification might be appropriate.[16] Thirdly, David is the universal penitent soul, a type realized anew in all sinners and, according to the *Imitation*, in the author himself and the French nation. But in spite of these possibilities there is a considerable difference between the types of the *Imitation* and those of the *Théorèmes*. Not only do the *Théoremes* use typological correspondences on a much larger scale, but the theme itself of revelation through temporal fulfilment is intrinsic to La Ceppède's exposition of the Gospel narrative.

The key to the fulfilment of the Old in the New Testament is seen in the sixth word from the cross ('consummatum est'), the point at which

> La verité succede à l'ombre des Figures:
> La vieille Loy fait place à ses nouueaux Decrets. (I. iii. 79)

The whole notion of revelation is intimately bound up with Christ's Passion. Both hinge on the doctrine of the Incarnation, and a number of the Old Testament types in the *Théorèmes* are not unnaturally concerned with the human nature of Christ. In I. ii (the narration of the trial and humiliation of Jesus) one finds, for instance, the figure Micah struck on the cheek by Pilate's forerunner Ahab (I. i. 11). But there are more complex types illustrating Christ's degradation, such as Reuben's crime against his father's concubine (Genesis 35: 22). This is linked with the Incarnation, which is traditionally metaphorized in terms of marriage:

> Qu'est-ce autre chose, ô Christ, ta saincte humanité
> Que l'Espouse, & le lict de ta Diuinité?
> Ce puant l'a poluë, & d'opprobres couuerte. (I. ii. 72)

The themes of sexual guilt, humiliation, revelation, and redemption come together in typological images of clothing and nakedness. In I. iii. 11 the first quatrain contrasts Christ's sacrifice with the ritual vestments of the Old Covenant. The new sacrifice strips

---

[15] All known extant copies of the 1612 *Imitation* are bound with, but following, the *Théorèmes*, so that the typological pattern is broken.

[16] Cf. Sponde, *Méditations*, ed. Boase, pp. 33–42.

away the veils of obscurity of the old; at the same time Christ's nudity paradoxically 'covers' the shame of Adam and Eve:

> Tout nud donc il exerce à ce coup sa Prestrise,
> Et couure la rougeur dont Eue fut surprise,
> Dont son mary rougit lors qu'ils se virent nuds. (I. iii. 11)

But the sonnet concludes by dwelling on humiliation as the instrument of redemption. The mockery of Noah's nakedness and drunkenness is the type of this:

> Puis tantost enyuré de l'amour de nos ames
> Dormant nud sur la Croix ces Chams, ces fiers haineux,
> Moqueurs le gausseront de cent brocards infames. (I. iii. 11)

More explicitly in I. ii. 71 on The *Ecce Homo* God is said to be 'hidden' in 'cet image hideux de nostre genre humain' adopted by Jesus in the Incarnation. It would be wrong, however, to assume from La Ceppède's emphasis on the suffering implicit in the Incarnation that his view of the human condition generally is pessimistic. The redemptive perspective of his typologies includes the elevation of humanity:

> Tout est donq consommé, grand Dieu de l'vniuers,
> Vous auiez consommé l'humaine architecture,
> Sathan l'auoit détruite, & malgré ce peruers,
> Vous l'auez rebastie en plus belle structure. (I. iii. 81)

Types are then used circularly to explicate the point in the Passion at which their own discovery and interpretation in the Old Testament becomes possible. In the above examples the type of Noah and the associated imagery demonstrate the sacrificial adoption of fallen humanity, by means of which humanity is recreated, previous time consummated, and Old Testament obscurities themselves revealed.[17] The representation of Christ's relationship to humanity, to the Church or the soul as a marriage, which is fundamental in mystical and devotional literature, is introduced early in the narrative of the *Théorèmes* and plays an important role throughout the work. It has already been seen how La Ceppède uses the typological themes of incest and marriage as metaphors also for the Passion and Incarnation (I. ii. 72). That

---

[17] Cf. also the types of Rachel (Genesis 35: 16–19; 31: 34) in I. i. 21 and I. ii. 71.

this is not merely a conventional use of traditional typology is
suggested by the fact that the next sonnet presents a contrasting
but related type: the royal marriage of Solomon:

> SIonides sortez, venez voir l'equipage
> Du grand Roy Salomon: le voicy couronné
> D'vn nouueau Diademe, au iour de son Nopçage,
> Qui luy fut par sa mere en partage donné.
> Ce plus que Salomon d'opprobres foisonné
> Sort couronné de ioncs (creus dans le Marescage
> De vostre Synagogue) à ce iour ordonné
> Pour consommer çà bas son heureux Mariage. (I. ii. 73)

Here is a link between the theme of Christ the king and the theme
of Christ the lover, and the typological basis for the erotic imagery
that is present in much of the work.

The emphasis on the fulfilment of the Old Testament sacrificial
rites is made quite strongly in the *Théorèmes*, and may reflect the
Tridentine reaffirmation of this aspect of the mass. The sestet of
I. i. 40 is, as La Ceppède points out, a paraphrase of the interpretation of the Passion in Hebrews 9: 7–12:

> Puis, outre la douleur dont son ame est outrée,
> Estant le vray Pontife, & proche de l'entrée
> Du nouueau Tabernacle, il luy faloit du sang.
> Il en verse, mais c'est, non du sang des victimes
> (Comme faisoient iadis ceux qui tenoient ce rang)
> Mais de cil qu'il espreint de ses veines intimes.[18]

With the glossators La Ceppède interprets the ritual of blood-
sacrifice prior to the pontiff's entry into the tabernacle as Jesus's
sweat of blood in Gethsemane. The progress of the narrative in
the *Théorèmes* from the agony to the Crucifixion is paralleled by
the high priest's procession from the initial sacrifice to his entry
into the inner tabernacle, which itself is realized as the cross. The
stripping of Christ is the inverse fulfilment of the priest's vesting
before the sacrifice in the sanctuary (I. iii. 11). But Christ's garment
is also related by its whiteness with the sacrificial vestment of the
Old Testament, and with the sacrificial lamb (I. ii. 54).[19] The
temple itself is fulfilled in the body of Christ (I. iii. 15, etc.), and

[18] Cf. also I. i. 12, I. iii. 44, for Christ as pontiff.
[19] The 'symphonie en blanc' (Bremond, *Histoire*, vol. i, p. 350); it is made up
of typological correspondences whose common attribute is 'blanc'.

with this notion one may link metaphors for Christ, such as 'cette belle structure' (I. iii. 16) and 'ta belle architecture' (I. ii. 72).

Typologies of this kind serve primarily theological and exegetic purposes. On the one hand the Passion provides the key to the obscurities of the past; on the other, the personages, events, and institutions of the past, once interpreted in the light of the Passion, are presented as proofs of the divine plan. But this group overlaps, particularly where the Crucifixion is concerned, with another class of biblical images. These, while being typological in so far as they are derived from the Old Testament, seem to have a mainly symbolic and emotive function at a very general level of religious feeling.[20]

The Crucifixion is the mid-point at which the old is converted into the new. But it is not only historically central. In La Ceppède the cross in its various symbolic and typological guises, including that of the temple, is situated at the centre.[21] More precisely, it is situated at the point where the earth intersects the vertical line between heaven and hell. The Christian sources for this are patristic. Taking up Augustine's 'ligni cuspide rumpitur Golgotha'[22] La Ceppède declares that the point of the cross penetrates to hell:

> Puis la leuant debout, la pointe on precipite
> Si roide dans ce trou creuzé sur le rocher
> Que le coup s'en va bruire au centre du Cocyte. (I. iii. 18)

And specific mention is made in I. iii. 28 of the fact that the cross 's'esleue du milieu de ce bas Element'. Moreover, the wider scene of the Crucifixion, the sacred city of Jerusalem, is also at the centre of the world (I. iii. 29, n. 4). Such symbols are, however, given a typological dimension by La Ceppède's reference to the prophetic utterance in Psalm 73: 12, 'operatus est salutem in medio terrae'. In a number of religions the sacred object of the centre is a column, ladder, tree, or mountain.[23] In La Ceppède similar objects occur as symbolic prefigurations of the cross. Thus in I. iii. 25 the 'belle Tour de David' is a type of the cross. Jacob's ladder is one such image with a typological basis. Without citing any authority,

---

[20] On the images discussed below and their occurrence in world religions cf. Eliade, *Le Mythe de l'éternel retour; Images et symboles*.

[21] On symbolic centrality of the temple, etc., cf. Eliade, *Images*, ch. 1, *passim*.

[22] See Migne, *Patrologia Latina*, vol. 39, col. 2038.

[23] Cf. Eliade, *Images*, ch. 1.

La Ceppède associates the mysterious location of the communicating ladder with the centrality of the cross:

> L'eschele Israelite est posée en ce lieu,
> Sur laquele auiourd'huy s'appuyant l'homme-Dieu,
> Nous fait iouir des biens qu'il promit à nos Peres. (I. iii. 23)

Although it is because of the identity of location that La Ceppède here relates the cross with the ladder, the ultimate motivation clearly lies in the fact that both symbolize the reconciliation of heaven and earth. Hence attention is drawn also to the Incarnation in the phrase 'homme-Dieu'.

The sacred mountain is another symbolic prefiguration used in the *Théorèmes* to link Old Testament events with the Agony, the Crucifixion, and the Ascension. The Agony takes place on a mountain, and here too La Ceppède lays great stress on the hypostatic union.[24] The beginning of the work describes the ascent of Christ to Gethsemane on the slopes of the Mount of Olives, which faces Calvary. Sonnet I. i. 5 is a eulogy of the former; the sonnet following contrasts it with the pagan Mount Helicon. And in I. i. 7 La Ceppède clearly shows that he is aware of the universality of the belief in the sacredness of mountains and of trees often associated with them. At the same time he points to the recurrence of mountains in the Gospel narrative itself:

> Sur la cime d'vn mont, dans le secret d'vn bois
> Nos ancestres ont eu cet honneur memorable
> De l'entendre parler, de receuoir ses loix,
> Qu'il graua sur la pierre, & saincte & venerable . . .
>   Et Christ mesme choisit vn mont pour enseignen,
> Fit briller sur vn mont esclairs de sa gloire,
> Et s'en va sur vn mont ses chauds vœux desseigner.

Typological motifs within the New Testament narrative constitute an essential part of the structure and unity of the two parts of the *Théorèmes*. The Ascension which is related in Part II takes place according to patristic authority 'Sur le mont qu'il baigna de sueurs precieuses' (II. iii. 9), that is, on the Mount of Olives described in I. i. All three major events in the reconciliation of humanity and divinity—the Agony, the Crucifixion, and the Ascension—are implicitly brought together in II. iii. 27 by means

---

[24] Cf. his excursus in I. i. 37, n. 3, discussed above, pp. 80 ff.

of the identification of Christ himself with the symbolic central
mountain (here derived from the prophetic symbolism of Isaiah 2:
2 with its patristic commentaries):

> DE la maison de Dieu la montagne mystique
> Preparée s'éleue au dessus des coupeaux
> Des Monts plus éleuez, & les nombreux troupeax
> Des gens y vont courants comme à leur Antartique.
> Céte montagne est Christ que l'humeur frenetique
> Des Iuifs a preparée à grand coups de marteaux . . . (II. iii. 27)

The mountain, then, is in the *Théorèmes* a symbol of the reconciliation of man with God through the Passion and Ascension.[25]

Probably the most clearly developed of the types and symbols of
the cross in the *Théorèmes* is the central tree—an image with parallels in many religious symbolisms. The identification of the tree
with the cross or with Christ himself has its justification in Nebuchadnezzar's dream of 'a tree in the midst of the earth' whose
height was great (Daniel 4: 7–15). It occurs in patristic writing,
particularly that of Origen and Chrysostom, and is firmly embedded in the iconography of the Middle Ages. The true fulfilment of
Nebuchadnezzar's tree is the cross. In interpreting this type in
I. iii. 28 La Ceppède emphasizes the height, centrality, and fertility of the cross. In the next sonnet images are developed independently of the biblical reference in order to stress the mediating
role of the incarnate Christ:

> IVsqu'au Ciel voirement, au comble de l'Empyre
> Cet Arbre de la Croix esleue sa hauteur,
> Et nul ne peut atteindre au Ciel de son Empire
> Que celuy, qui des Cieux est le supreme Autheur.
> . . . Bien sçauons nous que c'est dans le centre du monde
> Que cet Arbre est planté, pour marque que son fruit
> Est pour tous les bourgeois de la machine ronde.

An important feature amongst those which enable La Ceppède to
elaborate such parallels is the theme of fecundity. Sonnet I. iii. 30,
for example, is devoted to an allegorical exposition of its first
line: 'Cet Arbre est foisonnant en mille fruits diuers'. And it is
this theme that underlies certain other symbolic prefigurations of
the cross. In the Old Testament the tree of life tends to be identified as the vine. The vine and the winepress (derived principally

[25] Mountains represent the Apostles reflecting the light of the sun in II.
iv 28.

from Isaiah 63: 3) were, as La Ceppède points out, 'figuratifs de la Croix' (I. iii. 23, n. 4). The winepress image occurs in I. i. 56 and I. iii. 23 in such a way as to relate the focal points of the Passion as narrated in the *Théorèmes*—namely the Agony and the Crucifixion. This theme of the fruit of the cross (the blood of Christ) is in turn linked with the theme of the infertile vineyard (derived from Isaiah 5: 1–6), this time in order to contrast the Old Covenant with the new as an epoch of sterility followed by one of fertility (I. ii. 64).

Linked with this complex of imagery is the figure of Noah, who, fulfilled in the crucified Christ, is represented on the cross as 'enyvré de l'amour de nos ames' (I. iii. 11). Further, the blood-wine of the Crucifixion is associated with the stream of water from Christ's pierced side, and in I. iii. 94 this leads to the comparison of the body of Christ with 'l'autre Arche mystique', which was 'la figure du corps de Iesus-Christ, ouuert au coste, pour . . . receuoir & sauuer les bons de deluge des flammes eterneles' (n. 4); in I. iii. 22 it is the cross that is regarded as the antitype of the ark, and that floats on a 'mer de sang'. The flood-waters destroy, but also purge and regenerate. Other prefigurations of the water from Christ's side bring out the fertilizing and healing aspects. In I. iii. 25 the cross is linked with the 'Bois sucrin', the tree in Exodus 15: 25 cast by Moses into the desert water; in I. iii. 95 Longinus' stabbing of Jesus on the cross is said to be prefigured in Moses' smiting of the rock (Numbers 20: 11). La Ceppède develops this latter theme by means of images of food and healing, and explicates the typological relationship as a prefiguration of the cleansing rite of baptism (I. iii. 95). This theme in turn is associated with a series of related typologies through the figure of Longinus.[26] In the sources used by La Ceppède Longinus is believed to be blind until cured and converted by the water flowing from Christ's side. The conversion is recounted in the sestet of I. iii. 92 which is verbally linked with that of I. iii. 45 (both are paraphrases of Luke 23: 47–8). Sonnet I. iii. 45 itself points to the conversion and baptism of the Jews and Gentiles in the future, and back to the prayers of Christ in Gethsemane. The sweat of blood is a prefiguration of the shedding of blood at the Crucifixion, and is likewise associated with the cleansing and healing water. In one of the sonnets on the Agony (I. i. 39) La Ceppède compares the redemp-

---

[26] Cf. Wilson, 'Notes on a Sonnet by La Ceppède'.

tive blood of Christ with yet another biblical prefiguration—the healing of the man born blind in the waters of Siloam, which spring from the sacred Mount Sion:

> CEtte rouge sueur goutte à goutte roulante
> Du corps de cet Athlete en ce rude combat,
> Peut estre comparé à cette eau douce & lente,
> Qui la sainte montagne en silence rebat.
> L'aueugle-nay (qui mit tous les siens en debat
> Pour ses yeux) fut lavé de cette eau doux-coulante,
> Et dans le chaud lauoir de cette onde sanglante
> Toute l'aueugle race en liberté s'esbat
> Et l'vn & l'autre bain ont redonné la veue . . .

La Ceppède's manipulation of traditional types and symbols in connection with the Passion results in a dense network of imagery. The Agony and bloody sweat anticipates the symbolism of the Crucifixion with the references to the ritual curing of physical and spiritual blindness; there is a further typological perspective which relates Old and New Testaments on the one hand, and the New Testament and the practices of the Church on the other; at the same time this is closely bound up with the partly typological symbolism of the sacred mountain, and, it could be added, with the military imagery (cf. above, line 2 of I. i. 39).

The Old Testament types of Part II are also often inseparable from general patterns of symbolism. Indeed, the notion of rebirth bears a certain resemblance to that of typological correspondence. In I. iii. 100 the sepulchre is alluded to on the authority of Augustine as a parallel to the womb of the Virgin; in I. i. 36 Scriptural passages are adduced to show that 'la Resurrection est vne autre naissance'. The rebirth is symbolically linked not only with the nativity of Jesus but also with the birth of the universe, the creation. Nativity and Resurrection are typological repetitions of the creation, since they all occurred on the same day of the week (II. i. 45).[27] With the theme of rebirth is associated the primordial flood which is destructive yet regenerative. Amongst the Old Testament events listed in II. i. 38 which correspond to the forty hours between the Crucifixion and the Resurrection is the forty-day period of the Flood, 'l'horrible lauement . . . des mortels'. In II. i. 44 the Resurrection after 'ce grand orage De la Croix' is prefigured in

---

[27] Cf. the entombment described as 'repos . . . au bercail' in II. i. 37.

the return of the dove to the ark. Closely bound up with these types is the image of the flowering of the withered tree. In I. iii. 26 the cross was described as the 'bois sec' that cancels out the 'bois vert' that brought about the Fall. Now the cycle is completed with the reflowering of the tree in the person of the risen Christ:

> CHrist, aux yeux aueuglez de la Gent Hebraïque
> Paroist vn mauuais arbre . . .
> Mais lors qu'elle a cuydé tout à fait le seicher,
> Le voilà reuerdir, s'esleuer heroique . . .
> C'ét, cét arbre planté sur le moite riuage
> De l'eau proportionnée à son iuste breuuage,
> Qui iamais ne s'éffeuille, & porte en sa saison. (II. i. 39)

The image of the fertilizing water is taken up independently in the next sonnet in order to link the regeneration of the individual soul in baptism with the Resurrection (II. i. 40).

A similar combination of natural images and typological correspondences can be observed in the presentation of the culminating mystery in the work, the gift of the Holy Spirit at Pentecost. The Spirit appears in the first place in the form of breath or the wind: 'nous appellons vent ce que l'Euangeliste appelle Esprit' (II, p. 544). La Ceppède has already acknowledged on the authority of Basil, Génébrard, and Desportes that the term 'spiritus' in Psalm 77 can be read in the two senses of 'spirit' and 'the wind' (II, pp. 278–9). Along with the Church Fathers and medieval natural science La Ceppède continues to believe in the fecundating property of the wind. The series of sonnets II. iv. 2 to 7 draws on the lore surrounding this idea, which is linked in turn with the idea of creation, and prophetic and even poetic inspiration. These associations are for the most part expressed by means of typological correspondence. Thus II. iv. 2 alludes to Genesis 1: 1 and 2: 7:

> Cet Esprit halenant sur eux, va r'auiuant
> Leurs ames, tout ainsi que nostre terre seche
> Feut jadis animée auec vn peu de vent.

The creative aspect of the wind is linked with sexual love (as a metaphor for the soul's desire for God) by way of a typological allusion to 'l'Espouse au 4. des Cantiques verset 16 qui appelle à soy pour souffler en son jardin l'Aquilon, & l'Auster ou Meridional: Soubs le nom desquels vents elle entend le sainct Esprit selon les PP. & les modernes escriuains . . .' (II, pp. 548–9).

It is clear from cases such as these that it is natural phenomena that play a key role in providing images—images frequently regarded by La Ceppède as 'demonstrations' of the mysteries that constitute the primary themes of his work. However, two points should be noted. In the first place, some of these natural images, for example that of the mystic tree, do have sources in symbolic and prophetic passages of the Old Testament. In the second place, there is an essential similarity between typological correspondence and the use of natural phenomena in images in the *Théorèmes*: in both, the terms of the comparison are held to be literally true, and to be intrinsically related in some way; this being so, both are felt to be 'proofs' of the divine plan in creation and in history. There is no reason to oppose the one to the other, and consequently the question of contrasting parts of the *Théorèmes* in terms of either 'figural [i.e. typological] art' or 'descriptive realism' need not arise.[28]

(ii) *Pagan types*. As has been seen, La Ceppède justifies pagan as well as other profane images with the Christian and Platonic argument that the sensible can raise the contemplator to suprasensible mysteries.[29] As in biblical exegesis, the methods by which the spiritual sense could be extracted were, however, diverse. The three principal methods of interpretation that emerged during the Middle Ages and Renaissance have been expounded by Seznec: the euhemeristic interpretation; the interpretation in terms of natural phenomena; and allegorical interpretation in terms of moral and theological truths.[30] After the Council of Trent the dangers to be avoided are the literal sensuality of myth on the one hand, and on the other the heretical implications of neo-Platonic syncretic exegesis. The corresponding solutions, both of which are found in La Ceppède, are allegorization and the insistence on a typological schema which strictly subordinates the pagan figure or event (whether regarded as historical or fictional) to Christian revelation.[31] Certain mythological images are, of course, common-

---

[28] Cf. Evans, 'Figural Art' countered by Du Bruck, 'Descriptive Realism'.
[29] See above, pp. 104 f.
[30] Seznec, *La Survivance des dieux antiques*, Part I, *passim*.
[31] La Ceppède condemns the literal identification of Christ and pagan deities (I. ii. 78); myths are allegorized Old Testament history (I. iii. 22, n. 1) or allegorized theology actualized only through Christ: 'céte Theologie fabuleuse de l'antiquité est maintenant histoire veritable' (II. iv. 13, n. 1).

place, and independent of exegetic principles. In poetic contexts at this date the term 'Olympe', for instance, is so frequently found that it appears to be devoid of pagan associations. There is nothing in the particular contexts in which it is found in the *Théorèmes* to suggest that La Ceppède in any way revitalizes this metaphor. The use of classical synonyms for the Christian hell, however, may be more significant. It has been pointed out that Christ's death, descent into hell, and Resurrection in the *Théorèmes* are to some extent underpinned by types and symbols based on the theme of the destructive yet regenerative flood-waters. At the moment of crucifixion the term 'Cocyte' introduces the theme of the flood in I. iii. 18. The implicit typological significance becomes clear in I. iii. 22: the waters of hell, of the deluge, and the Crucifixion are all brought together in the 'bouillons stygieux'; the cross floats on the waters as the 'bois industrieux' of the 'true' Deucalion, that is, Noah. The descent into hell is associated above all with water, with the 'bords Phlegethontides', with the 'flots Acherontides' (I. iii. 86), the 'antres stygieux', and with the 'Auernal Corsaire' (II. i. 1).[32]

Mythological images used in this way are quite distinct from moral allegorization, which is employed by La Ceppède in particular connection with the theme of earthly and divine love. Thus the Magdalen's 'amour sacre-sainct', for instance, is contrasted with 'les feux de Cypris' (I. iii. 98; cf. also *Imitation* 37, 4). The conflict of the two loves is expounded in a more elaborate fashion by a discursive allegorical treatment of the story of Europa and the bull:

> On peut . . . Chrestienner la fable de la belle Europe que Iupiter transformé en Taureau enleua de sa terre & l'emporta où sa voluptueuse passion la desiroit. Elle se laissa voirement emporter, mais ce fut auec vn extréme regret de quitter le doux air de sa naissance . . . C'ét à dire que si bien nous sommes quelquefois emportez par le Taureau de la concupiscible loing de Iesus-Christ & du Ciel, en la terre de Satan, de la chair, & du monde, au moins deuons nous retenir, & auoir tousiours au cœur vn regreteux souuenir du bien que nous delaissons' . . . (II. ii. 41, n. 3)

With reference to the same theme La Ceppède speaks of 'les pieds

---

[32] Cf. also 'le lac de l'eternele nuict' (*Imitation* 142, 6); 'Coursaire des morts' (*Imitation*, 'Vexilla', 6); and Christ as 'Le Pilote discret' (I. i. 74).

de l'ame' in sonnet II. iii. 32—a phrase which is found in Augustine and others with the meaning of 'affections', but which is also in La Ceppède's sonnet apparently an indirect allusion to the myths of Eurydice and of Achilles interpreted allegorically from a moralistic point of view: 'A cecy se rapportent moralement les fables d'Eurydice, & d'Achille qui receurent la mort par le talon' (II. iii. 32, n. 1). In the same manner the seduction of Danae is moralized as a warning of the power of gold to corrupt.

The identification of pagan heroes with Christian figures, and especially with Christ himself, was, although present in the medieval tradition, a delicate matter in the atmosphere of Tridentine orthodoxy in which La Ceppède was writing. He is cautious of syncretic speculation; yet pagan figures of this type play a significant role in the pattern of secondary themes in the *Théorèmes*.

Although Peter is condemned along with Icarus in I. i. 13, he is in II. ii. 93 described as 'ce grand Achate'. This description rests, La Ceppède explains (n. 4), on Peter's relationship on the one hand with John and on the other hand with Jesus. But for this ambiguity the comparison might be thought evidence to support the view that some identification between Christ and Aeneas is intended in the *Théorèmes*.[33] This view is usually based on the work's opening paraphrase of the *arma virumque cano*, and La Ceppède's fairly frequent references to the *Aeneid*. However, it should be borne in mind that the figure of the heroic wanderer with his descent into hell and triumphal return is common to many mythical and religious forms, and there is no need to posit the epic alone as the primary source of this aspect of the *Théorèmes*. The fact is that La Ceppède's Christ-hero is compounded of firstly, the concepts of military chivalry discussed earlier, secondly, the Old Testament types of the military leader, and thirdly types from various sources in myth.

Orpheus was a well-established Christ-figure from the time of Clement of Alexandria to the Renaissance Florentine interest in the theological parallels in the Orphic hymns. La Ceppède's handling of the Orpheus myth, however, is strictly limited. He does not even exploit the traditional association of Orpheus with David, who is otherwise such a prominent figure in his work. Instead he uses those elements which are relevant to the central theme of

[33] Cf. Donaldson-Evans, *Poésie et méditation*, pp. 89–90.

redemption—namely Orpheus' descent into hell to recover Eurydice, interpreted in this context theologically as

l'Eglise proprement appelée icy Euridice (qui vaut autant dire que verité) nom tres-propre à l'Eglise de Dieu: faisant allusion de la fabuleuse descente d'Orphée aux Enfers, pour en r'amener son Euridice, à la veritable descente de Iesus-Christ aux Limbes pour en tirer son Eglise . . . (I, p. 386)

The same is true of his single use of the Prometheus myth: it underlines another essential aspect of the structure of the mysteries embodied in the narrative of the *Théorèmes*, the descent of the Son from heaven, his redemption of man, and his ascent:

> SI le Fils de Iapet n'eut jamais apportée
> La flamme Titannide en ce bas Element,
> Ses hommes n'eussent eu jamais d'auiuement,
> Et le vent eut sa terre, & sa forme emportée. (II. iv. 13)

Further, some of the elements involved in this parallel are thematically linked with more general patterns in the work. In the first place, the creative role of Prometheus reinforces the theme of creation and regeneration associated with the Resurrection and Pentecost; secondly, this theme is related to the image of the fecund wind (also described in classical terms as 'Zephyr' and 'Favonius' in II. iv. 2), and to that of the divine sun, the 'Pere des clartez' of whom the Holy Spirit is an emanation dispensed by 'notre diuin Promethée' (II. iv. 13).

Probably the best-known mythological type of Christ in Renaissance literature was Hercules—a figure who had acquired a complex range of significations[34] and who is best known from Nicolas Denisot's *cantique* on Hercules and Ronsard's *Hercule Chrestien*. In the *Théorèmes* there are no more than two explicit references, and only a few unobtrusive indirect allusions; but all of these merge with other images that make Christ the archetypal hero. That Hercules is here to be regarded as a type fulfilled in Christ is apparent from his association with Samson:[35] in I. i. 96 Jesus is addressed as 'Magnanime Samson Nazarien Alcide'. The accompanying note explains that Samson's betrayal by Delilah is a prefiguration of that of Christ by Judas; and there is a parallel,

---

[34] See Jung, *Hercule dans la littérature française du XVIe siècle*.
[35] Cf. Jung, p. 107.

implicitly alluded to in this sonnet, in Deianeira's betrayal of Hercules. This sacrificial aspect is complemented by his role of slayer of monsters:

Le nom d'Alcide conuient à nostre Sauueur, pource qu'Alcide fut le dompteur des monstres & des meschans, comme le rapporte amplement des anciens Noël le Comte . . . Et Iesus-Christ a esté le vainqueur des monstres du peché, & de l'enfer . . . (I. i. 2, p. 24).

This is the aspect that is brought out in indirect allusions to the myth. Although La Ceppède does not explicitly develop the traditional identification of Hercules with David,[36] the co-occurrence of the antonomasia 'cil par qui fut Anthée accrauanté' and the moral allegorization of Goliath's presumption in I. i. 14 may not be fortuitous. It is here Peter who is being accused of presumptuous emulation of the hero Hercules, but all the other indirect allusions to Hercules' labours imply a comparison with Jesus. The court of the high priest is compared with 'l'antre d'vn Cacus, d'vn Busire' (I. ii. 19) and by implication Christ with their slayer, Hercules. This identification is evoked each time the Jews are compared with Busiris. The reference to Jesus as 'Athlete sacré' (I. i. 19; I. i. 39), as 'ce fort' (II. iii. 1) might have a similar relevance. But the hero-image of Christ tends not to be confined to one myth: the multiplicity of mythical correspondences merely serves to bring out a more general notion of 'ce Guerrier eternel' (I. i. 83).

There is a further accepted interpretation of the pagan deities in the Renaissance which is relevant for the imagery discussed in the next chapter—namely, their association with natural phenomena. In the wake of the Pléiade such periphrases as 'le flot Neptunide' (I. iii. 24), 'les bourgeois Amphitrites' (I. ii. 2) are not unexpected, and probably have little significance. However, some of these images can be seen to play a more important role. The comparison of the Holy Spirit with Zephyrus or Favonius, and its contrast with Arcturus in II. iv. 2 provides a means of expanding the secondary theme of the Spirit's fecundity. La Ceppède comments on this and draws out the allegorical possibilities (n. 4):

Le Zephire est ainsi appellé pource qu'il porte & donne la vie, faisant germer & croistre les plantes & les fleurs (voyez Gel. au 2. liu chap. 22).

[36] Cf. Jung, p. 107.

Il est aussi nommé *Fauonius a fouendo*, pource qu'il fomante tout; *Et est genitalis spiritus mundi quo plantae hyberno frigore enectae reuiuiscunt* . . . Le raport de ces proprietez se fait de soy-mesme aux perfections de ce vent du sainct Esprit qui porte veritablement & donne la vie, qui fait germer, & produit en nos ames les plantes & les fleurs des vertus immortelles. Et qui est en vn mot, l'ame, et l'esprit vivifiant de l'vnivers.

The Spirit is thus clearly compared with the pagan wind-deities not for purely ornamental reasons but because of their connotations. This is not the only instance in which the deities are brought to life in connection with the theme of fertility. In the sonnet just referred to the Holy Spirit is 'cil dont Cybelle conçoit Les plantes & les fleurs dez qu'elle le reçoit', and Cybele by implication stands for mankind: This is also the case in II. ii. 62, where it is said

> ET Cybèle, & Titan hument l'eau ruissellante
> Des gros yeux de Iunon, mais bien diuersement . . .

and where the opposition of Cybele and Titan is meant to express the relationship of mankind to the divine sun, Christ. It is in fact the sun that most frequently among the natural imagery attracts classical names: Titan (e.g. II. ii. 10; II. ii. 62) and Phoebus (e.g. I. i. 96; I. iii. 13; II. ii. 46). This frequency is no doubt in part a function of the central role played in the *Théorèmes* by solar imagery of all kinds, and in particular by the image of Christ as the true sun. The use of the pagan gods of nature in the *Théorèmes* is thus partly allegorical (as in the case of the Holy Spirit); but the association of Christ with, for example, the sun-gods bears some resemblance to his quasi-typological identification with the heroes such as Hercules.

VI

IMAGES AND THEMES

B. THE SUN AND ASSOCIATED IMAGERY

THE typology of the *Théorèmes* already suggests two things that offer a means of unravelling the complexities of La Ceppède's imagery. On the one hand, the typologies rest on a relationship in time between the obscure and the revealed; and on the other, typologies are associated with solar, vegetative, and similar motifs. These are in fact interrelated dimensions in the structure of the imagery of the *Théorèmes* which are clarified by the identification of Christ with the sun. Solar images are susceptible of both forms of metaphorical organization distinguished at the beginning of the last chapter: they can, like typology, relate to a temporal cycle; or they can serve as analogies for other entities in the natural and supernatural hierarchy.

As for the provenance of the solar imagery, it is present, as is well known, in many religions. In Platonic, in neo-Platonic, and in Christian thought the sun symbol provides a tool for expounding numerous speculative concepts.[1] Tertullian uses sun imagery to define the Trinity, and, in conjunction with vegetative imagery, to justify the Resurrection. For Ambrose Christ himself is the 'Sol Novus', the true fulfilment of the pagan deities.[2] The Platonic and Plotinian traditions are represented most fully and are most effectively transmitted to the Middle Ages and the Renaissance in the works of the pseudo-Areopagite. The visible sun represents the invisible light of God; but the imagery, in spite of the insistence on abstraction, relies on the solar attributes of universal illumination, generative power, and attraction. It is the latter, the dynamic relationship between the earth and the sun, between the soul and

[1] See, e.g., Eliade, *Traité d'histoire des religions*, ch. 5; Dunbar, *Symbolism in Medieval Thought*, pp. 119 ff., 138 ff., 148 ff.; Kantorowicz, 'Oriens Augusti' and 'Dante's Two Suns'.

[2] Sermo VI: 'Hic igitur est sol novus . . .' (Migne, *Patrologia Latina*, vol. 17, cols. 635 ff.).

God, that is emphasized.[3] In Valeriano the sun stands for Truth,
and the popularity of the *Hieroglyphica* probably accounts for the
appearance of the image (alongside other natural 'hieroglyphs') in
the academies.[4] All this could not have come about without biblical justification. The designation of the Messiah as 'Sol justitiae'
(Malachi 4: 2) and as 'Oriens', as well as the wealth of light and
fire imagery in the New Testament, authorized the use of such
imagery. La Ceppède's sources in this as in other spheres are
primarily biblical and patristic.

(i) *The 'Imitation'*. The dominant image theme is the sun in its
various paradoxical aspects and in its hierarchical relations with the
elements of water and earth. These themes are present in the
original text; but La Ceppède makes them explicit and extends
their use in his own version. It is noticeable that it is his penitential
psalms proper which display this property. Jehovah is not, it is
true, explicitly equated or compared with the sun; but he is
designated by images of its various conflicting characteristics.

Destructive fire is amongst the characteristics which are most
stressed in the psalms. God is manifested in the thunderbolt(31: 3;
101: 3; 102: 5), his wrath is burning heat:

> Allumé de courroux, boüillonnant de fureure . . . (37: 1; cf. 6: 1)

The Last Judgement will be 'il feu prompt qui desertera ces lieux'
(37, 10). Meanwhile the suffering of the penitent is expressed in
terms of burning; his flesh melts 'au feu de ma misere' (6, 2; cf. 6,
4). The original text of Psalm 101 uses fire and smoke as an image
of reduction and evanescence. La Ceppède translates this into
alchemical terms in his prose version:

> . . . desia mes plus beaux iours sont éuaporez en subtile fumée (comme
> le Mercure au feu de l'Alchimiste) & mes os rostis aux braises de mille
> ennuis, s'en vont reduits en cendre. (101, p. 31)

The most common Old Testament image of the transience of
man is derived from vegetation. The sun-God evaporates the vital
humours (31, 3), withers the grass (101, 3, 7, 16), and (in 142, 5)

---

[3] See *De divinis nominibus*, cap. 4 (Migne, vol. 122, cols. 635 ff.).
[4] See Yates, *French Academies*, pp. 90, 149, 168 f. (on Du Perron's syncretic
view of the sun symbol); also Dagens, *Bérulle*, pp. 294 ff., 329 f.; Rousset,
'Images de la nuit et de la lumière' (on the mystical use of the symbol in Hopil).

withholds the fertilizing rain, the symbol of grace.[5] It is not only the actively destructive aspect of the sun that enters into the schema, but also its absence. God's withdrawal in displeasure is described as an eclipse (50, 9). The suffering of the sinner and of his people is 'la nuit des aduersitez' (129, p. 35). Death is an eclipse of the sun: 'la nuict de la mort va mon iour éclipsant' (37, 5). It is the fear of confusion, aberration, and chaos that La Ceppède's use of the Hebrew imagery seems to emphasize in the *Imitation*. He comes closest to identifying Jehovah with the sun when he expresses this fear:

Faites leuer sur les tenebres de mes forfaits la matineuse Aurore de vostre Clemence . . . & ne detournez point apres vostre Soleil de mon foible zenit; de peur qu'en l'aueuglement de son éclipse, ie ne me precipite dans le Lac infernal (142, p. 40).

The positive aspects of solar and vegetative imagery are linked almost exclusively with the doxology at the end of each verse paraphrase. On the one hand the Trinity is seen as the principle of universal fertility:

> Que l'Eternité saincte en son infinité,
> Grosse du triple los de la Trine-vnité,
> Feconde tout ce tout des surgeons de sa gloire. (50, 14)

On the other hand the Trinity is located in the realm of the empyrean (101, 18); the Holy Spirit is a 'Flamme durable' (142, 12), a symbol of illumination and guidance. Elsewhere the imagery of the storm, the flood, and darkness is complemented by the images of the pole-star (31, 6) and the 'phare' (50, 7; 142, 7), representing a principle of direction desired at a time of confusion.

These opposing aspects of the divinity expressed principally in terms of solar and associated images state a problem which was already that of Job and the Psalmists, but which also has obvious relevance to the historical circumstances of La Ceppède's paraphrase. Man suffers either because God is absent, or because, when present, he is angry and punitive. The problem is how to achieve the permanent divine presence, and at the same time to receive God's pleasure. Hence La Ceppède brings in (or brings out) images of mediation between the poles of divine beneficence and displeasure. The *miserere* supplies the image of the ritual cleansing

---

[5] But cf. fecundity linked with sin ('vne pepiniere feconde'), 50, p. 24.

of sickness and sin in water—an image with which La Ceppède associates the notion of grace through his own image, 'l'éponge de ta grace' (50, 1); and Psalm 31 provides the image of the flood which not only destroys but also purifies (31: 5). The paraphrase of Psalm 102 (not in the penitential series) has two images of mediation: the image of the rejuvenated eagle present in the text, to which La Ceppède adds the further paradox of the God 'Qui fait que ton printemps en hyuer refleuronne' (102, 3). Fire is used as an image of human passion (37, 4), which is in turn used as an image of divine love manifest in the Holy Spirit: 'Fay que de ton feu sainct les flammes amoureuses Me conduisent ça bas . . .' (142, 8). This feature is entirely due to the paraphraser's intervention, and is developed at the end of the psalm into a climax suggesting a mystical ascent to the realm of eternal light. It is now the purgative aspect of fire, its cleansing effect which it has in common with water, that is emphasized (142, 9 and 10). This transition from human suffering to the divinity is even clearer in La Ceppède's version of Psalm 101. As has been seen, an alchemical image is used in the prose version to express the reduction of man to nothingness at the beginning of the psalm. Paraphrasing verse 27 of the original he continues it in order to describe the prophesied redemption:

> Les iustes épurez au fourneau de ta grace,
> Dans le sacré Palais de ton Eternité,
> Verront briller vn iour les surgeons de leur race.[6]

Sublimation is here conceived in historical terms, but fire imagery elsewhere expresses mystical transmutation. The burnt offerings mentioned in Psalm 50 are naturally developed by La Ceppède not only as a type of the Crucifixion and the martyrs, but also as a symbol of the soul's ascent. The soul is compared with the pyralis, the insect which according to Pliny is attracted to but not consumed by fire: 'Fay moy la Pyralide éprise de sa flamme' (50, 9; cf. also 50, 13). Images of metamorphosis, fire, and love of this kind are so common amongst the mystics that there is little point in seeking a specific source. The point is that La Ceppède imports them into his paraphrases and that they are incorporated in the over-all schema of sun, fire, flood, and vegetation imagery, which

---

[6] 101, 17; cf. the similar image in 'Sur les sainctes Reliques', I, ll. 9–11 (*Imitation*, p. 54): 'nostre humanité Sublimée au fourneau de vostre authorité'.

expresses the ancient religious problem of reconciling apparent divine anger with divine favour. La Ceppède's christianization of the penitential Psalms consists less in bringing out the prophetic and typological interpretations than in resolving this contradiction by the use of mediating images which either combine the dual aspects of the sun, water, and vegetation symbols in a paradox, or express the idea of spiritual metamorphosis through suffering. More specifically it might be said that the complex of image themes in the *Imitation* points to a preoccupation with the problems of personal redemption and grace.

(ii) *The 'Théorèmes'*. In examining the system of Old Testament typologies in the *Théorèmes* above it became clear that they were inseparable from certain key images such as vegetation, fire, water. What did not emerge directly was the fact that these images are bound up with the sun imagery in the work. There are four fundamental aspects of such imagery that should be stated at this point, since in the poetry itself they are subtly interwoven. These are: the cyclical character of solar imagery with its inherent contrasts, and the characteristics of the sun symbol of heat, light, and generative power. Although similar aspects are present in the *Imitation*, the *Théorèmes* present a considerable advance in the richness of the organization of these images. In the first place, the *Théorèmes* have a narrative structure (suffering, death, Resurrection, Ascension, Pentecost) for which the sun- and season-cycle provides an analogue. In the second place, the sun itself is manifest in various other figures displaying the same cyclical patterns parallel to the narrative. Thus the warrior-king figure has links in the imagery with the sun; the vegetation symbols tend to merge with the figure of the gardener; the water and the sun are related in some of their symbolic functions (purifying and fertilizing); the function of the symbolic animals is defined with respect to their relation towards the sun; and even the figure of the lover, which to some extent constitutes a separate area of imagery, has some ground in common with the images just mentioned. All these tend to be applied in varying degrees to the protagonist of the *Théorèmes*.

The solar and related imagery in the work, then, is complex. But it is also carefully controlled. On the one hand, the whole of nature for La Ceppède appears to be open to symbolic interpretation (I. ii. 65). On the other hand, comparisons between Christ and the sun in particular have to be carefully justified in the notes. With respect to the risen Christ, for instance, an accompanying note points out:

Iesus-Christ resuscité est icy, & ailleurs en nos vers metaphoriquement appellé Soleil auec beaucoup de raison. Puis qu'il semble que le Soleil porte empreints les dons de gloire qui sont en nostre resuscitant. (II. i. 49, n. 5)

And the points of similarity in this context are specified at some length. Underlying this account is the desire to distinguish between symbol and reality. This may also be the purpose of his refutation in I. ii. 35, n. 5 of the early Manichaean heresies according to which Christ was materially identified with the sun, his body being regarded as assimilated to it at the Ascension. But the most important of the theological rationalizations of sun symbolism concerns the relationship between the persons of the Trinity. In II. iv. 15 La Ceppède explains how the Holy Spirit is to be regarded as mediating between man and God,

> Ainsi que les rayons de l'aisné de nature
> Fondent pour éclairer tous ces terrestres lieux
> Sans délaisser pourtant leur natale ceinture.

It is perhaps the use by the early Church of this argument to propound the unity of the Father and the Spirit that accounts for the central part played by the sun in orthodox Christian symbolism.[7] The sun is only rarely in the *Théorèmes* involved in theological argumentation as explicit and as conscious as this. Nevertheless it can be shown that La Ceppède does incorporate Christian sun imagery and its ramifications in an implicit but coherent structure throughout the work. It can further be said that this structure has two dimensions, which are closely bound up with the formal organization of the *Théorèmes* as a continuous cycle built out of discrete sonnet units. In the first place, the cyclical solar images underlie the phases of the narrative; in the second place, the reflective pauses within the continuing narrative correlate with the imagery of the divine sun in dynamic relationship with man and creation.

(a) *Sun and vegetation cycles.* It is the annual cycle of the sun that provides the imagery underlying the events from the Passion

---

[7] See Dunbar, *Symbolism*, pp. 144 ff.

to Pentecost. The times of the year at which they occur have a mystical significance, although the tradition is not always consistent in its interpretations. In I. iii. 2 La Ceppède points out that the sun was in Aries when the Lamb (that is, the *agnus Dei*, where 'agnus' is 'a young ram') was crucified. The image is introduced indirectly, and in contrast to the images of darkness and disease with which the Jews are associated (lines 1–4). In the remainder of the sonnet La Ceppède gives the image a typological dimension, by going on to assert that the sun was in the same position at the time of the Incarnation, and, he insists against one authoritative body of opinion, at the time also of the creation.[8] In II. i. 43 a slightly different scheme is offered for the cycle of Incarnation, lamentation, Crucifixion, and Resurrection, which is presumably intended to be metaphorical rather than calendrically consistent:

> CE grand Soleil, de qui l'autre n'est qu'vne flame
> Par quatre des maisons du grand Cercle a passé.
> Par celle de la Vierge, ou neuf mois sa belle ame
> A de son corps égal l'organe compassé.
>
> Par celle du Vers'eau, quand son œil a trassé
> Sa douleur par son pleur, en maint acte sans blasme,
> Par celle du Taureau, quand son corps terrassé
> S'est pour victime offert sur le gibet infame.
>
> Or à ce iour il entre en celle du Lion
> Perruqué de lumière, il darde vn milion
> De rayons flamboyans sur les deux Hemispheres.

Again in I. ii. 30 it is the metaphorical rather than the astronomical use of the zodiac symbols that is evident: Christ is here described as the 'Vierge Nourriçon', and hence as the summer sun (in Virgo) which melts the mountain snow (a symbol of spiritual intractability). These examples seem to show quite clearly that while the symbol and the reality are carefully separated, the sun is central to the way the career of Jesus is depicted in the *Théorèmes*, and that, furthermore, the annual cycle is a means of representing typological correspondences.

However, the details of the narrative depend not on the zodiacal cycle but on that of day and night (or eclipse), darkness and light, death and resurrection. The first book of Part I opens with an invocation to the Holy Spirit in the form of purifying fire (I. i. 1),

---

[8] The question is settled by reference to the *Georgics* (I, p. 354).

and the narrative proper is initiated in I. i. 2 by introducing 'cet Alcide non feint' as a hero associated with fire symbolizing the themes of love and purification (emphasized in the Johannine text that La Ceppède is following at this point):

> Il exhale soudain le feu qui le brusloit
> Sur les siens: les exhorte à l'amour fraternele:
> Les laue; les sublime au feu qu'il exhaloit.

This link between the hero-figure, love, and the communication of the fire of the Holy Spirit is one which persists throughout the work, and is finally epitomized in the solar figure of Prometheus (II. iv. 13).

But in the first book the imagery is primarily determined by the setting of the narrative in the garden, and by night. After the Last Supper Jesus goes out towards the rising sun (I. i. 5). The Mount of Olives is a symbol of fertility—indeed the mountain itself is envisaged as a tree ('Ce mont qui dans Cedron ses racines abreuue'), which bears fruit ('ô montaigne . . . Permetés qu'a ce coup ie gouste vostre fruit'). The point of the reference to the 'fruit' of the mountain becomes clear if one bears in mind that I. i. 7 explains that woods and mountains are locations of divinity, and that the divinity is in this case Christ, who is himself, as will be seen, associated with fruit-bearing vegetation. In I. i. 38 the sweat of blood in the garden is spoken of as 'sueur fructueuse', and is seen as a foretaste of the 'pressoir de la croix'. It is this symbolism of fertility and of the sacred mountain that is the basis of the complex of associated images which makes the Agony and the Crucifixion parallel events in the *Théorèmes*.

The nocturnal setting is made symbolic of Jesus's suffering by means of images of the sun's absence. The hero himself is said to give way to 'la grosse vapeur De la noire tristesse, & de la froide peur' (I. i. 18); and the disciples are said to sleep because of the absence of the divine sun (I. i. 42). The night is also symbolic of the Jews and of Judas. The sun theme becomes quite explicit on the capture of Jesus:

> . . . A ce coup les tenebres
> Ont pouuoir d'éclipser le Soleil radieux. (I. i. 73)

In I. i. 75 this symbolism is taken one step further to represent the Jewish failure to penetrate the obscurity of Old Testament pro-

phecies and prefigurations. The night of the Jews is described in
this part of the narrative as darker than the 'noirceur des nuicts
Cimmeroniques' (I. i. 77). But the dominance of darkness and the
obscuring of the sun is a part of the divine will: '... vous retirez de
ces tourbes iniques Vos rayons lumineux en vous mesme reduits'
(I. i. 77).

Jesus is not only the sun, but also vegetation: he is identified
with the vine, and with the flower of the stem of Jesse, 'pource que
selon la verité Hebraïque, on peut lire Nazarien au lieu de fleur; &
dire, *La fleur montera de sa racine*, ou, *Le Nazarien montera de sa
racine*' (I. i. 55, n. 5). He is also 'ce Jardinier celeste' (I. i. 85; cf.
also II. ii. 23, II. iv. 16, II. iv. 26). The eclipse of this composite
figure brings winter and sickness. In I. i. 85 the abandoned disciples
are now described as victims of 'la Bise funeste', the plague-
bearing wind. These images are drawn together at the end of
Book I in order to present the typological parallel between the
New Testament incident just described and the exit of Adam from
Eden. The 'bon Iardinier' of the first quatrain is more oppressed,
it is said, that the 'premier Iardinier' mentioned in the second
tercet; his disappearance leaves the garden 'vn noir desert sauuage',
not only because he is the gardener, but also because he is the sun
itself, and because

> Ce feconde Soleil, cet Aspect matinier
> Qui faisait refleurir vostre esmail printanier,
> Est ores esclipsé par vn espais nuage. (I. i. 99)

From now on La Ceppède has to sustain the paradox of the sun
amidst darkness, until radiance and extinction on the cross. In the
invocatory sonnet opening I. ii, therefore, he stresses the nocturnal
setting: 'Les erreurs, les horreurs de cette nuict m'esfrayent' (I. ii.
1). The portrayal of the humiliation of Christ appears to him to be
problematic; the difficulty is resolved since the mere rehearsal of
the incidents in his verse is seen as indicating the presence of the
fire of the Holy Spirit (I. ii. 1). It is the imagery of darkness and
light that enables La Ceppède to express poetically the paradox
of Jesus's triumph through humiliation—a paradox that is thematically related to that of the Incarnation emphasized in Book I.
Christ by his replies 'fait briller son iour dans la nuict qui l'accuse'
(I. ii. 20; cf. I. ii. 16). He is 'le Roy de l'vniuers', and like the sun
is obscured but never extinguished; hence even at this point in

the narrative light imagery is related to the theme of renewal
and resurrection through an allusion to the raising of Lazarus
(I. ii. 25).

In the sequence I. ii. 29 to I. ii. 31 the divine sun appears
momentarily in its full vigour to transform Peter's lack of faith into
penitence. The dynamic relationship between the divine sun and
the individual soul is a theme that belongs to the reflective dimension (rather than the narrative) of the work and is discussed more
fully below. Nevertheless this episode dominated by imagery of
light is integrated into the progressing narrative, which has
hitherto been dominated by darkness. It heralds the dawn, 'l'Aube
à regret sortant de la Marine' (I. ii. 32), after Jesus's arrest—an
appropriately muted dawn since the Christ-sun is at the same time
imprisoned beneath the earth by the Jews. The sun symbolism
involves the animals of the bestiaries at various points in the
Théorèmes. The Jews are, for instance, frequently represented as
vipers. Here the symbolic viper is primarily a chthonic creature
avoiding the light:

> Qui veid onq dans la nuict d'vn rocher cauerneux
> Roder pres d'vn flambeau, ses hostes veneneux,
> Non pour estre éclairez, mais pour haineux l'eteindre:
> Il void dés que le Christ entre dans le Conseil,
> Ces venimeux Rabins à la foule le ceindre
> Pour éteindre le iour de ce flambant Soleil. (I. ii. 33)

In the sonnet that summarizes the theme of the suffering humanity
of Christ (I. ii. 70 on the *Ecce Homo*) the imagery of solar eclipse
is still present beneath the Petrarchan rhetoric: his eyes are 'deux
Soleils éclipsez'. This coincides with images of withering and
infertility: 'les roses, & les lys de son teint sont flétris'. And the
crown of thorns, which has already in I. ii. 64 been explicitly linked
with the unfruitful vine (see Isaiah 5: 1–6), is now in I. ii. 70
described as 'vne haye exécrable'. Towards the end of Book ii,
however, the rising of the eclipsed sun-figure in the subsequent
parts of the Passion and Resurrection cycle is anticipated:

> Mais tous ces noirs efforts de leur aueugle rage,
> Dissipez, se perdront comme vn foible nuage
> Disparoit au leuer du Soleil radieux. (I. ii. 96)

It has already beenseen that the Crucifixion sequence is accompanied by vegetation imagery rooted in the Old Testament.

It remains to show how this is interwoven with solar images. The temporal progression of the narrative is indicated at the beginning of Book iii with reference to the dawning of the day of the Crucifixion, with the sun in the sacrificial house of Aries(I. iii. 2). In I. iii. 6 Christ is not merely associated with the sun, but actually identified with vegetation: he is the 'bois fertille, & vert' in contrast to the Jews who are 'bois sec, sans fruit, & sans verdure'.[9] And the intersection of this kind of image with typological symbols has already been seen with respect to the theme of the tree of the cross 'foisonnant en mille fruicts diuers' (I. iii. 30). The central tree reaching to the heavens is not surprisingly linked with the sky and the sun. Furthermore, the cross is the fulfilment of Old Testament obscurity. Hence light imagery is used when La Ceppède apostrophizes the King of Babylon who failed to give the true interpretation to his dream of the tree (I. iii. 28). In I. iii. 31 the apocalyptic cross itself shines:

> Et fay qu'à ce grand iour, qui te verra brillante,
> Dans les plaines d'azur, ta lumiere drillante
> N'épouuante mon ame.[10]

The account of the eclipse at the Crucifixion carefully separates the sun from Christ as creation from creator, although the contrast between the sun's 'brilliant diademe' and Christ's crown of thorns might also be seen as an implicit comparison (I. iii. 65). In any case, Christ continues to be closely indentified with the sun, since the Virgin prays (I. iii. 76) that her son will draw up her tears 'Comme le Soleil va les vapeurs attirant', and since the closing of his eyes in death is described as an 'eclipse' of their 'flame' (I. iii. 85).

Since the first part of the *Théorèmes* concerns the Passion, the image of the sun and light is constantly in tension with that of night and obscurity. The real significance of the sun cycle on the narrative level does not become plain until the Resurrection story in Part II. The first section of II. i. (sonnets 1–14) deals with the descent into hell, and there is only one reference to the light aspect of Christ (as the 'Père des Lumieres' (II. i. 8)). By definition

---

[9] Interpretation of Luke 23: 11.
[10] I. iii. 31. The Sibylline oracles are quoted as a source (I, p. 404); cf. also the paraphrase of the *Vexilla*: 'Arbre brillant & beau', 'La Croix mysterieuse éclate vn nouueau iour' (*Imitation*, pp. 50, 51).

hell is the place 'où iamais le Soleil à nuict s'oppose' (II. i. 2). But
the Resurrection section (II. i. 15–50) opens immediately with the
linking of the rising of the sun with the rising Christ. Not only is
it the sun's day cycle that is in question, but also the return of
vegetation after the winter and after the destructive flood (II. i. 16).
As the basis of his verse La Ceppède quotes a passage which he
attributes to Ambrose:

sic enim post hiemalis rigoris frigidam quodammodo sepulturam,
pullulare elementa omnia festinarunt, ut, resurgente Domino, et ipsa
consurgerent. Nam utique ex resurrectione Christi aer salubrior est,
et sol candidior, terra fecundior . . .[11]

As in Part I, images of this kind are not merely ornaments accompanying the narrative, but are also to some extent identified with
its content. Thus Christ is the 'fleuron Iessean' that withered at
the Passion but reflowers along with the tree of life at the Resurrection (see I. i. 34, 39). The cross is again presented as the sun, and
in much the same terms as in I. iii. 31 (to which he refers the reader):
Christ will raise 'son bois de rayons éclatant' (II. i. 35). His identification with the sun is related to biblical prefigurations. Psalm
56: 9 provides a prophecy of the Resurrection associated with
the dawn (II. i. 36). The reference to the rising of the 'sol justitiae'
in Malachi is used in the same way (II. i. 37). Just as the eclipse of
the sun leaves it essentially unchanged, so the divinity of Christ
is unaffected by death; moreover, he is the 'true' sun fulfilling
the Old Testament promises:

> La Diuinité donc ce brouillard dissipant,
> Et faisant de son iour ce corps participant
> Le rend or' reuiuant, plus beau, plus desirable.
>   En fin ce vray Soleil à nos yeux s'est ouuert:
> Se despouillant luy mesme, à ce iour admirable,
> Du nuage, & du sac qui le tenoit couuert. (II. i. 42)

The sonnet following describes the zodiacal course of the sun-
Christ, and the general context of II. i. 44 suggests the solar
characteristics of two Old Testament types of the risen Christ—
Noah, who arises from sleep and dons a 'robe glorieuse & brillante',
and Samson, who breaks out of prison into the daylight. Not only

---

[11] 'l'homel. 3. au Iour de la S. Pentecost'; but according to Migne it is
Homilia LX , 'De ascensione' of Maximus Taurinensis (see Migne, vol. 57,
col. 369).

sacred history but also the cycles of natural history furnish proof
for La Ceppède of the Resurrection:

> CE mystere est par tout marqué par la nature:
> La lumiere se meurt à l'abord de la nuict,
> Puis reuit, & reluit: le grain sous la culture
> De la terre se meurt, puis nombreux se produict. (II. i. 47)

The cycle is further reflected in a mythical story (derived from
Solinus, *De mirabilibus mundi*) of a spring in which a flaming torch
may be extinguished but withdrawn re-ignited (lines 9–11). This
no doubt reflects the sun's nightly mythical descent into the sea.
The point as far as the image structure of the *Théorèmes* is
concerned of the emphasis on the waters of hell now begins to
become apparent. In the opening sonnet of the Resurrection
sequence the images of the risen Christ are on the one hand the
type of Moses' passage through the Red Sea, and on the other
hand the rising of the sun. In the concluding sonnet (II. i. 50) the
image of the stag combines similar ideas. The stag is linked
traditionally with the sun and with the dawn,[12] and is a symbol
of Christ hounded by the Jews. Further, according to the natural
histories and bestiaries the stag plunges into water at the height of
the chase, just as Christ passed through the waters of hell, and
just as the sun sinks into the sea.

It is on the whole the case that the other symbolic animals
occurring in the *Théorèmes* are associated with the sun or with
the theme of renewal. Drawing on Aristotle and Pliny, on Basil,
Ambrose, and Origen, sonnet II. i. 26 lists the natural phenomena
that are felt to be demonstrations of the Resurrection. The pelican
is used as a symbol of renewal through sacrifice;[13] the eagle was a
solar creature because it was believed to be alone capable of looking
into the sun, and La Ceppède uses it as a symbol of rejuvenation
and as a 'preuue de la Resurrection' on scriptural and patristic
authority; the serpent, which as has been seen may represent the
antithesis of the sun, is here associated with it as a symbol of
renewal (lines 10–11). The lion is another important symbol with
a dual role. On the one hand it is the Jews who are compared with

[12] Cf. Hebrew title of Psalm 21 'victori super cervam aurorae' and Génébrard's Christological interpretation, quoted II, p. 143.
[13] On other cases in literature cf. Graham, 'The Pelican as Image and
Symbol'.

beasts of prey destroying the sacred lamb: they are described, for
instance, as 'les rageux Lyons ioüissant de leur proye'.[14] On the
other hand, not only is the lion of Judah a symbolic Old Testament
type (Genesis 49: 8–10) of Christ, but Leo is the zodiacal sign
under which the Resurrection is said to take place, and according
to the bestiaries and patristic authority it is precisely the Resurrection that the lion symbolizes. Moreover, sonnet II. i. 34 in which
this image occurs is of the type which lists parallel types and
symbols, and sets in formal correspondence the lion brought to
life after three days (first quatrain) with the return of 'Ce Soleil
éclipsé par vn obscur tombeau' (second tercet). This parallel
becomes much closer in the synaesthetic comparison that is made
in II. i. 43 between the light of the sun and the lion's roar: 'Le
Soleil entrant au signe du Lion darde ses rays furieusement ardens,
comme vn Lion rugissant les feux de sa colere' (n. 4).

At this point, too, the theme of Christ the King reappears in
a way which may be highly significant for the relationship the
Théorèmes bear to their background. Medieval and Renaissance
political theology conceived the discontinuity within continuity of
kingship with the aid of two key images: the two bodies of the king
analagous to the two natures of the incarnate Christ, and the cyclical constancy of the sun.[15] Now the lion, which as has been seen
has strong solar connections, was also a symbol of kingship, as
La Ceppède was plainly aware. The bestiaries presented the lion
sleeping with open eyes as a symbol of vigilance; La Ceppède
explains that this further represents Christ in the tomb, since
although his physical body was dead, 'sa personne Royalle, c'ét à
dire le Verbe diuin veilloit tout à fait, & pouuoit partant bien dire
Ego dormio, & cor meum vigilat. au 5. des Cantiques vers. 2' (II. i.
34, n. 1). It appears that the notion of the two persons of the king,
the one which dies and the one which never dies, is being applied
to Christ, though originally the converse was the case. The following sonnet (II. i. 35) adds to this complex sun-king figure the image
of the phoenix, which was well established as a symbol of the
risen Christ,[16] but also in the sixteenth century was common as
a symbol of monarchy. In describing the phoenix as 'de ce grand

---

[14] I. ii. 15; cf. I. ii. 37; also Jews as tigers (I. ii. 86, etc.).

[15] See Kantorowicz, *The King's Two Bodies*; Jackson, 'The Sleeping King'.

[16] The best-known source was the phoenix poem attributed to Lactantius;
but La Ceppède cites also Tertullian, Ambrose, Bede, Epiphanius, Pliny, and
Tacitus.

Héros le symbole asseuré' La Ceppède now links it with the theme of the heroic warrior which plays an important role in the Passion sequence of Part I. The fact that several strands of image themes should converge at this point is hardly surprising. They all exhibit inherently cyclical characteristics, and the account of the Resurrection is the climax of the cycle in the narrative.

(b) *The sun, love, and grace.* The solar images discussed so far relate to the linear progression of the narrative. But this dimension is integrated with a second dimension—the dimension which reflects on certain topics arising from the action. Corresponding to this dimension, and frequently accompanying it, is the imagery of the sun, not in its cyclical, temporal aspect, but in its hierarchical aspect according to which it contrasts with the earth and its attributes of coldness, darkness, and inertia. The primary theme to which these images give expression is that of the relationship between God and mankind, a theme which clearly from the theological point of view merges with the narrative theme in Part II of the bestowal of the Holy Spirit.

Man is constantly in the *Théorèmes* compared to or identified with earth ('O ma terre, ô mon corps', I. iii. 90), with the shifting and infertile sand (I. i. 50; I. i. 63; I. ii. 4), and with slime and dirt ('ce monceau de fange', I. i. 35; 'vil monceau de bourbier', I. iii. 80). On the one hand, this aspect of humanity is redeemed in the person of Christ at the Incarnation and Ascension, and in the 'sanglante fange' (I. ii. 67, 68) of the Passion. On the other hand, the question of the continuing communication between men and God after the Ascension has to be solved by the theology of grace, and in La Ceppède this is dependent to a considerable degree on the imagery of the effects of the sun.

The absence of the divine sun leads to coldness and inertia. The disciples in the garden sleep because Jesus is absent from them. La Ceppède adds a personal reflection applying this lesson to the individual meditator:

> Ne m'esloignez donc, point, ô Soleil de mon ame;
> Car perdant la chaleur de vostre sainte flame
> Me voila Lethargique aux Enfers tresbucher. (I. i. 42)

Similarly, Peter's infidelity is compared with ice (I. ii. 5), with the hard snow which melts only under the effect of the divine sun. The melting snow is then associated with tears of repentance, and this in turn with the purifying flood, with the sacrament of baptism which cleanses 'sa mortelle soüilleure' (I. ii. 30). The shifting reference of the images underlines the theme of metamorphosis. In the next sonnet the images are explicitly related to the doctrine of divine grace:

> L'Apostre n'eut iamais veu l'horreur efroyable
> De l'abysme, où sa chair l'auoit precipité,
> Si du Soleil Diuin ce rayon pitoyable
> N'eut faucé de sa peur l'épaisse obscurité . . .
> Cet Astre seul nous verse au cœur la Penitence:
> Et si de son aspect l'influente assistance
> N'opere avecque nous, vains sont tous nos efforts.
> O flamboyant Soleil, foudroyez les deffenses
> De ma chair, & rendez mes desirs assez forts
> Pour me tirer du monde, & pleurer mes offenses. (I. ii. 31)

The source is Augustine.[17] La Ceppède avoids commitment on the question of the priority and scope of grace and free will. But in the second tercet it is the attractions of the flesh and the world that prevent the 'desirs' from turning to God; and it is God alone, represented in wrathful solar guise, who can suppress the obstacle of the flesh. The notion of the right orientation of the will is outlined in I. i. 85, where La Ceppède addresses the disciples who have 'withered' in the absence of 'ce Jardinier celeste' and of 'ce Soleil'. Since he prays that like the heliotrope he may be turned constantly towards the sun, he seems to regard the disposition of the soul towards God as natural but in need of divine reinforcement. This depends on the idea of the conflict between the two delectations.

Other elements in La Ceppède's view of the matter become evident when he is led in connection with the Judas episode to consider the problem of the failure to receive divine grace. Whereas Peter's ice melts in the rays of the sun-Christ, Judas is

> . . . vn monceau de fange
> Qui s'endurcit au iour du Soleil radieux.[18]

This image of natural cause and effect would seem to suggest that some souls might be predisposed not to respond to grace, indeed

---

[17] Sermo LXXIX (Migne, vol. 5, col. 1899).
[18] I. i. 44; cf. this image also in Du Bartas, *Judit*, ll. 201–3.

that the divine source causes this predisposition. The implications are countered in I. i. 46, which emphasizes the notion of the attractions of the human will by God without constraint on human freedom:

> Bonté qui par bien-faits l'homme au salut conuie,
> Sans forcer toutesfois sa libre volonté,
> Pour ce que la vertu gist au chois de la vie

Again in I. iii. 80 salvation comes only through freely willed submission to God: 'Rends ta volonté libre à la sienne asseruie.'

The problem of mediation between man and God, and the role of grace are clearly important in La Ceppède's work, but he is careful to avoid controversial extremes in his overt remarks on the subject. There are two different components in his view, which are not in all respects explicitly reconciled. It is clear, on the one hand, that on occasion he will stress the role of free will, effort, and active co-operation. On the other hand, he will elsewhere stress a notion in which spontaneous orientation of the affections is at some point indistinguishable from the divine attractive forces—a notion ultimately based on the Augustinian opposition of love of the world and love of God.

Similar ideas underlie another current of imagery that has some connections with sun imagery—namely the current centring on the image of Christ as lover. That love is to be a dominant image, and is to be linked with that of military heroism, is clear from the first sonnet: 'Ie chante les amours, les armes, la victoire' (I. i. 1). In I. i. 5 'nostre Amant' enters the Garden of Gethsemane as if it were a Petrarchan wilderness, and from here on throughout both parts of the *Théorèmes* Christ is recurrently referred to as the 'parfait Amant' (I. iii. 71),[19] as the 'fidele amoureux' (I. iii. 69), and even as 'ce Beau' (II. iii. 11). But love, along with generative power, is an attribute of the sun. It is not just that images of fire and warmth are associated with sexual love. Certainly the references to 'priere enflammée' (I. i. 34), to the 'feu de son amour extreme' (I. i. 39) help to establish the association between Christ as lover and Christ as sun.[20] But there are more direct links. The heliotrope, this time representing the Virgin, follows the sun's path and is said to hitch 'Son amoureuse vmbelle au char de son Amant' (II. iii. 11). More

---

[19] Cf. also I. ii. 67, 73; iii. 20; II. ii. 37, 88, 89.
[20] Cf. also I. i. 71; iii. 50, 51.

clearly still, Jesus is described as 'ce Soleil de Iustice . . . brulant
d'affection' (II. i. 37). The theological and mystical significations of
this imagery as expounded by La Ceppède are threefold: they
centre around the Incarnation, the consummation of the Crucifixion, and the union of the soul with the Godhead. In all cases the
image of the marriage union is bound up with Christ's suffering
and death. In I. i, with its concern with the problem of the union
of the two persons of Christ arising from the account of the Agony,
the emphasis is on love as the motivation of the Incarnation. This
theme is repeated with almost obsessive insistence throughout the
work.[21]

But the Passion is not merely an act of love in the sense that it is
motivated by love; it is also an act of love in the sense that the
events are associated with images of sexual union. The degree of
Jesus's humiliation seems to be regarded as directly proportional
to his love for man; hence it is at the climactic points of his physical
suffering that erotic images for his relation with the individual
soul are evoked. The episode of the binding of Jesus has a mystical
significance of this kind. Jesus is literally bound, but theologically
it is precisely by this suffering that man is released from the bondage of sin:

> O liens, ô trauaux, ô mystiques estreintes . . .
> Déliez nos liens, soulagez nos miseres . . . (I. i. 91)

The bonds are also taken as a symbol of the marriage of Christ to
humanity and to the Church: 'Chers cordeaux, c'est par vous que
cet Espoux maintient Son Epouse' (I. i. 93). His passive suffering
is paradoxically active redemption. The word 'étreinte', which in
I. i. 91 was used mainly in its passive sense, is now placed in an
ambiguous context to express the delight of the devout soul in
Jesus's pain: 'Hé! Combien vostre estreinte est douce & desirable'
(I. i. 93).

That sexual imagery is implicit in the Old Testament types
of the Crucifixion has already been demonstrated: the image of
incestuous rape (I. ii. 72) is complemented by the image of royal
marriage (I. ii. 73); the image of Christ's nakedness redeems the
nakedness of Adam and Noah (I. iii. 11). These paradoxes are
essentially the same as that found in the narrative of the binding

---

[21] See in particular I. iii. 20; cf. I. i. 27, 71; ii. 53, 66; iii. 5, 20; II. i. 3; ii. 75.

of Christ. But the relationship between the death on the cross and the individual soul is worked out in a somewhat different manner. The imagery accompanying the typological figures just mentioned points implicitly to the cross as the ritual marriage-bed where the union between Christ and the Church is consummated.[22] The role of the Virgin, as the symbol of the Church and of the supreme mystic union, is essential at this point. She is no longer simply the mother, but also the bride of Christ. Christ is described as 'enyuré de l'amour de nos ames Dormant nud sur la Croix' (I. iii. 11), when the Virgin approaches, 'l'embrasse, & pleurante marie Ses larmes à son sang, & ses pieds à sa Croix' (I. iii. 12). This union is elaborated in the next sonnet in terms of an overtly sexual image familiar to the Pléiade:

> ACheuant ces propos, d'vn long baiser iumeau
> De la Mere, & du Fils les leures sont colées,
> Et leurs bras enlassez comme on voit accolées
> Les branches de la Vigne à celles de l'Ormeau.
> Comme n'esteints tu point, ô Phoebus, ton flambeau . . .
>
> (I. iii. 13)

This draws together not only the erotic images but also the sun image, and the image of Christ as the vine and the fruit of the vine—the wine of love with which it has just been said he is inebriated, and through which he is further linked with Noah.

But the Virgin is also an exemplar whom the Church or the individual soul should imitate. Her response to the cry of thirst from the cross, interpreted symbolically as an invitation to penitence and union (I. iii. 74–6), should inspire the meditator:

> POur t'esmouuoir, mon ame, à ce piteux deuoir
> Medite la douleur de la Vierge eplorée. (I. iii. 76)

The union that is urged on the soul is with the mystical body, and again depends on erotic imagery:

> . . . on fabrique
> Des logettes pour vous dans la pierre mystique
> De son corps, & sa voix vous semond d'y venir.
> Belle, venez y donq, vostre Espoux le commande.
>
> (I. iii. 21, cf. I. iii. 30)

---

[22] Cf. Rabanus Maurus on Jacob's ladder (a type of the cross) as a symbol of *charitas*, 'quod charitas nos et per compassionem societ proximo, et per desiderium copulat proximo' (quoted by Dunbar, p. 392).

But the preoccupation underlying the development of such imagery in the *Théorèmes* is with neither penitence nor ecstatic union alone, but with the conflict of love of the world with the love of God. La Ceppède exhorts his soul thus: 'Ne soy plus Philanthrope, & deuient Philotée' (II. ii. 96). It is the human passions that hinder the ascent of the soul. However, it is not by reason that they are overcome. The ideas about grace conveyed by the solar imagery, and discussed above, are also worked out with the more familiar theological image of transcendent love. Free will is not denied, but it is in danger of being overshadowed by the appetites without divine aid. La Ceppède uses the Platonic image of the two horses of the soul:

> De mes fiers appetits le coursier indompté,
> Entraine maintefois ma libre volonté:
> Et si ne puis sans vous arrester sa carriere.
> Donnez nous donc, Seigneur, pouuoir de l'arrester,
> De peur qu'il donne en fin dans la noire barriere
> Où (sans vous) ie me voy des-ja precipiter. (I. i. 84)

On the other hand, a similar image is used to state the power of sacred love. Commenting on Peter's presumptuous promise of fidelity, La Ceppède explains it as excess of love. He goes on to say that love of this kind transcends reason and has no limits:

> L'amour, de la raison enfonce la barriere . . .
> Rien ne peut arrester l'amoureuse carriere . . . (I. i. 13)

This does not of course mean that La Ceppède rejects right reason.[23] Furthermore, the assumption behind the technique of creatural symbolism and exegesis in general is that truth is accessible and intelligible, albeit through a veil of obscurity. The dilemma is that while creation is essential as a means of information about God, creation itself and its attraction for man must be constantly overcome.

At the end of the first book of Part II, which relies so heavily on natural images to explain the Resurrection, La Ceppède employs the image of the sphere. This definition of God, usually attributed by those who cited it to Hermes Trismegistus, was common amongst medieval theologians from whom it was borrowed in

---

[23] Cf. I. iii. 44:
> Maint d'entre les mortels definit au compas
> De la droite raison, les preceptes Ethiques . . .

Renaissance poetry.[24] The sphere whose centre is everywhere and whose circumference is nowhere provided a metaphor for the divine perfection, universality, and infinity. La Ceppède clearly admits this interpretation in his note (II. i, 'voeu', n. 1). But the notion of the ubiquitous centre has a particular significance for the devout humanist concerned with the reconciliation of secular life and a life of piety. Thus there is especial emphasis in the sonnet itself and in the accompanying notes[25] on two related points: the conflict in the soul between love of the world and love of the divine centre; and the incomprehensibility of this centre:

> Mon ame s'en écarte, & pource elle patit;
> Et veut s'en approcher: mais l'appast détestable
> De céte volupté, faussement delectable,
> Par mille obiects trompeurs tousiours l'en diuertit . . .
> Donne luy tant d'Amour pour te faire adherance
> Qu'il passe par de là tout humain iugement,
> Comme on ne peut iuger de ta circonferance. (II. i, 'voeu')

God is ultimately only knowable through union with him, that is, through 'vn Amour si grand qu'il excede tout ce que l'homme peut comprendre, comme Dieu est infiny & incomprehensible'.[26] The underlying problem becomes apparent. God is omnipresent in creation—an idea that accords with the use of natural symbols; yet he is also outside creation. The soul's relation to God on the one hand and to creation on the other is thus problematic, and is expressed as a conflict between divergent attractions. It is not only a moral, devotional problem; it is also a problem of knowledge and of poetic symbolization. Hence the constant need in the *Théorèmes* for the invocation of grace, by means of which alone the right relation (in both a moral and an epistemological sense) between creation and the divine may be achieved.

(c) *Images of Revelation*. While Christ is at the centre of sun and light imagery, the Jews are at the centre of the images of night and darkness. Besides its role in the narrative this opposition has an obvious application to the theme of human inability to glimpse and recognize divinity when it reveals itself.

The overwhelming majority of the images connected with the Jews in the *Théorèmes* derive from the iconography of the bestiaries.

---

[24] See Poulet, 'Poésie du cercle et de la sphere'.
[25] Cf. above, pp. 82 ff.
[26] II, p. 152, conflating Isaiah, Hilarius, Nilus, and Plato.

When the images of the viper, the beast of prey, the owl (I. i. 48), or the ostrich (I. ii. 44) are used to represent the Jews, their significance is largely defined by their antithetical relationship to the Christ-images—the celestial sun, the sacrificial lamb, the eagle of the Ascension. However, there are other relevant associations deriving from the tradition. The Jews are 'loups affamez' (I. i. 61), 'mastins herissez que la rage bouffit' (I. i. 64), a 'Canine race' (I. iii. 41). These beasts are not only associated with the solar opposites of winter, night, and coldness, but also with the unbridled appetites of the flesh. Similarly, when the image of the lion is used of the Jews, it signifies violence, and more particularly profanity and lust (I. ii. 37, and n. 3). The main point of such images is not the antagonism between the Jews and Jesus in the Passion narrative, but the Pauline association of the sins of the flesh with spiritual blindness. It would seem to be primarily because they fail to recognize in Jesus the prophesied Sun of Justice, that the Jews are said (e.g. in I. i. 75, 77) to have 'cœurs aueuglez', and to be symbolized by the night. Corresponding to this blindness of the Jews is that of the disciples on the road to Emmaus and thus of all Christian souls (II. ii. 47, 49, 52). La Ceppède himself prays for vision: 'Hé! désille mes yeux pour voir' (II. ii. 47). Since the Crucifixion is the central point at which the Old Testament obscurity is finally clarified and mediation between man and God achieved, the Redemption is said to be a 'Collyre contre l'aueuglement'.[27] The Jews as representatives of the forces of darkness and material reality are particularly clearly opposed to the light of divine reality in I. ii. The whole of this book could be interpreted on the level of imagery as a confrontation between the Old Testament and paganism on the one hand and the New Testament on the other. More generally it is a symbolization of the tragic inability of man to perceive God directly.

Mediation is metaphorized as the half-light, shadow, and illuminated cloud, that is, in images of darkness mingled with light. A frequent synonym for Old Testament type or figure was 'umbra'. La Ceppède uses it apparently not as an alternative substitute but as a metaphor in such phrases as 'l'ombre des figures' (I. iii. 79), and 'l'ombreux estat . . . des figures' (II. i. 19). The images of penumbra associated with the key events of the Crucifixion and

[27] II. iii. 22; cf. also 'Imitation du Stabat Mater', *Imitation*, p. 53.
[28] Cf. Auerbach, *Scenes*, pp. 44 ff.

Ascension can be added to the solar and typological images of mediation already discussed. One of the aspects of the symbolic tree of the cross is its shade, the Hebrew symbol of divine favour, of mediating grace: 'Son ombrage amoureux sous lequel on repose Est sa grace' (I. iii. 30). It is, however, at the Ascension that the problem of mediation between terrestrial and celestial becomes acute. And it is here that La Ceppède states most clearly that he regards divine mysteries as manifest in enigmatic form only. Again he uses an ancient Hebrew image—the paradoxical image of the 'brillante nue', the 'nue luisante':

> Aux Mystères Diuins la nue sert tousiour,
> Car elle tient vn peu de la nuict, & du jour.
> Selon que plus ou moins le Soleil la penetre.
> Ainsi (comme a trauers vn nuage entre-ouuert)
> Le Seigneur des Seigneurs manifeste son étre
> Ny trop obscurement, ny trop à decouuert. (II. iii. 10)

It has been seen that certain types of Christ centre around ritual vesting and divesting. In fact, images of garment and nudity constitute a coherent network expressing the themes of revelation and incarnation. The Jews' attachment to the Law, to the flesh, and the letter is conveyed in the image of the ritual vestment. Their refusal to see Pilate on legalistic grounds is described as 'ce bel habit . . . De la religion', as the vain plumage of the symbolic ostrich (I. ii. 44). However, just as Christ loosens the knots of bondage, so he removes the garment concealing the naked truth and preventing man's ascent from the world. The garment is identified with the human flesh. Through the Incarnation Christ is 'affeublé d'vn nuage' (I. iii. 1); at the Agony his prayers are 'quelques traits que la chair habille à sa façon' (I. i. 24); at the Crucifixion he wears only 'le sacré Manteau de son humanité' (I. iii. 11). It is in this web of imagery that the sonnet 'Blanc est le vestement . . .' (I. ii. 54) and the sonnet 'Aux Monarques vain-cueurs . . .' (I. ii. 63) should be seen. The sonnet on the Pharisaic 'habit de la religion' (I. ii. 44) anticipates these two poems both in its images of colour and in its image of the garment. The white robe of Christ is in contrast with the 'Sepulchres blanchis' who wear the 'bel habit' in I. ii. 44; it is in I. ii. 54 the typological fulfilment that replaces the sacrificial robe of the Old Covenant. The symbolism of the garment as such is somewhat clearer in the

preceding sonnet (I. ii. 53), where La Ceppède makes it clear
that Christ's garment is not a symbol of hypocrisy or superficiality.
He says of Christ 'Que son Ame, & son Corps sont parez d'vne
sorte', thereby implying that the white robe of Christ is a genuine
symbol of what is written and not merely an external ornament
without signification. These ideas are, however, taken much further
in I. ii. 63, where by word-association and ambiguity La Ceppède
makes explicit the identification of the garment with the flesh. Since
sin is symbolized by the colour red it is associated with the red
robe; so, playing on the senses of 'endosser', he addresses the robe
itself, thus: 'ce Christ t'endossant se charge de nos crimes'; the
fusion of garment and flesh is even more complete in the final line
referring to 'les sanglans replis du manteau de ta chair'. The garment thus becomes all a symbol of incarnation, of the total
union of divinity and humanity. Indeed, this sonnet initiates a
sequence that develops the sonnet's images, and leads to the *Ecce
Homo*, the presentation of Christ as man, as 'Dieu se cachant sous
l'éncore mortele' (I. ii. 71), or as the annotation on this line has it,
'soubs le manteau de l'humanité'.

　　There are further ramifications of this symbolism of clothing,
which point to the recurrent theme of the conflict of flesh and spirit
in the devout. While the garment signifies the hypostatic union in
Christ, in man it relates to a conflict. Mark (14: 51–2) recounts
the flight of the young man naked at the arrest of Jesus. He is
regarded as an antitype of Joseph who left behind his coat in order
to avoid sin (I. i. 87). La Ceppède explains the coat further as
representing 'les habits, ou habitudes au mal qui nous fait souuent
prisonniers de Satan' (I, p. 179), that is, as a 'habitus', a disposition
of the whole being, which, if directed towards the world, leads to
sin. The notion of orientation implied here is similar to that expressed in terms of solar and love images.

　　It is significant that La Ceppède should state that it is only by
divesting himself of the seductions of the flesh that he can write
his *Théorèmes*, which are themselves concerned with unveiling in
another sense:

> Ores que sainctement vostre Esport me conuie,
> De retracer vos pas, par les pas de ces vers,
> Ce monde, ce charmeur, cet ennemy peruers,
> Me prenant au manteau veut frustrer mon enuie . . .
> Faites donc (s'il vous plait) ô Seigneur desormais

Que de l'Adolescent imitant l'exemplaire
Ie quitte ces habits au monde pour iamais. (I. i. 88)

The question of poetic composition is integrated in the thematic
structure of the *Théorèmes*. Although a connection between the
image of divesting for spiritual purity and the image of unveiling
for poetic exegesis is never made explicitly, it could be said to be
present in the traditional symbolism used by La Ceppède. The
obscurity of Old Testament Scripture is frequently referred to
metaphorically as folds concealing the truth. Just as La Ceppède
refers to the 'replys du manteau de ta chair', so he also refers to
prophecy 'caché dans les replis De tant d'Oracles vieux' (I. iii. 77),
to the 'reply de ces difficultez' of Scripture (II. iii. 24), and to the
'reply, Des vieux siecles' (I. iii. 61). These metaphors become clear
in the light of the established symbolic interpretation of the episode
of the rending of the veil of the Temple at the Crucifixion. This
veil, 'Ce voile grand, & riche artistement tendu', conceals the
sacred mysteries, and thus symbolizes the textual obscurity of the
Old Testament; at Christ's death the prophecies and prefigurations are fulfilled and, hence, revealed: 'Tout est déuoilé donq
a ce cour memorable' (I. iii. 91). The image recurs whenever La
Ceppède mentions actual prefigurations in phrases such as 'cette
figure est ores deuoilée' (I. i. 83).

It is possible to take the function of garment imagery one step
further. La Ceppède's poetic theory employs the image of the
garment to designate the substance, not merely the style, of his
work: 'ce fort drap d'or ne se manie pas aisement à tous les plis
qu'on veut'.[29] This can be taken as simply referring to the complexity and difficulty of the concepts and language used by his
theological sources. But the image itself may have further signification. It is clear from what has been seen of La Ceppède's use of the
garment as an image that it can be used to express a relationship
between two spheres of being. By virtue of its very structure the
garment stands at the border between inner and outer, between
invisible inward truth and visible external appearance. As such
it is precisely the image of the image—that is, an image which
pinpoints the whole problem of symbolization, the relation between signifier and signified. But the scheme is applicable to
moral and theological ideas. The devotional problem of the conflict

[29] I, p. 10; see ch. IV above on the garment of style and the Incarnation in
linguistic speculation.

between the two loves can be represented by means of the garment image as a conflict between specious externalities and the naked innocence of the spirit. More fundamentally, in the thematic preoccupations of the *Théorèmes* it symbolizes the theological solution to both these problems—the doctrine of the Incarnation in which the two opposing principles are united.

The structure of the imagery—that is, the various relationships between the images—may be thought of as having two dimensions:[30] the one is sequential, and based on the cyclical relationships inherent in the meanings of certain images; the other is static, and based on hierarchical resemblance. The two intersecting dimensions are both characterized by the opposition and mediation of extreme terms. Thus some of the themes associated with this framework are the reconciliation of world and divinity, the corresponding conflict within the devout soul, the harmonization of order and disorder, even the duality of signification. In the *Imitation* such oppositions appear primarily as problems. The *Théorèmes* seem to seek solutions: the cyclical narrative structure is a means of transcending conflicts, and mediating images abound at the appropriate points. It is this profoundly Christian schema of images and concepts that underlies the rich symbolic texture of the poetry. These meanings are, of course, in the first instance theological and devotional. But embedded in the texture, and itself a product of the underlying schema, is the theory of religious poetic creation. Poetry reveals the obscure, and, in so doing, acts as an instrument of communication between the divine and man in his historical situation.

[30] See Appendix II for a schematic summary.

VII

VOCABULARY, SYNTAX
AND RHETORIC

THE foundation of any religious style within the western
Christian tradition, including the style of the meditative
manuals, is the language of the Bible—but the Bible as
transmitted through centuries of exegesis and translation within the Graeco-Roman literary culture. The Hebrew and Greek
Scriptures were latinized by Augustine and Jerome through
the application of the rhetorical and interpretative traditions of
the Roman world. Conversely, the received literary culture was
christianized by this very process—a process which for Augustine
was tantamount to a 'redemption' of language and literature. The
aesthetic and civic functions of rhetoric are transformed into
cognitive functions, which interpret the Scriptures, rehearse their
inherent truths to the faithful, or aim to convert the unfaithful
through persuasive eloquence. All this is possible because the
Scriptures themselves are held to exhibit the schemata, the tropes,
and even the *dispositio* of pagan literature.[1]

In sixteenth-century France the situation is somewhat similar.
A reinvigorated classical culture with its literary and rhetorical
norms coincides with, and in the second half of the century to
some extent confronts, a heightened religious sensibility. There is
a movement away from the profane and formalistic rhetoric of the
Petrarchist Pléiade poetry, towards a utilization of the acquired
literary techniques in sacred contexts. There is an attempt to
convert the language of the revived classical literature to the
persuasive and cognitive ends of religious discourse. On the one
hand, there is the development of Reformation and Counter-
Reformation sermon rhetoric with its evangelizing aims. On the
other hand, there is the rhetorical analysis of the Bible by such
humanists as Génébrard, whose work on the Psalms was for La
Ceppède a reference book in the matter of Hebraisms. Thus in

---

[1] Cf. Curtius, *Europäische Literatur*, ch. 4; Colish, *Mirror of Language*, ch. 1.

certain respects the position of the devout literary humanist in the late sixteenth century is a repetition of that of the rhetor Augustine in the fifth century. There is already at hand for a poet like La Ceppède an established Christian theory and practice of 'redeemed' language, in which the intellectual framework of Graeco-Roman rhetoric is bound up with the hebraized Latin of the Bible.

1. *Archaism and the Biblical Element*

The books of the Bible most commented on and most familiar throughout the Christian tradition were the Psalms. It is with the Psalms that La Ceppède began his devout literary career, and with which he apparently occupied himself concurrently with the composition of the *Théorèmes*. There is good reason, therefore, to assume that the biblical influence on the vocabulary and syntax of La Ceppède's style in both the *Imitation* and the *Théorèmes* is far-reaching. It will be seen further that the *Imitation* in particular shows clearly the merging of biblical language with classical humanist rhetoric. It is first necessary to examine the non-rhetorical aspects of La Ceppède's style from the point of view of their relationship to contemporary secular literary developments on the one hand, and to the requirements of Christian style on the other.

It cannot be denied that there is a hard core of words and syntactical constructions which are archaic or provincial by Malherbian standards:

—conjunctions, adverbs, and prepositions condemned as provincialisms, archaisms, or *chevilles*, such as: *ores, oncques, jaçoit, meshui*[2]

—nouns, adjectives, and verbs condemned by Malherbe or known from other sources to be moribund, including *ardre* (e.g. II. ii. 52),[3] *acravanter* (e.g. II. ii. 100), *bellesse* (e.g. I. i. 76), *isnel* (e.g. II. iii. 26)

—morphological features, like the form *cil* of the demonstrative, which, according to Malherbe, 'ne vaut du tout rien',[4] the verb forms *je prins* and *lairra*,[5] and the adjectival forms

---

[2] Cf. Brunot, *Doctrine de Malherbe*, pp. 254, 265 f., 463; *Histoire de la langue française*, vol. iii, pp. 95 ff.

[3] Cf. Brunot, *Histoire*, vol. iii, p. 13.   [4] Ibid., p. 290.

[5] Ibid., p. 322.

records (I. iii. 87) and the old feminine form of *grand* (I. i. 42), with its comparative *greigneur* (I. i. 77).

The evidence seems to suggest that La Ceppède's style is to some extent characterized by the persistent habits of his 'ramage natal' and of the literary language of the sixteenth century. This is contrary to the tendency implied in the *Imitation* variants: but there is no reason to expect absolute consistency in this matter. Moreover, it is still possible that certain 'irregularities' are related in some way to the hebraized Latinity of Christian writing. To support the hypothesis of a convergence of this kind one can adduce in some telling instances quite explicit evidence from La Ceppède's own annotations. These are remarkable in that they appear to show a feeling that certain features of his style can be justified in terms of devotion and exegesis, but not in terms of the most advanced literary norms.

The sources for such justification are varied—a fact which may suggest some confusion on La Ceppède's part. In the matter of the Latinism *feres* Malherbe had noted in his commentary on Desportes: 'c'est un mot qui se trouve assez dans Ronsard, mais il ne vaut rien.'[6] The same tension between the old and new styles is implicit in La Ceppède's comment on the same word, although the emphasis is complementary:

Feres. l'aduouë que ce mot est écorché du Latin, & non guieres receuable; ie l'vsurpe neantmoins pour ce coup, & sans consequence puis que i'ay à garent Ronsard qui au 97. Son. du 1. liu. de ses Amours dit ainsi . . . (II. i. 43, n. 3)

La Ceppède evidently realizes that the word, and Latinisms in general, are not in fashion, and knows that they are typical of Ronsard. But unlike Malherbe he retains sufficient respect for the Pléiade to justify to himself the isolated use of a useful rhyme-word.

But for a more frequently used Latinism La Ceppéde relies on more solid argument derived from the etymological tradition in biblical exegesis. The word *alme* was greatly favoured by Ronsard and his champions, but had fallen into disrepute by the time of Malherbe.[7] It is used freely, however, in the *Imitation* and *Théorèmes*. La Ceppéde is evidently aware of its status: in a short

<hr/>

[6] Ibid., p. 112.   [7] Ibid., pp. 4, 105.

philological essay (I, pp. 489–91) he defends the word, and by emphasizing its etymology he gives it a new precision in the devotional context.

The word was, he says, common amongst the Latin writers and had been naturalized by the Italians and subsequently by the French. As an example of the French usage he cites, of course, Ronsard.[8] He is undisturbed by the fact that its use is often in connection with the pagan goddesses Ceres and Venus; illustrative quotations from Virgil, Columella, and Cicero enable him to discern three basic meanings of the word which he employs in order to justify specific examples from the *Théorèmes*. In the first place, the word is 'donné pour epithete a Cerés pour l'appeler nourriciere' (I, p. 489). This sense is used in I. i. 99: 'Puis qu'on vous a priué de vostre alme Rosée'. In the second place,

Ce mot signifie encor belle, & sainte; & en ce sens Virgile appele Venus Alme en l'Epigramme de Venus, & du vin; & Ciceron (apres Ennius) au 3. des Offices, donne cet epithete à la foy: c'est en ce sens que nous auons cy-dessus donné cet adiectif à la prouidence de Dieu au 3. vers du Sonnet 63. du 1. liure. (I, p. 490)

In the third place, 'Ame signifie encor tranquile & serain', and is commonly found in association with the sun. Thus in I. ii. 97 the Virgin speaks of her son as 'Belle Ame de mon Ame, Alme iour de mes yeux'. In all three senses the adjective can be appropriately applied, he maintains, to the Virgin herself, as in the case on which he is here commenting: 'Alme Mere du Christ'.[9] The pagan associations are not denied: they are all part of the background notions of syncretism and conversion in which La Ceppède's writing is based. But the philological explanations do not stop here. Quite apart from the fact that the word is common in the hymns of the Church, the word *alma* in Hebrew and in translated forms means 'virgin'. To establish this La Ceppède appeals to a wide range of opinion from Jerome to Robert Estienne, while seeking to refute contentions of Aquila and Cajetan that the word is the antonym of 'virgin', 'vne ieune femme deflorée' (I. p. 490). The discussion on the propriety of the word is closely bound up with exegetic method. Several translations of the key biblical passages (Genesis 24: 43,

[8] *Premier Livre des Amours* (1584), sonnet 80 (see *Œuvres*, ed. Laumonnier, vol. iv, p. 61), 'alme Soleil'; cf. Petrarch, *Canzoniere*, 188, 'Almo Sol'.

[9] I. iii. 88; cf. the antiphon 'Alma redemptoris mater', and Petrarch, *Canzoniere*, 366, l. 87, 'Vergine sacra et alma'.

Isaiah 7: 14, Proverbs 30: 19) are drawn on. La Ceppède points out that the Septuagint with Jerome's approval renders the Hebrew word as 'virgin' in Isaiah 7: 14; and that in spite of the claims of Aquila and Cajetan 'l'ancienne, & commune lecture' of Proverbs 30: 19 is 'viam viri in adolescentia', not 'adolescentula'. But even if it were read, as in 'la vieille traduction', 'viam viri in adolescentula', it is proper, according to the established exegetic principle of allegorizing the unacceptable, to interpret the passage mystically as a prophecy of the Incarnation. But recent scholarship enables him to retain the prophetic sense, 'se tenant au sens literal mesme', because the translation of the Hebrew Bible published by Robert Estienne in 1557 has 'Vestigium viri in Virgine'. This detailed argument illustrates the extent to which an apparently simple stylistic feature is rooted in Scriptural philology.

Certain other lexical departures from the Malherbian canon might be explained as the transposition of biblical Latinity. The cases of *lac* (for 'hell' in *Imitation* 142, 6) and *dol* (for 'guile' in *Imitation*, p. 13) derive from the Vulgate text. Similarly, *bénin*, though rejected by Malherbe as archaic, [10] is found frequently in La Ceppède to denote the quality of divine liberality: e.g. 'Verse benin sur luy ta douceur nompareille' (*Imitation* 101, 1). Again it is probably the Vulgate source that is responsible. The same argument applies to such deprecated words as *oindre* ('vostre Oinct', *Imitation*, p. 23; 'l'Oingt du Seigneur', I. ii. 33), *ire* (e.g. I. ii. 86), *dextre*.[11] All these are words intrinsic to biblical devotion.

The Malherbian demand for logical consistency may lie behind the justification of the rendering of Psalm 101: 18, which runs:

> Le souuerain Seigneur voit d'vn œil gratieux . . . (I. i. 29)

La Ceppède concedes that 'ces termes de voir la priere ne semblent pas bien à propos'; but significantly he forestalls criticism by adducing his duty to remain as close as possible to the biblical mode:

> Toutesfois on en a icy vsé pour rapporter plus naifuement les mots de l'Escriture saincte: & puis que Salomon & Dauid ont ainsi parlé . . . il n'y a icy que reprendre. (I. i. 29, n. 2)

Aspects of La Ceppède's syntax too may be bound up with the influence of biblical Latinisms. The substantivization of adjectives

---

[10] Brunot, *Doctrine*, p. 256.
[11] e.g. I. iii. 50; for Malherbian disapproval of these terms see Brunot, *Doctrine*, p. 256; *Histoire*, vol. iii, pp. 103, 110, 114, 160.

and participles, a well-known Pléiade practice based on Greek and Latin models, is justified in II. ii. 39, n. 3 commenting on the phrase 'ce grand Salutaire':

Ce mot, fait substantif, passera tel pour ce coup en François: d'autant que c'ét vn des noms propres de nostre Sauueur.

The principle that the sacredness of the subject permits what La Ceppède evidently feels to be an unacceptable practice has wide implications. In fact, this is not an isolated instance. Substantivized adjectives designating the Godhead may have acquired special association with religious discourse in view of the vernacular Bible translations utilizing the expressions 'L'Eternel' and 'l'Immortel'. The *Théorèmes* use both these, as well as the following substantivized adjectival attributes: 'le benit de Iacob' (I. ii. 85); 'l'Oingt du Seigneur' (I. ii. 33); 'l'Enuoyé du Monarque supreme' (I. ii. 85); 'cet Humanisé' (II. iv. 12); and 'ce Beau' (II. iii. 11), an example that illustrates the convergence of the devout with the profane poetic style.

Quite apart from this particular principle La Ceppède apparently absorbs the Vulgate substantivized forms denoting moral categories.[12] The expression 'le craignant Dieu' (*Imitation* 14, 3), for example, is a direct translation of 'timentes Deum'. There are several similar cases which are stylistically significant: 'les obstinez' (*Imitation* 31, 5; II. iv. 10); 'les humbles' (*Imitation* 101, 12); 'mes haineux' (I. i. 72), which combines a syntactical solecism with an archaic word condemned by Malherbe; 'des iniques' (I. ii. 100); and the compound forms: 'les destinez a la campagne noire' (II. i. 28); 'des mieux philosophantz' (II. ii. 76); 'les marquez a ton coing' (I. iii. 31).

The distinction between vernacular poetic discourse, paraphrase and, indeed, directly translated biblical text itself is frequently so tenuous that La Ceppède frequently comments on features of the sonnets as if they were themselves objects for exegesis. Thus, relying principally on Génébrard's commentary on the Psalms, he explains the unusual plural abstract 'justices':

Ce mot en plurier, & en singulier est prins maintesfois en L'Escriture saincte pour les œuures de l'homme, & le plus souuent pour les bonnes (comme en ce vers). (II. i. 23, n. 2)

It is not so much the morphology that La Ceppède finds it neces-

---

[12] Cf. Leblanc, *Poésie religieuse*, pp. 330 ff.

sary to elucidate here as the precise biblical meaning of the expression. This transfer of the semantics of Vulgate hebraized Latin goes so far as to retain in one instance, where the presumed actual words of Christ are paraphrased, what is supposed to be the elements of the Hebrew tense system and adjectival degree system (II. ii. 77, n. 6). It is perhaps significant that Génébrard in his commentary pays particular attention to tenses, and it was well known from patristic commentaries that the Hebraic 'past' signified the 'future' especially in the prophetic books. The result for La Ceppède's language in the *Théorèmes* is that the reader is asked to read, where specified, the French perfect (e.g. 'Heureux ceux qui . . . Ont creu', II. ii. 77) as the future tense, and to read a French positive adjective (e.g. '& bien heureux encores Seront ceux qui . . .' II. ii. 77) as comparative. This type of literalistic paraphrase doubtless arises from La Ceppède's concern with the letter, the Hebrew letter, as the basis of exegesis.

Since such cases as the above suggest a firm biblical Hebraic substratum in La Ceppède's style, it is perhaps valid to consider the possibility that other features may be so explained, even though they are not explicitly acknowledged. The old periphrastic conjugation of verbs, for instance, was criticized during the seventeenth century; Malherbe affected not to understand it in Desportes. It did however, have its champions and Maupas and others insisted that the present participle of the verb conjugated with *aller* or *être* expressed 'une perseverance et continuité d'action'.[13] In other words, this form was felt to have an aspectual value which later scholars have recognized as playing an important role in Hebrew grammar.[14] La Ceppède's use of the form seems almost exclusively to have a durative, progressive, or inchoative value:

Plus ie suis abbatu, plus ils vont s'éleuant (*Imitation* 37, 9)

Jamais le doux sommeil ne vient siller mes yeux.
Ie ressemble à l'oiseau qu'on nomme solitaire,
Je vay cerchant retraicte aux plus funestes lieux.

(*Imitation* 101, 5)

---

[13] Brunot, *Doctrine*, pp. 446; *Histoire*, vol. iii, p. 337.
[14] Cf. Joüon, *Grammaire de l'hébreu biblique*, pp. 385 ff.; Barr, *The Semantics of Biblical Language*, pp. 73 ff. For a Renaissance view cf. Bellarmine, *Institutiones linguae Hebraicae*, p. 94; Hebrew is regarded as lacking a 'present', having instead a form '*Benoni* id est intermedium, quod nos vocamus participium actiuum, siue praesens, praesentis temporis . . . Quinetiam hoc Hebraei verbum ipsum praesentis temporis . . . circumloquuntur.'

The frequency of this form in the *Imitation* may therefore be linked with the themes of endurance and long-suffering. In expressing the idea of the eternity of God the periphrastic form appears almost inevitable:

> Cette gloire a roulé par tous les siecles vieux,
> Et comme elle est encor elle sera brillante. (*Imitation*, 37, 10)

Similarly, in the *Théorèmes* the characteristic Hebraic–Latin durative aspect is retained, for example, in the paraphrased words of Jesus: 'J'estoy . . . enseignant' (I. i. 73), 'Niniue fut pleurante Quarante iours' (II. i. 38), and the inchoative nuance in:

> . . . si tant soit peu ses yeux sont arrestez
> Sur les yeux maternels, leurs pruneles parlantes,
> S'entredisant Adieu, vont perdant leurs clartez. (I. iii. 10)

The latter illustrates how the function of the periphrastic form in the *Théorèmes* differs from that in the *Imitation*: instead of being employed to express personal endurance it is now used to highlight objectively the emotional climaxes of the narrative of the Passion, and to create the illusion of presence for the devout reader. The flexibility of sixteenth-century usage thus accommodates a stylistic trait that is essential to devotional practices.

It became clear in Chapter V that a major feature of La Ceppède's manner is the use of a very wide spectrum of metaphors and images; the grammatical presentation of these images is also revealing. They are of course presented in a variety of ways, including explicit comparison by means of expressions (*être*) *comme*, *ressembler*, and their equivalents. But more typical is a particular kind of genitive construction (noun+*de*+noun) corresponding to a Hebraic form (the 'construct state'), which was rendered in the translating languages by means of the genitive case or equivalents. It was a construction that has something in common with the rhetorical trope hendiadys. In the proliferation of this formula La Ceppède shows his relative freedom from Malherbian constraint. But it is a commonplace in psalm paraphrases and other biblical poetry from Marot to d'Aubigné and beyond.[15]

---

[15] Cf. Leblanc, *Poésie religieuse*, pp. 333 ff.; Trénel, *L'Élément biblique dans l'œuvre de d'Aubigné*, pp. 93 ff.; Weber, *Création poétique*, pp. 706 f. The construct state is defined as the form of the noun before another noun used attributively; it is the noun modified (not the modifier) that is in 'construct state'. See Joüon, *Grammaire*, pp. 385 ff., and Barr, *Semantics*, pp. 89 ff.

The best-known example of the Hebrew genitive is the absolute superlative which is met in French from an early date. The qualified noun is repeated in the genitive plural. La Ceppède uses, for instance, 'le Saint des Saints' (I. iii. 91), 'le vainqueur des vainqueurs' (II. iii. 28), spontaneously and not as translation. But other relationships may exist between the two nouns in this construction, and these may be provisionally drawn up into three groups. The first comprises the normal French use of the genitive, or of 'de' between two nouns, expressing possession, origin, cause, etc. Some of these are stylistically striking only because their content is peculiarly biblical: for instance, 'ce fils de l'Homme' (I. ii. 35), and 'les œuures de tes mains (*Imitation* 142, 4), which is a direct translation of 'facta manuum tuarum' (Psalm 142: 5). In 'ministres d'iniustice' (*Imitation* 6, 5), which follows the same pattern, La Ceppède is being more Hebraic than his Vulgate model, which has the circumlocution 'omnes qui operamini iniquitatem' (Psalm 6: 9).

In the second type the second noun is attributive, that is to say, it qualifies the first of the nouns (usually concrete), thus functioning as an adjective: 'Prince de la clemence' (*Imitation* 142, 1) paraphrasing 'Dominus', and 'chansons d'allegresse' (136, 3), which is not a translation. Some superficially similar cases are difficult to analyse in this way, however. Even the familiar 'dies irae'—'iour de son ire' in La Ceppède's version of the *Stabat mater* (strophe 8)—would require a lengthy paraphrase; similarly 'Dieu de mon Salut' (*Imitation* 50, p. 25). Both examples are no doubt models for less commonplace yet complex cases, such as 'cloux d'amour (*Vexilla* 2), which seems to embody a combination of meanings.

In the third type the qualified word is the second noun, which is generally abstract, while the attributive noun may be either abstract or concrete. This construction is a very active means of producing metaphors, and can generally be paraphrased as a noun adjective, or 'A is (or resembles) B'. This type is thus distinct from the Hebraic genitives so far discussed, and is found rarely in the Bible. Nevertheless it bears an obvious surface resemblance to the biblical cases, and this fact may go some way towards accounting for its prevalence in La Ceppède's style. In the case of 'Les traicts de ta rigueur' (*Imitation* 37, 1), 'éclairs de ta . . . cholere' (*Imitation* 101, 3), 'le burin d'amour, sur le roc de mon cœur' (I. iii. 31) there is either an implicit comparison or a personification of the qualified nouns as autonomous agents. The bold image 'l'éponge de ta grace' (*Imitation* 50, 1) may be analysed in the same way. A number of converted erotic metaphors are presented in this way: 'feu de ton Amour' (*Imitation* 50, 13), 'feu de mon martyre' (I. iii. 76), 'feu de mes sanglots' (*Imitation* 6, 4). In less familiar expressions the metaphorical element is more apparent: 'bourbe des vices' (*Imitation*, 1, 3); 'l'infiny de tes . . . années' (*Imitation* 101, 15), and its opposite 'point de ce bas Element' (101, 13); 'cizeau de nos peines feruentes' (101, 10), 'fourneau de vostre auctorité' (*Reliques* I); 'prison de ces fumeuses Citez' (*Reliques* II); 'le dongeon de l'eternele vie' (*Imitation* 142, 3); 'la barriere . . . de la raison' (inverted, I. i. 13); 'le baston de sa Croix' (I. ii. 92); 'l'Auerne de mon ame' (*Imitation* 37. 6); etc.

This extremely frequent metaphor formula can be related to La Ceppède's characteristic style and outlook in three ways. Firstly, its superficial structure links it strongly with the Hebrew genitive, and thus with the other Hebraic stylistic features already observed. Secondly, it can be linked with La Ceppède's desire to provide a clear exposition of scriptural meaning, for the second member of the phrase often serves to clarify what would otherwise be an obscure translation. For instance, translating 'de profundis' (Psalm 129: 1) he glosses 'de l'abysme' with 'de ces calamitez': 'De l'abysme profund de ces calamitez (*Imitation* 129, 1), thereby interpreting the text allegorically or prophetically in terms of contemporary upheavals. In such cases the genitival formula compresses the letter of the text and its interpretation into one whole. Finally, there is a certain dualism in the construction which is reflected in the repetitive principle of rhetorical parallelism that is also characteristic of La Ceppède's style.

2. Christian Rhetoric

While modern criticism of the Psalms has tended to approach their style in terms of types of 'parallelism' (basically, 'synonymous', 'antithetic', and 'synthetic'),[16] the Middle Ages and Renaissance described biblical style more specifically in terms of Graeco-Roman rhetoric. The link between oratory and exposition of biblical texts was declared by Augustine in the *De doctrina chri-*

---

[16] Cf. Oesterley, *The Psalms Translated*.

stiana. With this authority for the application of the secular arts behind him Cassiodorus systematically compared the Psalms with the rhetorical forms of profane literature. For him Psalm 69: 1, for example, is an *epitrochasmos*; Psalm 41: 16–17 he took to be a 'quinquepartitum syllogismum, quem Cicero oratoribus aestimat applicandum';[17] Psalm 43: 15 employs *anaphora* or *relatio*. In the sixteenth century Gilbert Génébrard takes his authority directly from the text of the Psalms. He glosses Psalm 77: 2 thus:

Stylo parabolico, tropico et figurato, non simplici et vulgari, sed artificioso et eleganti. Loquar parabolas, insignes, memorabiles, figuratasque sententias et propheticas.[18]

At the Counter-Reformation the role of eloquence increases in importance; during the seventeenth century it comes to hold a central place in Jesuit education. It is hardly surprising, therefore, that La Ceppède, who was immersed in patristic, medieval, and contemporary theological writings, should adopt a rhetorical approach to the Bible and to the Psalms in particular. As an advocate and humanist he would in addition probably be familiar with the rhetorics of Aristotle, Quintilian, and Cicero, and perhaps with the sixteenth-century French compilations based on them.[19]

The part of rhetoric that is most relevant in examining La Ceppède's style at the level of sentence-structure is *elocutio*, and within that the 'figures of diction' or 'schemata'. Various patterns may be set up by the repetition of sound, the repetition of ideas, and the opposition of ideas, and may comprise particles, words, phrases, or whole sentences. Word-repetitions are classified according to the position of the repeated words within the sentence.

Alliterative repetition of single sounds occurs in the *Imitation* relatively rarely. When it does occur the words involved are also often in some way related in sense, as for example, in: 'Que de honte, & d'horreur mes haineux soient couuerts' (*Imitation* 6, 5). The alliteration here may be intended to replace the rather different repetitive device of the original: 'Erubescant et conturbentur vehementer omnes inimici mei; convertantur, et erubescant valde

---

[17] *Expositio in psalterium*, Migne, *Patrologia Latina*, vol. 70, col. 306; cf. Curtius, *Europäische Literatur*, pp. 48 f.

[18] *Psalmi Davidis*, 1600, p. 463.

[19] Cf. Nostredame's tribute to his civic eloquence in *Entrée*, ed. Boy, p. 32; on the rhetoric of his speech to Marie de Médicis cf. Quenot, 'Un discours inconnu', pp. 356 ff.

velociter' (Psalm 6: 11). La Ceppède's version approximates to the combined chiasmus, synonymy, and alliteration not only by employing three nouns whose initial sounds are similar, but also by using nouns which, if not precisely synonymous, at least belong to an area of the vocabulary associated with notions of moral revulsion.

The simplest of the repetitive devices is the repetition of a particle. In the *Imitation* the prefix *re-* appears to be particularly prominent. Its functions vary according to context, but are all ultimately related to the themes of the penitential psalms. In the first place, since *re-* can be prefixed freely to a large number of French words, it creates the possibility of facile rhetorical repetitions. But its use in the *Imitation* probably has a definable emotive role in expressing the Psalmist's theme of endurance of moral and physical trials. Secondly, this is possible because of the rich variety of meanings it can convey in specific instances: it can denote one or more repetitions of an action; it can denote a morally or physically retrograde movement; it can intensify. In the *Imitation* its use partakes of all these nuances, but most generally it seems to be used in such a way that it refers both to iterated action and to moral backsliding. Both the foregoing points are illustrated in the following description of long-suffering combined with recalcitrance:

> Las! mes vlceres vieux, desia cicatrisez,
> Maintenant repourris, maintenant recrusez
> M'apprennent que souuent la recheute est mortelle.
> Accablé de tristesse & de douleur recuit
> Comme vn tendre bourgeon que l'orage martelle
> Elangouré ie traine & le iour, & la nuict. (*Imitation*, 37, 3)

But it is not only negative change that is suggested by this pervasive prefix. The tedium of the Psalmist is not a steady journey to destruction; it consists rather of bouts of relapse and elation; continual error is accompanied by repeated atonement and pardon. Thus when La Ceppède uses a verb such as *laver* or *purger* in the *Imitation* it is almost invariably prefixed by *re-*. Verbal repetition may to some extent be connected here with the repetition intrinsic to ritual:

> Bon Dieu tu m'as souuent mes offenses quitté,
> Mais tes pitiez n'ont pas vn nombre limité
> Sus, relaue moy donc & me repurge encore . . . (*Imitation* 50, 2)

> Tu me nettoyeras de ma lepre rebele:
> Tu me relaveras . . . (*Imitation* 50, 6)

It is not easy to find similar thematic explanations for La Ceppède's evident predilection for word-repetition and word-play in the *Imitation*. Homonymic and partial homonymic repetitions in biblical language were recognized and praised by rhetorical exegetes.[20] But rhetorical categorization is apt to obscure the significance of this aspect of the style of the *Imitation*—an aspect which was coming to be regarded as distasteful by court-poets by the time the second edition of the work was published. It is more revealing to examine on the one hand the contextual function of the kind of rhetorical device in question, and on the other the possible sources and stylistic associations of such devices.

There is one striking though isolated instance of the onomatopoeic use of paronomasia and polyptoton:

> Il tend ore ses mains tend ses deux pieds aux cloux,
> Tandis les clous d'amour clouent dans sa poitrine
> Son cœur tout amoureux, qui s'immole pour nous.
>
> (*Vexilla*, strophe 2)

The words 'cloux' and 'clouent' have here an obvious imitative and evocative role, the effect of which is possibly supported by the repeated sounds 'tend', 'tandis', and 'tout amoureux', 'pour nous'.

Most similar devices, however, cannot be justified in these terms. The most important thing seems to be the pattern. A word at the beginning of a phrase may be echoed at the end (epanalepsis): 'En faueur de ton nom sainctement fauorable (*Imitation* 142, 9); 'Il est temps, ô Seigneur, ô Seigneur, il est temps' (*Imitation* 101, 9), which outbids the original in formal symmetry. The repetition may be ternary: 'O Gentilin gentil, où les ames gentilles'.[21] 'Les fleurons mieux fleuris au premier vent s'éflorent' (*Imitation* 102, 8). Chiasmatic arrangements are common: 'Auec le baume doux de sa douce mercy' (*Imitation* 102, 2); 'Ta puissante iustice, & ta iuste puissance' (*Imitation* 50, 10). Other repetitive figures may stretch over several lines:

> Pource donc qu'à toy seul appartient la mercy
> (Mercy que ta bonté nous départ tout ainsi
> Que le Pere à l'enfant) ta mercy ie reclame. (*Imitation* 129, 3)

---

[20] Cf. Cassiodorus on Psalm 102: 8 (Migne, vol. 70, col. 721): 'haec figura dicitur paranomasia . . . quae similitudine sermonis concitat audientis affectum.'
[21] 'Sur la dévotieuse retraicte du monastère de Gentilin', *Imitation*, p. 56.

There is no need to extend the list. The question is whether there exists any intrinsic link between this type of style and the genre of psalm paraphrase as it is developed in the sixteenth century. As has already been pointed out, one of the above examples derives from a repetition in the original. The repetitive element in biblical style may be strong, but its origin in Hebrew grammar has not necessarily anything to do with embellishment. Western commentators nurtured in the rhetorical tradition merely interpreted appropriate features as ornament.

One such apparently repetitive construction which is very common in biblical Hebrew and which also finds its way into the Hebraic Latin of the Vulgate, is the so-called internal object of the verb.[22] The most influential type is that in which the grammatical object has in Latin the same stem as the verb: 'peccastis peccatum maximum' (Exodus 32: 30), 'cantabimus canticum Domini' (Psalm 136: 4), 'concupierunt concupiscentiam' (Psalm 105: 14). Sometimes the Vulgate replaces the internal object by co-ordinated synonyms: 'concupiscit et desiderat' (Proverbs 21: 26). It is easy to see how cases such as these could sanction forms of synonymy and paronomasia in vernacular paraphrases. This in part explains why biblical translation was so readily adaptable as a literary genre: the strong rhetorical element in sixteenth-century poetry would reinforce, or be reinforced by, the rhetorical structures read into the Bible.

The *Imitation* naturally continues and exploits this style in the first place through direct translation in, for example: 'chanter des chansons d'allegresse', 'Comme chanterons nous du grand Dieu les Cantiques' (*Imitations* 136, 3); 'Qui ne sied auec eux en leurs sieges pestés' (*Imitation* 1, 1). In the case of 'chanter des chansons' the phrase as a whole is tautological and logically intransitive; the relationship between subject and object is not one of opposition. But if certain verbs are treated in this rhetorical formula the result may be a genuinely transitive phrase with an antagonistic (though phonetically similar) object. This quasi-Hebraic device then provides the opportunity for concise antithesis and paradox, as in: 'Ils forceront le fort de mon courage';[23] 'Vous, qui forcés l'effort de ces flots agités' (*Reliques* II); 'Je ne puis plus porter ce faix

---

[22] Cf. Joüon, *Grammaire*, pp. 373 ff.
[23] *Imitation*, 37, 9; 'fort' is used ambivalently as 'stronghold' and 'strong part'.

insupportable' (*Imitation* 129, 1), 'A fin de n'abboyer a ces cruels abbois' (*Imitation* 37, 7).

  There is a strong antithetical element in all these examples that is brought out more clearly if they are compared with the more explicitly paradoxical repetition that La Ceppède uses in order to present his image of the just sacrifice:

> Au feu de ton Amour mille peuples nouueaux
> Brusleront sans brusler comme ieunes Pyraustes.
>
> (*Imitation* 50, 13)

This type of repetition in which formal similarity embodies some opposition might then be related to the central themes of the *Imitation*—the themes of conflict and patient endurance through adversity. This can be further illustrated from a passage in which the words 'honneur' and 'honny' are employed in a construction superficially and rhetorically similar to the paradoxical 'internal object' repetition just discussed: 'Qui sa paix a troublée, ou son honneur honny' (*Imitation* 102, 3), where words from the same area of ideas (moral appraisal) are forced into oxymoron through an accidental phonetic similarity.[24] The figure may in some sense reflect the moral conflict at the heart of the Psalms—indeed the moral and psychological paradox of the penitent's self-justification through self-accusation, and even the confrontations and confusions of the civil wars. The context provides some support for this last possibility since it may be an indirect allusion to the troubles:

> C'est luy [Jehovah]
> Qui fait grace, & iustice, & qui prend la defense
> De cil qui patient va suportant l'offense
> Qui sa paix a troublée, ou son honneur honny.

More generally, the rhetorical collocation of similar-sounding words may be compared with the process of relating objects in metaphor, and hence to the principle of analogy that governs so much of La Ceppède's thought and writing.

  The figure complementary to homonymy (similarity of sound combined with disparity in sense) is synonymy (disparity in sound with similarity in sense). The patristic and medieval commentators on Scripture often note the prevalence of tautological repetition,

---

[24] Cf. also the alliterative linking of 'honte', 'horreur', 'haineux', quoted above, p. 167.

frequently seeking to establish nice distinctions between pairs of words such as 'ira' and 'furor' (Psalm 6: 2; 37: 2).[25] This particular example triggers off a series of synonyms and periphrases in La Ceppède's versions:

> DEsarme ta fureur, attiedy ton courroux,
> Recalme ton visage, & te monstre vn peux doux
> A tancer, à punir mes crimes deplorables. (*Imitation*, 6, 1)

> ALlumé de courroux, boüillonant de fureur
> Ne m'examine pas, ne punis mon erreur. (*Imitation* 37, 1)

Virtual synonyms in the original are often given more rigid rhetorical form in the paraphrase. Thus 'miser factus sum et curvatus sum' (Psalm 37: 7) is transformed into the elegant chiastic figure: 'Accablé de tristesse & de douleur recuit' (*Imitation* 37, 3). Similarly, 'miserere mei, Deus, secundum magnam misericordiam tuam' (Psalm 50: 3) becomes 'I'implore tes pardons, ta clemence i'embrasse' (*Imitation* 50, 1). Cases like these occur in large numbers, but many of them are to be accounted for less as rhetorical ornament and emphasis than as explanatory expansion.[26] A synonymous word or phrase may be used to literalize a metaphor (and conversely) or to clarify a theological point believed to be implied. This is consonant with the role of exegesis in La Ceppède's poetry. In some cases both members of a synonymous pair are metaphors, as in 'Il a fendu le Ciel, il a percé la nuë' (*Imitation* 101, 13). More often only one is metaphorical. On the whole, if it is the second part that is metaphorical the arrangement is a purely decorative elaboration. However, in many similar cases there is a progression from the general to the more precise statement. When two isolated nouns are involved the process is akin to the genitive constructions discussed above: in 'De ton Feu, ton Amour ne me priue iamais' (*Imitation* 50, 9), the second noun explains the symbol 'Feu'. Similarly, in the synonymous phrases 'Qui suit son Testament, qui fait ses volontez' (*Imitation* 102, 9), the second half of the line clarifies the first, which is a literal translation. It would therefore be mistaken to say that synonymy in the *Imitation* is mere rhetorical ornament. It seems rather to be a product sometimes of the style of the model and sometimes of a desire for clarity.

---

[25] e.g. Cassiodorus (Migne, vol. 70, col. 61).
[26] Synonymy is also termed *interpretatio*: cf. *Ad Herennium*, 4, 28, 38.

While Malherbe rejects excessive synonymy in the name of logic and economy, and while he studiously avoids it in his rendering of the Psalms, La Ceppède utilizes it for the sake of exegetic exposition and clarification and, more obviously, for the sake of fidelity to the style of the original.

The repetition of syntactic patterns, that is, 'parallelism', is an extension of the figures already discussed. In addition to this the chief syntactic characteristics of the biblical sentence are a comparative absence of subordination and marked repetition or marked absence of conjunctions. In general these are also characteristics of the *Imitation*. They may even be exaggerated where the text suggests them, and are often introduced spontaneously where there is no textual guidance.

The repeated members of the phrase may begin with the same word (anaphora). If this is an important noun (rather than a conjunction or a pronoun) it will suggest a mode of elevated incantation that is not only biblical but also liturgical; suppression of the conjunction is an intrinsic part of this mode:

> Gloire soit au grand Dieu qui ce Tout façonna,
> Gloire soit à son Fils, qui ce Tout rançonna,
> Gloire à son Esprit sainct, qui fomenta les ondes.
>> (*Imitation* 129, 5)

Not only the suppression of conjunctions but also the transposition of the elliptical syntax of the Latin text may contribute to the broken character of the sentence or phrase series. The following is influenced by the syntax of the model 'Beati quorum remissae sunt . . .' (Psalm 31: 1). It also illustrates the way some of the types of repetition discussed above combine with syntactical repetition reinforced by asyndeton:

> DE tous les dons gratuits la grace est le Greigneur,
> Heureux le criminel qui l'obtient du Seigneur.
> Bien heureux, qui tapit sous l'abry de sa grace.
> Tres-heureux qui pour voir abolir ses pechez
> Ne les colore point, ne les tient point cachez,
> Ne flate point son tort, ne dement point sa trace.
>> (*Imitation* 31, 1)

Similar examples occur in the *Imitation* which are not necessarily due to direct translation. Psalm 31: 16–20, for example, is organized in the Vulgate by means of co-ordinating conjunctions and connective adverbs:

> 16 tu exaudies me . . .
> 18 Quoniam ego in flagella paratus sum:
> et dolor meus in conspectu meo semper.
> 19 Quoniam iniquitatem meam annuntiabo:
> et cogitabo pro peccato meo.
> 20 Inimici autem mei vivunt, et confirmati sunt super me . . .

La Ceppède transposes the verbal repetition of conjunctions into rhythmical and syntactical repetition—a change which seems to have a deliberately expressive function. A series of disconnected affirmatives is disrupted by an even more disconnected series made up of exclamation, imperative, and interrogation:

> Pour moy ie me dispose au supplice ordonné,
> I'ay pour iamais mon ame au deuil abandonné.
> Je veux prescher par tout l'horreur de mon ofense.
> Je ne veux rien penser qu'au mal que i'ay commis.
> Mais qu'est-ce que ie voy? Seigneur, pren ma defense
> He! voicy l'escadron de mes durs ennemis. (*Imitation* 37, 8)

The conjunctions are omitted and the antithesis implied in the Vulgate's 'autem' is emphasized by more emotive constructions. La Ceppède's treatment of the text indicates the dramatic and dialogic quality of his paraphrase with which the persuasive use of rhetoric is closely connected.

The style of the *Imitation* consistently avoids subordination, but subordinate clauses tend to be arranged in the Vulgate manner in parallel series with a repeated introductory word. The Vulgate's repetition of 'ut', for example, is closely followed in:

> Afin que ces captifs chantent leur deliurance,
> Qu'ils perfument Sion du los de sa clemence,
> Que dans Hierosolyme ils annoncent ses loix:
> Que mille nations diuerses en ramage,
> S'vnissent en son Nom . . . (*Imitation* 101, 14)

Syntactic units thus coincide with the rhythmic units in a way which emphasizes the similarity in sense between the different parallel members. The examples quoted show how La Ceppède's rhetoric translates both the emotive and the ritualistic aspects of his original. But are his paraphrases mere literary exercises? It is worth bearing in mind that during the civil war period public penitential ceremonies were common, and that the chanting of psalms seems to have been an important part of this acting out of collective distress and guilt.[27]

The functionality of La Ceppède's rhetoric can be clarified further. Rhetoric was fundamentally concerned with influencing in practical terms the attitudes and behaviour of the hearer or reader, and the theory defined three rhetorical genres with reference to the particular aims in view—namely, the 'demonstrative', the 'deliberative', and the 'judicial' genres. The last was primarily the forensic speech designed to defend past action, a situation which is similar in structure to that of the penitent before his God.[28] It is the prose paraphrases of the *Imitation* in particular which reveal the clearest convergence of the rhetoric with its prime function in judicial pleading and the language of supplicatory prayer. This convergence rests ultimately on an interpretation of the Psalms that goes back to the Fathers. Augustine, for instance, is fond of playing on the ambiguity of the word 'oratio' meaning both 'speech' and 'prayer'. Similarly, the *Imitation* (1594) gives the title 'oraisons' to its prose paraphrases. Cassiodorus's expositions of the Psalms frequently assume the framework of the forensic speech, referring to the sinner as 'reus'.[29] La Ceppède's prose version of Psalm 50 is a good example of the utilization of the divisions of the advocate's speech into exordium, narration (statement of the facts), proofs, and refutations (or where relevant *deprecatio*, plea for mercy), and peroration. The exordium of La Ceppède's 'oraison' requests compassion for 'ce criminel miserable', who is of course the 'je' represented in the speech. The next section constitutes the *narratio*, a confession that is an ordered enumeration of transgressions arrived at by listing the possible interpretations of the text, 'tibi soli peccavi' (Psalm 50: 6). Each point is made distinctly and emphatically by reiteration of the word 'seul'. This

---

[27] Especially at the court of Henry III. Cf. the *Journal* of L'Estoille, e.g. p. 53, on the king and processions in Aix, December 1574; and Yates, *French Academies*, ch. 8, and 'Dramatic Religious Processions'; Jeanneret, *Poésie et tradition biblique*, pp. 350 ff.

[28] On the expression of this through the imagery see above, p. 108.

[29] See his commentaries on Psalms 6 and 50; and Smalley, *Study of the Bible*, p. 49. On the ambiguity of 'oratio' in Augustine cf. Baldwin, *Medieval Rhetoric and Poetic*, p. 67. In the sixteenth century 'oraison' also commonly means 'prose work': cf. Du Bellay, *Deffence*, ed. Chamard, p. 36. The sense 'oration' was learned and Latinate.

section merges with the next, the argument of the defence and its refutation. La Ceppède's interpretation of the text on which he bases the exculpation adheres to the orthodox Catholic gloss. Taking the verse 'in iniquitatibus conceptus sum', he tentatively argues that he is not responsible for his sins. This is rejected, since he must admit that free will concurred with natural predisposition (*Imitation*, p. 24). All argued defence is then abandoned and the plea is made for mercy:

i'abandonne (comme je dois) toute excuse, & recours simplement à vostre Clemence . . . (*Imitation*, p. 24)

A long peroration now ensues which returns to the original appeal for clemency. According to rhetorical theory the peroration should be a final incitement of the hearers by means of striking metaphors and passionate diction. This is indeed the case here: there is a general movement away from the rational tone, the indicative moods of the Ciceronian sentences that have preceded, to a string of parallel rhetorical interrogatives, imperatives, and hyperbolic metaphors which enable him to relate his own case and the troubles of his time:

Comblez mon ame de liesse par le rétablissement de la paix, que la guerre ciuile de mes sens luy auoit dérobé . . . Faites fondre sur moy cette langue de feu, & je prescheray si viuement de parole, & d'exemple les deuoyez, que maint, reuenant à bon sens se conuertira, & fera penitence de ses reuoltes. Encore, encore, mon Dieu, grand Dieu de mon Salut, ie vous supplie deliurez moy de mes sanglantes attaches, & repurgez mes veines du sang corrompu dont elles brunissent, lors mon gosier enflé de ioye rechantera vos bontez iustifiantes . . .

Forensic rhetoric thus accommodates the paradox in which self-accusation is the ultimate defence. Yet the persuasive techniques of human eloquence seem here to be intrinsic to abject confession. This may be explained by the fact that prayer (directed to God) and sermon rhetoric (directed to men) are traditionally confused, and that the Psalm paraphrases have a didactic as well as personal devotional function. More fundamentally, persuasive rhetoric in prayer may reflect the primitive element of coercion deeply buried in the practice of supplicatory prayer—an element perhaps brought into prominence by the nature of the civil war penitential movements.

The most general characteristics of the language of La Ceppède's poetry can be seen in terms of two forms of convergence. On the one hand, certain latinized Hebraic elements of the Bible are transposed into the vernacular where they have an archaic aspect by the linguistic standards of the seventeenth century. In some instances they merge with the style of the Pléiade. On the other hand, the biblical tradition merges with the rhetorical tradition, not only perhaps because of historical circumstances, but because of the religious relevance of rhetorical devices. Rhetoric systematizes the means of ritual repetition, expository synonymy, verbal symbolism; it systematizes the double-edged means of communicating with and influencing both men and God.

VIII

THE STRUCTURE OF THE *THÉORÈMES*

1. *Sonnet Form*

THE use of the sonnet by La Ceppède for doctrinal and devotional ends is entirely comprehensible in the light of its history.[1] The form was cultivated in Provence both by revivalist dialect poets like Bellaud de la Bellaudière and by the French poets in the circle of Henri d'Angoulême.[2] Because the sonnet had become inextricably associated with the themes of profane but spiritual love, its utilization in an explicitly religious manner naturally arises as a result of the notion of poetic 'conversion'. From the love-sonnets of Du Bellay to those of Desportes there is an inherent ambiguity in the use of erotic and mystical images. Indeed, certain sonnet cycles in French describe or imply a spiritual development from profane to sacred love.[3] In the later years of the sixteenth century devout provincial poets such as Chassignet, Lazare de Selve, Anne de Marquets, Gabrielle de Coignard at Toulouse, Louis Gallaup de Chasteuil at Aix, and others, turn to the sonnet form, no doubt partly because of its literary prestige, but also because it lends itself thematically to 'conversion'.[4] But in the course of its development the sonnet had acquired other thematic associations besides the erotic. In particular it was not uncommon among the Italian sonneteers to use the form as the vehicle for philosophical and theological ideas.[5] The primary dyadic structure of the sonnet appears to have been

---

[1] On the history of the sonnet cf. Colletet, *Traitté de l'epigramme et traitté du sonnet*, ed. Jannini; Jasinski, *Histoire du sonnet*; Mönch, *Das Sonett*.

[2] Cf. Fromilhague, *Malherbe. Technique . . .* , p. 176.

[3] The *Olive* ends with a religious sequence; Desportes includes anti-Petrarchan religious sonnets from 1577. On the thematic organization of French sonnet cycles cf. Rousset, 'Les recueils de sonnets'.

[4] J.-B. Chassignet, *Le Mespris de la vie*, Besançon, 1594; Lazare de Selve, *Les Œuvres spirituelles*, Paris, 1620; Anne de Marquets, *Sonets, prières et devises*, Paris, 1566; Gabrielle de Coignard, *Œuvres chrestiennes*, Tournon, 1595. On Gallaup see above, p. 18.

[5] Cf. Mönch, p. 61.

appropriate to dialectical argument. Moreover, the sonnet was typically directed towards an individual (real or fictitious) and was intended to demonstrate, persuade, and propitiate, as well as to express the author's feelings. In the early seventeenth century the demonstrative and intellectual nature of the sonnet was recognized.[6]

The dialectic and persuasive potential of the sonnet's form is, of course, dependent on its rhyme-schemes, which can be themselves regarded as repetitive rhetorical devices. The variation of rhyme-combinations within the primary divisions of octave and sestet determines, of course, the relationships between the secondary divisions of quatrain and tercet. La Ceppède makes use of four different octave schemes:

> (i)   *abba abba*
> (ii) *abba abab*
> (iii) *abab baba*
> (iv) *abab baab*

Since each of these may be combined with tercets *ccd eed* and *ccd ede*, there are altogether eight different sonnet schemes in the *Théorèmes*. In other words, the schemes that La Ceppède does *not* use are those in which there is alternation of rhyme between the quatrains (i.e. *abab abab* and *abab abba*). Of the four octave schemes, (ii), (iii), and (iv) were innovated and popularized by Desportes,[7] and taken together they account for 361 of the 520 sonnets comprising parts I and II of the *Théorèmes*. However, if the quatrain categories are taken separately, type (i) is slightly more frequent than each of the others.[8] More significantly, if the eight over-all schemes (i.e. quatrain+sestet) are taken separately there is a high proportion of the type *abba abba ccd ede*.[9] This form is the scheme approved by Malherbe,[10] and it would appear that although still far from total conformity La Ceppède is tending to adopt the fashionable form.

As far as the rhymes themselves of his sonnets are concerned he is on the whole as strict as Malherbe in the use of supporting

---

[6] Cf. Colletet, p. 190.

[7] See, e.g., Elwert, *Traité de versification française*, pp. 178 ff.; Jasinski, *Histoire du sonnet*, pp. 194 ff.

[8] Type (i) 159, (ii) 79, (iii) 142, (iv) 140.

[9] 118; of the seven other schemes the most frequent is *abab baba ccd ede* (101 occurrences), the least frequent *abba abab ccd eed* (31 occurrences).

[10] Cf. Fromilhague, *Malherbe. Technique . . .* , pp. 176 ff.

consonants before the rhyming vowel. Indeed it is possible that the proportion of rich rhymes in La Ceppède's sonnets exceeds that in Malherbe's.[11] However, there are certain peculiarities in his rhymes, some of which affect the style and general form of the sonnet. He continues to use, for instance, the archaic or provincial rhyme *heure* with *nature*, *couverture*, etc., although there is a slight decline in the use of this rhyme in Part II of the *Théorèmes*.[12] In the sestets of the sonnets he occasionally uses only two sets of rhymes instead of three, and on inspection it appears that the four resultant words with the same rhyme are divided between the tercets according to their supporting consonants: e.g. 'abatuës'—'combatuës'—'d'embas'—'estenduës'—'combas'—'entenduës' (I. iii. 27); 'arrogant'—'brigant'—'teste'—'tonnant'—'tempeste'—'retenant' (I. ii. 66); 'partage'—'dauantage'—'contentement'—'engage'—'truchement'—'langage' (II. iv. 9). It is not clear from these examples whether La Ceppède would have regarded the four grouped *c* rhymes as essentially two different rhymes. There is some ambiguity here which may suggest a compromise between the two-rhyme Petrarchan sestet sometimes used by the Pléiade (*cdc cdc*) and the more usual French forms already mentioned. But more probably La Ceppède is undertaking the virtuoso task of using yet another four rhyming words in a way that parallels the quatrain form of the octave. In II. iv. 9, for instance, this effect is reinforced by the fact that the quatrain *b* rhyme is identical with the sestet *d* rhyme, so that the whole sonnet employs in all only three rhymes. By relaxing or tightening the rhyme-links in this manner, contrasts between the quatrain and sestet divisions can be modified with accompanying stylistic effects.

A further factor in La Ceppède's rhymes is a noticeable degree of semantic coherence. This is not merely due to the subject-matter, nor to the element of rhetorical paronomasia in rhyming, but apparently in many cases to a deliberate attempt to utilize rhyme in order to stress significant aspects of the narrative and their relationships. Both rhyme and rhetorical repetition serve the function of revealing the devotional implications of scriptural narrative in II. ii. 74. In this partly narrative, partly analytic representation of the disciple Thomas's state of mind the parono-

---

[11] Cf. above, pp. 45 ff., on La Ceppède's use of rich rhyme in the *Imitation*.
[12] Part I: out of 42 rhymes in -*ure* 16 involve *heure* or *meure*; Part II: out of 34 such rhymes 8 involve *heure* or *meure*.

masia in the hemistich ('il creut qu'ils le croyaient', line 2) and the rhymes ('mensonge'—'songe', ll. 1 and 4) serve to highlight a distinction between delusion and mendacity.[13] In the piece of direct speech that follows, the verbal and syntactical repetitions do not in themselves have any obvious role beyond ornamentation:

> Ie n'en croy rien (dit–il) si mon doigt ne s'alonge
> Dans les trous de ses mains que les clous étaioyent,
> Si ma main dans son flanc entamé ne se plonge . . .
>
> (ll. 5–7)

But in the last three lines of the poem, having succinctly narrated in the first tercet the interval of time between Thomas's words and the disciples' assembly behind closed doors in Jerusalem, La Ceppède takes the unusual step of repeating the rhyme-words of the quatrains:

> Puis monstrant à Thomas ses mains, luy dit alonge
> Ton doigt dedans ces trous: & dans mon costé plonge
> Ta main: & ne sois plus mécreant desormais.

The most fundamental principle of the sonnet—dissimilar rhymes in its two primary divisions—is here broken for a specific purpose which the author himself makes explicit in the accompanying annotation (n. 5, II, p. 337):

Les rithmes, & les paroles de ces vers 12. & 13. sont icy affectées, semblables à celles du premier quatrain, où nous auons couché & paraphrasé le dire de sainct Thomas, afin d'exprimer céte obseruation notable des PP. que Iesus-Christ luy dit les mesmes paroles dont il auoit vzé en son absence, afin qu'il s'asseurat par céte preuue de sa Diuinité. Puis qu'il sçauoit iustement ce qu'il auoit dit, ores qu'il n'y fut pas present corporelement.

The implications of this statement are, firstly, that La Ceppède is concerned with a 'preuue' of the Resurrection, and, secondly and more importantly, that he regards this proof as embodied in the form of his sonnet. A repetition in time regarded as significant by his patristic sources is transferred to the formal patterns of the sonnet's rhymes.

2. Functions of the Sonnets

(i) *Narration.* Since Scripture has in La Ceppède's view multiple layers of meaning it is often necessary for him to indicate in an

[13] Cf. I, p. 263, II, p. 245.

annotation when he is adhering to the letter of the text. Neither translation nor simple linear narrative is possible without a kind of self-exegesis in the sonnets themselves or in the accompanying annotations. However, it is clear that textual paraphrase, historical reference, and, in addition, an invented narrative literary framework, although scrupulously distinguished by La Ceppède, constitute the fundamental elements of the *Théorèmes*, as the following makes clear:

> MAis oyons le progrés de nostre Historien.
> Christ ayant accoisé quelque peu ces vacarmes,
> Demande encor' vn coup. Qui cerchez vous gendarmes?
> Ils respondent encor IESVS NAZARIEN. (I. i. 53, ll. 1–4)

In the accompanying note the 'historian' is identified, and it is pointed out with precision that only lines 3 and 4 are a translation of the Gospel text (John 18: 7). Line 2 and the first hemistich of line 3, on the other hand, constitute the invented means of recapitulating and linking the narrative between separate sonnets. Such participle phrases belong to a class of similar devices including classic epic narrative formulas like 'il eut dit', and various temporal clauses, which ensure narrative cohesion between isolated sonnets. Two further principles can be discerned. In the first place, La Ceppède frequently uses the expression *exaggeratio*, in the rhetorical sense of amplification, and in conjunction with reference to orthodox examples, in order to justify embellishment of otherwise faithful paraphrases. Thus in II. ii. 30, in contradistinction to the direct translation in I. i. 53 just quoted, the text (Matthew 28: 9) is said to be 'exageré suiuant les paraphrases ordinaires des Peres' (II, p. 212). That is to say, it is amplified by means of rhetorical repetition, parallelism, and rhyme. In the second place, the principle of 'pious meditation' permits the addition of new narrative details. This is the case, for instance, in I. ii. 98, where La Ceppède describes the procession to Calvary and invents the details of the mocking of Christ. A note comments as follows:

> bien que ces paroles & iniures en ce Sonnet, & en plusieurs des precedans & suiuans, ne soient escrites dans les Euangelistes; si est-il licite de les mediter ainsi pieusement, à l'exemple des anciens Peres Contemplatifs . . . (I. ii. 98, p. 342)

A further condition for this kind of addition to the scriptural paraphrase is that it be 'vray-semblable'—a consideration that illustrates La Ceppède's concern to establish a consistent and realistic narrative framework in the *Théorèmes*.

Where the introduction of visual detail is in question La Ceppède occasionally has recourse to traditional iconography, and there is evidence to suggest that painting techniques influence certain of his descriptions. Certain aspects of the *Théorèmes* suggest general comparisons with contemporary pictorial art: the imagery of light and darkness is paralleled in the technique of chiaroscuro.[14] But these aspects have explanations independent of the influence of painting. More reliable are the explicit indications in the annotations to the work. In some cases La Ceppède relates pictorial evidence to literal exegesis. For the problematic 'dispertitae linguae' he prefers the interpretation 'distributed' rather than 'cloven' not only because it seems more 'vray-semblable' and is supported by authority, but also because 'les vieilles peintures de l'Eglise le marquent ainsi' (II. pp. 564–5). It is not clear here exactly what La Ceppède is referring to; but it appears in other passages that he is also concerned with contemporary painting. In his iconography of the Virgin he rejects the portrayal of her as

transportée iusqu'aux extremitez coustumieres aux femmes communes, impatientes, & foibles, ainsi que ... plusieurs Peintres ignorans l'ont figurée, & la representent encor ... (I, p. 382)

It would appear that it is exclusively ancient paintings that La Ceppède finds authoritative, which is consistent with his humanist concern for textual and historical authenticity. Thus on a second occasion (I. iii. 97, n. 1) he justifies his own verbal depiction of the swooning Virgin by allusion to 'Les anciennes Images des sepulchres aux Temples' (I, p. 505). Since this information is acknowledged to be derived from Suarez the influence is probably not strictly pictorial.

These facts do not mean, however, there are no visual and spatial elements in the narrative schema of the *Théorèmes*. The clearest evidence is the note on the word 'reaux' in the lines describing Christ's death:

Voila de ses beaux yeux tout a coup enfoncée
L'vne & l'autre prunele, & leur flamme éclipsée,
Leur paupiere abatuë, & leurs reaux se cacher. (I. iii. 85)

---

[14] Cf. Buffum, *Studies in the Baroque*, p. 121.

La Ceppède's interest in medicine may lie behind this anatomical account, which merges both with the language of painting and with mystical Petrarchan imagery. He is aware of the techniques of three-dimensional illusion in painting by highlighting:

Reaux. Les rehauts sont les iours de la superficie, ou circonferance des yeux, du nez, de toute la face, & autres parties eminentes du corps humain, en termes & langage des Peintres, qui disent communement, que par ces rehauts, & les ombres, la peinture fait ses reliefs, & combien que le visage, & les membres d'vn corps mort ayent aussi leurs rehauts, ils sont toutefois sombres, & bien differens de ceux d'vn corps viuant, qui sont clairs, & bien égayez . . . (I. iii. 85, n. 3)

The essential elements in these remarks are lighting, depth, illusion, and a realism that seems to some degree to confuse physiological fact with pictorial representation. All these elements suggest the Caravaggiesque manner in painting. While no further direct comparisons seem possible, it is arguable that the principles of perspectival coherence and realism are present in the narrative structure of the *Théorèmes*. The discrete sonnet unit is an apt instrument for highlighting objects and events in relation to a panoramic whole, while the careful presentation of relationships between consecutive and simultaneous events is analogous to the organization of three-dimensional space in the pictorial plane.

In I. i. 86–8 the incident in Mark 14: 51–2 of the adolescent following Jesus is turned into a detailed narration and exposition parallel to that of Jesus's arrest, the simultaneity of which is carefully indicated in the surrounding sonnets. The first quatrain of sonnet 86 makes the transition from the group of Jesus and the Apostles who are the subject of the preceding sequence to a general description of the pursuing crowd, which, by means of a reference to their cries, facilitates a further transition to the more localized subject of the sonnet, the rousing of the adolescent:

> Vn ieune adolescent s'esueille matinier,
> S'affeuble d'vn linceul, hors du chalit se iette,
> Ouure vn peu la fenestre, espie, escoute, guette,
> Sort, s'approche, & craintif tallonne le dernier. (ll. 5–9)

The narration here is brief but dense compared with the more diffuse sequence of the main episodes of the Passion. Each of the four lines corresponds to a distinct phase in the subject's actions, and within each line the string of verbs represents the details of each phase. The sonnet thus returns the narrative line to the principal subject, Jesus and his captors. It might seem that there is a shift here in the narrator's viewpoint which would contradict the fundamental prerequisite of perspective. But there is an explicit relating of major and minor episodes: the one is subordinated to the other, marked by the initial phrase 'Mais cependant' of I. i. 89. It is this rational organization of events in linear verbal narrative in order to create an illusion of simultaneity that suggests the analogy with plane perspective.

There are other respects in which concepts of temporal relationships and history are significant in the structure of the *Théorèmes*. Types are brought into the principal narrative line in a variety of ways. Sonnet I. iii. 8, for instance, utilizes the octave–sestet divisions in presenting the type of Jonathan in the form of an explicit epic simile. Without any prior explanation the octave paraphrases 1 Kings 14: 1, 13 in the habitual asyndetic style of the realistic narration. The first tercet then introduces the literal theme of the simile with the classic device 'Non autrement le Christ . . .', while the final tercet reflecting the rationalizing element in La Ceppède's thought turns the comparison into a distinction with the phrase 'Ils different d'vn point . . .' The tendency to identify type and antitype in the narrative is here carefully qualified. But on other occasions the merging of separate historical persons or events is more complete. Sonnet I. i. 96 apostrophizes Christ in an ambiguous manner that combines two, possibly three historical allusions by means of double antonomasia:

> MAgnanime Samson Nazarien Alcide,
> Souffrez-vous ces liens, ces fers iniurieux?
> Où sont de vos cheueux les faits victorieux? (ll. 1–3)

The Jews are apostrophized in the following quatrain in a similarly ambiguous combination which draws together the circumstantial details of separate historical events, although La Ceppède is careful to elucidate the ambiguity in the accompanying note. Another method of achieving this dual vision of historical realities is the use of paraphrase and verbal allusion. Thus in I. iii. 61 the principal subject of the narrative verbs is the Virgin, but the typological lament of Naomi is brought into the narrative present not only by the overt phrase 'Auecques Noemi, cette chetiue Mere . . .' (l. 1), but also by the fact that the speech attributed to the Virgin is a paraphrase of Ruth 1: 20.

Not only is the historical gap reduced between the Old Testament narrative and the Passion narrative, but also between the Passion narrative and the historical present of the reader (or writer). The typological schema is essentially three-dimensional: type and antitype point to a further eschatological fulfilment and thus demand a moral response in the present from the devout soul.[15] The simultaneity of sacred events is possible through the self experiencing them and recounting them as real and present. It is the ubiquitous persona of the self illuminated by grace or poetic inspiration in the *Théorèmes* on which this depends.

The narrative tenses in I. ii. 1 first of all place the persona as contemporary in time and space with the events recounted. In a manner reminiscent of the Jesuit technique of 'application of the senses' La Ceppède represents his presence in a series of syntactically parallel but otherwise unlinked lines in the narrative present:

> LEs erreurs, les horreurs de cette nuict m'esfrayent . . .
> Mon Sauueur, ie n'ay point à vos iuges d'accés,
> I'ay perdu le sentier que vos ennemis frayent,
> Je n'oy rien que glapir ces chiens qui vous abbayent.

The first tercet is an invocation to the Holy Spirit for guidance such as was granted the Israelites in the pillar of fire (Exodus 13: 21). But the final tercet is related in a more complex way to what has preceded:

> Ainsi parmy les feux en despit des tenebres
> Et la gloire, & l'opprobre éclateront celebres:
> Vostre gloire en Horeb, vostre oprobre en ces vers.

La Ceppède here continues the parallel between himself, the Israelites, and the Passion of Christ one stage further in the narrative, and draws together temporally separate events as the subjects of a single verb in the future tense ('éclateront'). The paradox of the light amidst darkness at the lawgiving on Horeb (following the Israelites' wandering) is thus identified with the paradox of the judgement of Christ by Pilate, but both are also implicitly identified with the progressive writing (or reading) of 'ces vers' to which the Spirit inspires the narrator. Rhythmically reinforced parallelism is here essential in metaphorically relating the key words that

---

[15] On the ethical element in typology cf. Charity, *Events and their Afterlife*.

make the tercet comprehensible: 'feux'—'tenebres': 'gloire'—
'opprobre . . . celebres': 'Horeb'—'oprobre en ces vers'.

La Ceppède's narrative style is dependent for its content on
strict literal interpretation of the biblical text, and is characterized
by its visual intensity and its verb-based, conjunction-free syntax.
But the structure of the narration is ambivalent: it not only presents a rigorously coherent line for the Passion story, but also
presents a coalescence of separate time scales. The intense feeling
for the present and the resolution of temporal barriers can be
related to the typological schema of redemption, the theology
centred on the Incarnation, and the search to unite man with God.

(ii) *Exhortation and supplication.* The distinguishing feature of
apostrophe is that it presupposes a relationship between first and
second persons. It has an important function in the judicial and
deliberative genres of rhetoric which La Ceppède exercises to
some extent in the *Imitation*. In the *Théorèmes* it is the mode of
preaching and prayer, but is also integrated with narration and
theological exposition.

Because rhetoric is above all the language of the law courts it is
perhaps not surprising to find the narrating persona intervening
as if present in the account of Jesus's trial in I. ii in order to apo-
strophize the participants. For instance, Pilate's interrogative
recounted in the last tercet of I. ii. 79 elicits a counter-question
in the octave of the following sonnet:

> SI ton pouuoir est tel, pourquoy si longuement
> Detiens tu ce pauuret, qui n'a point fait d'offense? (I. ii. 80)

The justificatory reply is given by the speaker in the second quatrain and is based on his knowledge that Pilate subsequently affirms
belief in the accused's innocence. The point is reinforced rhetorically by means of paronomasia and paradox:

> Mais l'interest mondain ta iustice balance,
> Et te fera iuger ce Iuste iniustement.

The remainder of the sonnet continues the historical narrative—
that is, Christ's own reply to Pilate, apparently within the same
time scheme as the interpolated speech of the narrator. Here the
apostrophic interruption of the narrative constitutes a dialogue

within a dialogue, and the boundaries coincide with the formal divisions of the sonnet. But frequently the narrative line modulates less obviously into apostrophe. Thus I. ii. 24 is narrative in the octave and apostrophic in the sestet, but both parts describe the same event:

> Qui luy voile les yeux, qui luy crache au visage . . . (l. 5)
>
> Ah! Tigres vous soüillez, vous meurtrissez la face. (l. 9)

Similar parallelism can occur between separate sonnets and can serve more than one purpose. The octave of Sonnet I. i. 89 recounts the binding of Christ. But in the following sonnet apostrophe is used throughout to introduce an interpretation of the action as the fulfilment of Old Testament prophecy:

> ASsassins, garrotant ces mains officieuses,
> Vous rendez accomplis tous ces oracles vieux. (I. i. 90)

Sonnet I. i. 91 continues the narrative in a series of ambiguous imperatives which are only partly ironic, because the actions referred to are part of the divine plan: 'Or sus donc serrez fort, liez fort, ô canaille . . .' Further, the recipient of the apostrophe may abruptly change. In the sestet of the same sonnet La Ceppède turns from the actors in the binding to the bonds themselves, and exclaims, 'O liens, ô trauaux, ô mystiques estreintes' (l. 9). He even invokes their mediation—for they are both metonymically associated with Christ's redemptive Passion and metaphorically representative of the bondage of human sin. In general, however, what these three sonnets illustrate is the fact that the various means of approaching Scripture (literal narrative, theological and allegorical analysis, affective prayer, etc.) do not necessarily appear in specialized styles. On the contrary, the different levels of interpretation are unified in the common mode of the effective apostrophe, although the foundation of straightforward narrative usually precedes it.

The most characteristic use of the apostrophe in the *Théorèmes*, however, is the exposition of a moral lesson derived from the biblical text. In I. ii. 3 the bipartite composition of the sonnet corresponds to narration of the episode in which Peter warms himself at the doorkeeper's fire (John 18: 16, 18), and to the related moral allegorization. The narrative is interrupted by an exclamation and

an interrogative; the significance of the event is indicated by means
of metaphors in the characteristic genitival form:

> Ha! que fais-tu pauuret? tu entres dans la cour
> Des pieges de ce monde . . .
> Tu as resourse au feu de ton amour charnel.

The devout reader is clearly meant to generalize from this moral
address to Peter. But there are occasions when apostrophic rhetoric
provides a natural means of extending the text to include moral
exhortation of quite specific groups. Sonnet II. iii. 7, for instance,
attacks the deterministic notions of astrology in an apostrophe (ll.
12–14) directed against 'Vains Mathematiciens'. More obviously
linked to the situation of the post-Tridentine Church in France are
the exhortations to prelates (II. iv. 18), to the rebellious 'ambicieux'
(I. i. 67), and to judges and magistrates (I. ii. 81, 89). These are
moral lessons that are abstracted not from allegorizations of the
text as in I. ii. 3 but from the literal account of Jesus's arrest
and trial.

While narrative can give rise at one level to sermon-like apostrophe, at another there may be a natural transition from sermon-
like rhetoric to prayer. The manner in which such shifts are
worked out within the sonnet form is often intricate:

> SI le Pere Eternel son cher Fils abandonne
> A ce cruel trespas, pour s'estre ioint à nous:
> Quand nous trespasserons que sera ce de nous
> Si desioints de son Fils: son Fils nous abandonne.
>
> Si ce parfait Amant que son Pere abandonne
> Veut estre abandonné, pour estre auecques nous:
> Pour estre auecque luy, sus que chacun de nous
> Et Sathan, & le Monde, & la Chair abandonne.
>
> O bon Christ, bon JESVS, helas! ne souffrez pas
> Qu'ores, ny desormais, mesmes à mon trespas
> Le peché diuiseur de vous me dés-unisse.
>
> Faites que par sus tout vostre amour me soit cher:
> Que ie quitte le Diable, & le Monde, & la Chair:
> Qu'en vous seul ie renaisse, & qu'en vous ie finisse.
>
> (I. iii. 71)

The intrinsic divisions of the sonnet are here utilized so that the
octave embodies an exhortaion in which the stressed inclusive

'nous' indicates its general application, while the sestet contains a response in the form of a prayer in the first person singular. The unity of the octave is furthermore emphasized by the restriction of the rhymes to two significant words. Within the major divisions themes are associated with one another by means of the formal rhetorical devices of syntactic and semantic parallelism (synony-mous and antithetical) and various degrees of verbal repetition. Each quatrain is a conditional sentence, the first being interroga-tive and the second imperative; each half of the conditional is in both cases symmetrically distributed over the quatrain, a fact which corresponds to the *abba* rhyme-scheme. Moreover, the rhyming first and last lines of the two quatrains are thematically or syntactically arranged in progressive parallels, so that each line ending in 'abandonne' advances from the exemplary abandonment of the Son by the Father to the morally desirable renunciation of the world by man. Within and between the lines repetitive and polyptotic devices link the key words in the central notions of union and separation (*avec, joindre, abandonner, trespasser*). In spite of the shift from 'nous' to 'je' certain echoes of the first quatrain are introduced: 'diuiseur' and 'dés-unisse' (thematically related to those associated with *abandonner*); and the almost com-plete repetition of line 8 in line 13. The final tercet strongly marks with the repeated 'je' the transition to personal prayer, and is clearly meant as the final resolution of the doubt expressed in the first quatrain.

This shift between the collective and the individual[16] is frequent in the *Théorèmes*. It reflects not only a preoccupation with personal salvation, but also the claim in La Ceppède's Preface that the *Théorèmes* speak for France as a whole, and the implication that personal piety is the key to national well-being. The rhetorical structures in which successive transitions take place can also be seen as an interpretative instrument, in the sense that the parallel-isms form a metaphorical progression from the unobtrusive allusion to the letter of the text (l. 1), to the moral imperative (ll. 7–8), and finally to the responsive supplication expressed in the tercets. The sonnet and its rhetoric thus provide a means of interpreting the biblical text, of relating the devout reader with the events described, and of evoking his moral response.

---

[16] Only occasionally is 'je' identified exclusively with the author, e.g. II. iv. 1: Et rendez La Ceppède à bien parler appris'.

Certain of the sonnets seek to establish union between self and the narrated events on the one hand, and on the other between self and divine transcendence. In addition the self appears as the addressee of its own apostrophe. A conventional feature of the meditative exercise was the reflexive invocation of the devout soul's attention to the scene described. This may derive from the fact that the genre seeks to combine the didactic with the subjective. In the *Théorèmes* the aim seems to be to induce the devout to experience the narrative subjectively; but symbolically the addressing of the self suggests the notion of human duality. The way this function is reinforced through the rhetoric of the sonnet can be illustrated from I. i. 38, which has a primary division between the narrative mode of the octave and the apostrophe to the self in the sestet, the transition being made by means of an apostrophe to the body of Christ ('ô sacre-sainte Chair . . .') in lines 6–8. The sestet is divided first into an imperative to attend to the spectacle:

> O mon ame, contemple icy ton Redempteur,
> . . . voy combien il endure,

and then an exhortation to compose the soul in expectation of the subsequent events of the Passion. The 'composition of place' and the composing the orientating of the soul, are inextricably linked in meditative practice:[17] hence the tendency to create the impression that the meditating soul and the described events are co-present.

The correlation between the meditating soul and the scene meditated may be symbolically referred to within the apostrophic mode by means of schematic rhetoric linked with the sonnet form. Thus sonnet I. iii. 90, which follows the account of the earthquake at the Crucifixion, proceeds from line 1,

> SI la Terre à regret ce Gibet soustenant
> Tremble . . .

to the formally parallel line in the second half of the quatrain,

> O ma Terre, ô mon Corps dois tu pas maintenant
> Trembler . . .

From this moral analogy drawn from the narrated event to the self there is a further progression to an appeal to the affections in the

---

[17] Loyola speaks of 'composición viendo al lugar'.

second quatrain. The sestet develops into an appeal to the soul to transcend the body:

> Veux tu pas bien mon ame enfoncer tes clostures,
> Pour auec ton Sauueur t'en reuoler aux Cieux? (ll. 10–11)

As frequently in this type of sonnet where a personal and spiritual resolution is arrived at by means of successive metaphorical transformations of the initial literal text parallel conditional clauses assigned to each of the sonnet's subdivisions create a quasi-logical progression.

The direct address to God or 'colloquy' constitutes the final section of the classic devotional exercise.[18] La Ceppède's 'collo-quies' display a variety of tones corresponding to degrees of familiarity. He is to be found addressing God in the emotional tones of the lover (e.g. I. i. 94) and especially in Part II where dialogue tends to become dialectic, in the sober tone of the scholar. What is characteristic of the *Théorèmes*, however, is the juxtaposition and implicit interrelating of apostrophe to God and apostrophe to the self. The sonnet is used, as in the cases discussed above, to symbolize through the formal patterns of its structure the union of disparate elements. Parallelism can be seen as a form of implicit metaphorical identification. Hence, where God and the self co-occur as the recipients of a rhetorical apostrophe, the theme of the union of the soul with God is never far away. This tendency is most clearly seen in I. i. 94, which centres on the symbolic binding of Jesus and thus involves the theme of the binding of the soul to God. The first eight lines are addressed to Christ as lover, and the last six to the soul. The relationship between Christ and the soul is represented schematically in various ways: by partial repetition in the opening line:

> O L'amour de mon ame, ô nom-pareil Amant;

by means of antithesis across the hemistichs of the lines of the second quatrain in particular:

> J'ay commis le forfait, vous aurez la potence;

and by the echoing of the first line of the octave in the sestet:

> O trop ardant amour . . .
> O mon ame, à le suiure à ce coup sois hastiue,
> Que ton corps soit du sien maintenant prisonnier,
> Qu'en luy tu sois tousiours heureusement captiue.
>
> (ll. 9, 12–14)

[18] Cf. Martz, *Poetry of Meditation*, pp. 37 ff.

The parallelisms of the tercets thus draw together in the explicit reference to union the two elements, the soul and Christ, that are in tension in the octave.

The most noticeable feature of apostrophe is that it is interpersonal, direct, and urgent in tone. The wide variety of its uses in the *Théorèmes* can be explained in terms of a desire to establish a sense of direct communication with the biblical text regarded as historical action in which the actors, events, and objects themselves can be addressed. But it is also directed outwards to contemporary readers and inwards to the self, in order to effect some kind of moral conversion, as well as to God in the form of supplication. Further, schematic rhetoric, which naturally plays a role in the persuasive intention of apostrophe, also acts on a formal and symbolic level within the sonnet structure to interrelate the sacred historical narrative, the self, others, and God.

(iii) *Proof and persuasion.* The mode of proof and persuasion most closely resembles that of emotive apostrophe at the point where the meditator engages in colloquy with the Godhead. But the difference in tone is marked, as is the attitude of mind it reflects. Instead of the rhetorical questions and non-indicative verbs there is a logical question-and-answer pattern. Even where there is an element of personal emotion—as in I. i. 17, where the first quatrain recounts the choice of three disciples to accompany Jesus to Gethsemane, and the second indignantly queries the choice—the question is theoretical and expects an objective answer:

> Mais quoy! ces trois ont-ils le cœur plus espuré
> Que les autres? qui cause, ô prudence infinie,
> Que vous auez à vous cette triade vnie?

The sestet provides the answer, and, as is frequently the case in these question-and-answer schemes based on the formal sonnet divisions, the answer is introduced by an interjection, presumably to suggest the impact of the revelation: 'Ha! Ha! vous choisissez ces ames . . .', etc. On the other hand, the tone may be familiar but polite:[19]

> PErmettez-moy, Seigneur, de vous rementeuoir
> Que tout est descouuert au iour de vostre veuë. (I. i. 31)

---

[19] Cf. I. ii. 79: Jesus is 'le plus familier des hommes plus affables'.

Upon this reminder is based the question in the second quatrain as to the reason for Christ's prayer in Gethsemane, while each tercet provides an alternative solution. Just as the apostrophizing of persons and objects in the narrative seems to be intended to establish an affective relationship between the meditator and the events of the Passion, so the insistent questioning and searching for explanations seem designed to establish an intellectual involvement.

The answers given to questions are stated cautiously and in terms giving the impression of thought gradually unfolding, conceivably in order to encourage the devout reader to continue to pursue his own line of speculation. The sestet of I. i. 19 replies to two symmetrical questions (divided over the octave) by offering an interpretation of Christ's fear introduced with a tentative 'Peut estre vous auez . . .', etc. In I. i. 30 the first quatrain asks the reason why Jesus prays in both Hebrew and Latin, insisting that the question is answerable, for

> Tous vos faits, tous vos dits, out vn sens heroïque.

The second quatrain answers with a further question: 'Est-ce pas pour monstrer . . . ?' The sestet introduces a subsidiary question on the use of the word 'calice', to which the response is again in the form of an internal dialogue:

> Mais ie ne sçay pourquoy vous appelez calice,
> Parmy vostre priere vn si cruel supplice:
> Ce mot est-il bien propre à marquer vos douleurs?
> Voire; car . . .

Although the speculation in this type of meditation appears tentative it does suggest that La Ceppède attaches some importance to the discovery of hidden significances in sacred history, and, more importantly, that he regards them as accessible to the ordinary reader through the exercise of his human rational powers.

The rhetorical tradition, and in particular the Ramist system, encouraged the orator and poet of the late sixteenth century to 'invent' his material with the aid of logical forms (*topoi*), which in the resultant discourse show through more or less clearly.[20] In the

---

[20] On the role of the 'places of invention' in literary composition cf. Tuve, 'Imagery and Logic' and *Elizabethan and Metaphysical Imagery*; Ong, *Ramus*, pp. 281 ff.; Varga, *Rhétorique et littérature*.

Théorèmes La Ceppède apparently employs logical commonplaces to compose his sonnets, using them explicitly to prove a point, and even using them to analyse his own sonnets.

One such *topos* is the argument from cause[21]—an argument that could be said to be typical of the search in the *Théorèmes* for the consistency of the divine plan as revealed in history. This form yields an answer to a question that is not actually stated in the sonnet itself. A hint as to this underlying process is given in the notes to I. iii. 41, which state that the octave and sestet contain respectively 'la premiere des raisons pourquoy . . .' and 'la seconde raison . . . pourquoy . . .' (I, p. 421). It is a procedure commonly found in the meditative exercises (La Ceppède here cites Bruno and Guevara), particularly where the response leads to the rhetorical repetition of a single significant word. In I. iii. 20 each line of the octave begins with the word 'l'amour' in answer to some such suppressed questions as 'what was the cause of the Incarnation?' La Ceppède himself makes quite clear in his notes what form of argument he has been using:

Tout ce Sonnet n'est qu'vn rapport de tous les principaux points de la Passion cy-dessus descrits, à l'ardante amour dont Dieu nous a aymez, comme des effets à leur cause . . . (I. iii. 20)

Clearly, La Ceppède has much in common in such instances with the rhetoric of meditation. However, it is possible to argue that his use of the logical basis of rhetorical invention goes further than this. He speaks frequently of the 'proofs' contained in his sonnets. It is true that he speaks also of 'hiéroglyphiques', and this term in general refers to the images and symbols discussed in Chapter V. But logical demonstrations, as opposed to analogical demonstrations using imagery, occur in two major dialectical forms: assertion based often on Scripture or authority, progressing through successive definition and redefinition; and, more strikingly, syllogistic inference.

The method of dialectical definition and counter-definition may occur in a dialogue form and may involve verbal repetition serving an expository rather than a rhetorical function. In II. i. 28 the question is raised of the final resurrection of the damned. The proposition is first denied:

Resusciteront-ils? non, le resusciter
Est vn bien, que les bons seuls peuuent meriter (ll. 2–3)

[21] Cf. Varga, *Rhétorique*, pp. 42 ff., on the commonplace 'cause'.

to which the second quatrain responds with the synthesis:

> Ils resusciteront. mais non pas à la gloire. (line 5)

This conclusion is modified further in the second tercet in a more definitive but paradoxical statement:

> Disons plus hardiment, ils ne reuiuront pas,
> Réuiuans pour mourir d'vn eternel trépas . . . (ll. 12–13)

The dialectical structure here becomes transparent through the personalized form of interrogation and answer. But a more abstract form is found in, for instance, I. iii. 68, where the first quatrain states the problem to be explicated and the remaining metrical units of the sonnet embody the solutions. Each section highlights the logical links in the argument: 'Que jaçoit que . . .' (l. 5); 'Il est vray neantmoins que . . .' (l. 9); 'Mais pourtant . . .' (l. 12).

There is clear evidence that La Ceppède could be even more systematic. His overt use of the syllogism in the prose annotation on the Agony (I. i. 37, n. 4) has already been discussed. It can also be seen that the syllogism in its various guises is employed in the sonnets. In a note to II. i. 26 he states precisely the relation of the major premiss, minor premiss, and conclusion to the sonnet form, when he speaks of

La conclusion de ce tiercet, rapportée à la maieur proposition faicte aux deux premiers vers de ce Sonnet, & à la mineur discouruë aux vers suiuans. (II, p. 69)

While this clearly hints at the logical structure of the syllogism underlying the sonnet, the final result would no doubt be described rhetorically as an *epicheirema*, by which Renaissance rhetorics understood a looser, literary form in which subsidiary arguments support the premisses.[22] The argument of II. i. 26 runs thus: it is a hypothesis that if nature can revivify, then *a fortiori* (this too is a familiar commonplace of invention) the creator of nature can be revivified (ll. 1–2). The minor premiss is the assertion that nature can indeed resurrect itself; but this takes the form of a series of analogous natural symbols (pelican, eagle, serpent, silkworm) linked by rhetorical repetition (ll. 3–11). Since they fulfil the condition made in the opening lines, the last tercet infers the validity of the belief in the Resurrection, although this conclusion

---

[22] See Varga, *Rhétorique*, pp. 64–5.

is presented in the form of an aggressive rhetorical question addressed to the sceptical. This is an illustration not only of the combination of dialectic with rhetorical ornament, but also the combination of two modes of thought, the analogical and symbolic with the sequential and logical.

The syllogism is not always so heavily disguised in rhetoric. In certain cases the different stages in the argument are clearly marked by their coincidence with the metrical units of the sonnet:

> SI par le seul peché la mort fut introduite,
> Où le peché n'est point la mort n'a point de droict:
> Christ ne pecha iamais: C'estoit donc de la suite
> Que le traict de la mort iamais ne l'atteindroit. (II. i. 46)

This is again a hypothetical syllogism in which the first two lines constitute a complex premiss, the hemistich of the third line the minor premiss, and the remainder of the quatrain the conclusion. This conclusion is then utilized in the rest of the sonnet to prove that Christ must have died voluntarily (ll. 5–8) in order to demonstrate the fact of the final resurrection of all men (sestet). The whole sonnet is referred to in the 'Table' as a 'raisonnement'.

Again the basis of the apologetic argument against the Jews in I. ii. 85 is not only Scripture but the syllogism. The whole of the sonnet is occupied by a dense and not immediately obvious chain of reasoning drawing its premisses from the Old Testament. The first quatrain argues that since the Jews acclaim Caesar they deny their own sovereignty. Once this is established it is taken up into the argument contained in the second quatrain:

> Or si Iuda ne peut par vostre Oracle mesme
> Estre iamais priué du Sceptre merité
> Que l'Enuoyé ne vienne, il est donc verité
> Que Christ est l'Enuoyé du Monarque supreme.

The sestet concludes this argument, which is evidently meant to combat the Jews on their own ground, by quoting the Old Testament prophecy (Genesis 49: 10) on which the premiss of the first quatrain is based, and by indicating the prefiguration of the Jews' acclamation of Caesar (Numbers 14: 4). These two supporting arguments are produced with a triumphant note ('Ha! pauurets, il est vray . . .', l. 9) in order to clinch the point. The rhetorical apostrophe mode in which the logic is cast is aimed at the Jews

and is aimed apparently to persuade and prove. In Part II of the
Théorèmes this function becomes more marked and less bound up
with meditative techniques. Some arguments, not necessarily all
syllogistic arguments, are concerned with fundamental points of
doctrine such as the divinity of Christ and the immortality of the
soul. A sonnet which illustrates this clearly is II. i. 23, referred to
by the author in the 'Table' and in the annotations as an 'argument'
or an 'inference':

> SAns receuoir icy le loyer merité
> Maint Juste meurt pressé de cent morts violentes,
> Maint inique descend dans les tombes relentes,
> Sans estre icy puny de sa temerité.
>   Or soit inique, ou iuste, il est bien verité,
> Que tout cét homme entier éclot etincellantes
> Ses iustices (L'honneur de sa posterité)
> Comme entier il éclot ses coulpes insolentes,
>   Croions doncques céte Ame exempte du trépas,
> Et ce corps reuiuable: ou ne soustenons pas
> Que Dieu soit, qu'il soit iuste, & plein de prouidence.
>   Dieu fit de rien ce tout. Il peut donc aysement
> Redonner l'estre à l'homme apres sa decadence,
> Comme il le luy donna miraculeusement.

The content of the argument is patristic and well established,[23] and
it is to some extent a continuation of the preceding sonnet in which
the heresies of Porphyry and others are refuted. The intricate
interaction of logical form and sonnet form is characteristic of the
Théorèmes. The first quatrain (repeating one of the rhymes of the
preceding sonnet) exploits the parallelism of the rhyme-scheme to
state and to formalize the notion of the dual injustice of life. La
Ceppède does not now proceed immediately to the anticipated
conclusion—that a just God must mete out justice after death.
Instead he returns in the second quatrain to a point already made
in II. i. 22 with greater clarity: 'L'Ame, & le Corps ensemble
operent sur la terre' (II. i. 22, l. 12). Compounding the earlier
sonnet, he then arrives at the conclusion that both body and soul
must resurrect together, adding the fundamental linking premiss of
God's existence and intrinsic justice (ll. 9–11). The final tercet
introduces yet another patristic 'proof' of the Resurrection. The

---

[23] Chrysostom, Tertullian, and others are cited in II. i. 23, n. 3.

order in which the sonnet unfolds the argument is practically the reverse of the naturally expected order that is given in the summary of the poem in the 'Table': 'Que la confession d'vn Dieu iuste & plein de prouidence infere & conclut necessairement la resurrection des ames & des corps.' This fact is no doubt due in part to the compression of two separate arguments, but the effect of allocating to each quatrain apparently unconnected statements is to set up an expectation that is eventually resolved in the sestet. In fact the sestet is frequently handled in La Ceppède's work in such a way as to act as a logical key and clarification of the octave. The sonnet form is thus manipulated in a dynamic manner, not just as a means of logical exposition, but as a form which progressively reveals what is initially obscure. It will by now be plain that the idea of revelation of the concealed is fundamental to many aspects of the *Théorèmes*. But it is perhaps in the combination of logical demonstration and revelatory sonnet form that the full implications of the mathematical metaphor in the title can be understood.

3. *The Divisions of the* Théorèmes

(i) *Relationships between the sonnets.* It has been seen that in the *Théorèmes* rhyme is used within the sonnet in order to highlight important associations; it is used also between separate sonnets for the same purpose. Since certain rhymes occur very frequently it is perhaps fortuitous that certain pairs of sonnets containing similar rhymes should occur consecutively—although even chance co-occurrences of this kind can appear significant when reinforced by other links. But the co-occurrence of three or more sonnets linked in this way must almost certainly be a conscious device.[24] It is a device that is used in many parts of the work, but the following examples will illustrate the coherence it can give to groups of sonnets.

The concluding three sonnets of I. ii describing the procession from Jerusalem to Calvary are a homogeneous stretch of narrative. The sestet of each sonnet includes the following rhymes: 'affronteur'—'seducteur' (I. ii. 98); 'voleurs'—'douleurs' (I. ii. 99); 'clameurs'—'murs' (I. ii. 100). Even more significantly, for reasons that will become apparent, the last two sonnets of I. i,

---

[24] Cf. the systematic repetition of words, rhymes, or lines in certain Italian sonnet cycles; described by Mönch, pp. 29 ff.

which are a description of the flight from the garden that parallels
the exit from Jerusalem, also contain rhymes in -*eur*. Some of these
rhymes are, moreover, not without associations of meaning:
'pleur'—'fleur' (I. i. 99); 'peur'—'trompeur' (I. i. 100).

Groups of sonnets are often linked by means of not one but two
rhymes that have acquired thematic importance: one or both may
be repeated in successive sonnets. The most striking example of
this is found in the climax of the Crucifixion in I. ii. 74–99, where
the rhymes -*ieux* and -*oix*, associated with key words like 'Hebrieux'
'Cieux', 'croix', and 'roys', recur at intervals.[25] The importance of
this principle can be seen from the fact that it affects the less
central portions of the work. For example, the narration of the
apostles' violence in Gethsemane (I. i. 58–70) is unified by means
of two, perhaps three, related rhymes: -*ant* (-*ent*); -*ante* (-*ente*);
-*ance* (-*ence*). The key word of I. i. 58 is 'tradiment', which rhymes
in the same sonnet with 'Amant', 'aimant', and 'vaillamment'. The
following sonnet uses rhymes in -*ance* in the quatrains which will
recur in later sonnets, as well as a rhyme in the tercet that is
a near rhyme with the rhyme of the preceding sonnet's quatrains:
'tranchans'—'meschans' (I. i. 59). From the point of view of
meaning these form a transition for the quatrain rhymes of I. i. 60.
These are parallel to but largely antonymous with the quatrain
rhymes of I. i. 58: 'Galant'—'insolant'—'estalant'—'violant' (I. i.
60). Sonnets 61 and 62 also have rhymes in -*ant* and -*ent*, but this
time there appears to be no thematic link in the words themselves:
'cependant'—'respondant'—'secondant'—'respondant' (I. i. 61);
'ressentiment' — 'attouchement' — 'souuerainement' — 'largement'
(I. i. 62). In sonnet 63 the quatrain rhymes in -*ence* rhyme with
those of 59, and there is a certain thematic congruity, since 59
treats of the apostles' resistance to divine decree, and 63 of the
creator's governance of the universe: 'souuenance'—'apparte-
nance'—'ordonnance'—'conuenance' (I. i. 59); 'intendence'—
'prouidence'—'euidence'—'abondance' (I. i. 63). Sonnet 64 does
not repeat any of the previous rhymes as such, but the tercets do
contain as rhymes the feminine forms of the two key words of 60:
'insolente'—'violente' (I. i. 64). Sonnet 65, however, returns to the
rhymes of 63: 'tance'—'resistance'—'assistance'—'potence' (I. i.
65), and provides the actual rhyme-words for 68 'assistance'—
'constance'—'tance'—'resistance' (I. i. 68). The alternating rhymes

[25] Discussed by Donaldson-Evans, *Poésie et méditation*, pp. 54 ff.

of this octave recapitulate not only the rhyme but some of the meaning-associations of 58, 59, and 60: 'doucement'—'rudement' —'commandement'—'hardiment' (I. i. 68). Sonnet 69 recalls not only previous rhymes and associations but two of the key words in 58 and 60: 'violence'—'eslance'—'balance'—'vaillance' (I. i. 69). The remaining gaps in the network are filled by the repetition in 66 of the tercet rhyme-words of 59, by the repetition in the quatrain rhymes of 67 of the -*cieux* rhyme of the tercets of 64, and by the presence of -*ant* rhymes in the tercets. There is apparently no systematic ordering of these repeated rhymes nor do they define any complete narrative or thematic whole within the work. But the associations and correspondences that are set up are an aspect of the complex texture of the *Théorèmes*, and suggest La Ceppède's universe of hidden analogies.

In practice La Ceppède is not systematic in establishing links between sonnets in a group. Sonnets I. iii. 77–82 form a unified sequence on the sixth word from the cross, the 'consummatum est', which constitutes a focal point in the work for the development of the idea of the redemptive fulfilment of history. Sonnet 77 opens by marking the narrative link with the preceding account of the fifth word:

DEZ qu'il eut dit, I'AY SOIF, vn Iuif prend vne esponge

thus introducing a separate narrative unit. The commentary on this piece of the Gospel text dwells on typological and prophetic correspondences between the bitter vinegar on the one hand and the sweetness of the paradisial tree of knowledge, the sour grapes of the vineyard in Isaiah 5: 4, and the prediction of the Erythrean Sibyl on the other. These themes are epitomized in the tercet rhyme: 'lambrusque sauuage' and 'cet ingrat breuuage'; and these rhymes recur in the slightly altered context of the quatrains of the following sonnet 'rauage' [verb]—'breuuage'—'rauage' [noun]— 'seruage'. The context consists of a medical simile for the atonement: just as a fever is cured by diet, sweating, bleeding, and potions, so 'la fievre du peché' is cured by Christ on behalf of man. The tercets explain how each of these allegorical stages in the 'cure' have been achieved in the Passion, the final stage being the vinegar:

Il restoit (pour finir cette cure admirable)
Ce breuuage, & le Christ, tout à fait secourable,
Le prend, l'auale, & dit que TOVT EST ACCOMPLY.

(I. iii. 78)

The transition between the fifth and the sixth words from the cross is thus made by a gradated interweaving of themes and formal repetition. Sonnet 79 is linked by means of paraphrase and verbal repetition with the last phrase of 78: 'Tout est donq accomply', and the rest of the sonnet consists of metaphorically and logically related parallelisms derived from this initial phrase. Furthermore, the tercet rhymes 'augures' and 'Figures' of 79 echo those of 78: 'nourriture' and 'l'ouuerture'. Sonnet 80 has no such formal links, but illustrates the use of thematic relationships to link separate sonnets. The notion of consummation developed in the preceding poems leads to a recapitulation of the whole scheme of divine fulfilment in the creation, fall, and redemption. However, the tercets are associated by verbal repetition with what has gone before and more noticeably with the quatrains of the sonnet following:

> . . . il a tres-volontiers
> Consommé patient trente trois ans entiers:
> Et puis pour le parfaire a consommé sa vie.
>> (I. iii. 80, ll. 9–11)

> TOut est donq consommé, grand Dieu de l'vniuers,
> Vous auiez consommé l'humaine architecture.
>> (I. iii. 81, ll. 1–2)

The remainder of 81 progresses by means of synonymy and self-paraphrase to the work of the *Théorèmes* itself:

> Vous qui seul consommez toutes choses parfaites,
> Acheuez, consommez ce petit œuure . . . (ll. 12–13)

Sonnet 82 thematically initiates the next step in the Passion narrative, but as usual the transition is blurred, the relationships between one step and the next being suggested by formal repetition. The first line of 82 virtually repeats the first lines of 79 and 81: 'Tout estant consommé . . .' Moreover, the characteristic rhyme in -*age* of the first two sonnets of the group (77 and 78) are echoed in the tercets: 'courage'—'encourage'. Finally, it should be added that not only is there a high degree of cohesion between consecutive sonnets within a single narrative unit, but also there is some correspondence between the first sonnet of the present group (I. iii. 77) and a more distant group in which the image of the bitter vine is anticipated and developed (I. ii. 62–7, and principally 64). The narration of events in the *Théorèmes* is explicit and coherent.

The exact point in time relative to the narrative as a whole at which a particular action takes place is nearly always marked at the beginning of the sonnet by some such term as *tandis que, dès que, à peine*, etc. It is true that in the *Théorèmes* exclusively narrative sonnets are rare. But there are sonnets of which at least part serves to introduce the next step in the narrative; and there are sonnets which are exclusively commentaries, and which depend on the narrative sonnets as their point of reference. Certain primary divisions in the collection as a whole can thus be discerned on the basis of the principal narrative episodes, and, as will be seen, such divisions correspond well with the formal and numerical divisions of La Ceppède's 'partie' and 'livre'.

But are these primary divisions organized internally in a systematic manner? The narrative and commentary subdivisions naturally suggest the influence of the meditative exercise and its progenitor, scriptural exegesis. The application of the three powers of the soul to sacred history theoretically gives rise to three corresponding sequential divisions. In the *Théorèmes* it has been clearly seen that in general the different possible modes of representing and interpreting the Passion merge into one another. Nevertheless it is arguable that some sections of the work that take a concrete event as a point of departure do correspond in the 'commentary' subdivision to the patterns of meditative practice. This applies particularly to what is probably the oldest section of the *Théorèmes*, namely the stretch I. iii. 10–31, where three subdivisions, 10–19, 20–30, and 31, appear to match respectively the phases of 'composition', 'analysis', and 'prayer'.[26] A less diffuse illustration would be the sequence of three sonnets on the flight of the adolescent (I. i. 86–8), where each sonnet roughly rresponds to the three phases.

However, the meditative pattern by no means fits all parts of the *Théorèmes*. The 'commentary' subdivision of the section on the Resurrection, for instance, can be divided into two further groups of consecutive sonnets which seem to correspond respectively to a logical, intellectual approach and to a largely allegorical approach to the basic text. The narration of the Resurrection as an event occupies only sonnet 15. The next section comprises sonnets 16–33, all of which can be said to be concerned either with textual and historical problems arising from the letter of the Gospel, or with

[26] Cf. Cave, *Devotional Poetry*, pp. 216 ff.

dogma based on it. The method of approach therefore tends to be discursive and expository. Thus the historical details of the time interval between the Crucifixion and Resurrection are placed in doubt and debated in 17–19; more fundamentally, the reasons for a resurrection at any time are argued out in 20–1; then the precise Catholic dogma concerning those who shall rise on the last day is expounded and 'proved', and objections are refuted (22–33). The continuity between the sonnets is frequently made by means of logical connectives placed in the first line. While this section is predominantly linear and logical, the next (sonnets 32–50) could be said to be predominantly analogical and symbolic. Its main theme is the Resurrection as such, rather than the doctrine and doctrinal problems it entails, and the relationships between individual sonnets depend on metaphorical parallelism. Each sonnet presents one or more analogies, be they types from Scripture or 'hieroglyphs' from the natural world: sonnet 34 proposes in succession the parallel Old Testament symbols of Christ (the lion of Judah, the *sol justitiae*); 35 is devoted to expounding the phoenix symbol; 36 is partly a paraphrase, partly a Christological interpretation of a series of texts from the Psalms and other Old Testament books; 37 relates the *sol justitiae* to the natural sunrise accompanying the Resurrection.—What is essentially a list of symbols relating to the common central theme continues in this way up till sonnet 50, which concludes II. i. Throughout the whole of the sequence 16 to 50 emotional, prayer-like passages are to be found; but they are not apparently ordered in any way that might correspond to the classic meditative patterns.

One concludes, therefore, that La Ceppède classified the sonnets on the Resurrection into two approximately equal parts: the first is concerned primarily with theological matters and is logically organized, and the second is made up of symbolical analogies and repetitions. It is possible that this differentiation is quite independent of the theoretical meditative divisions of 'analysis' and 'prayer'. It could be claimed that the operative criterion is in fact exegetic, that the first group of sonnets corresponds in manner to the medieval *quaestio*, or ratiocinative excursus on a biblical text, and that the second separately exploits the possibilities of allegorical interpretation.

However, it would be no more accurate to insist on the general applicability of an exegetic schema at this level than it would be to emphasize the meditative patterns. Both are fused in the rhetoric of the sonnet. Such an amalgamation, no less than the web of repetitive, narrative, and logical links between the sonnets, is what would be expected from La Ceppède's encyclopedic and integrative view of things. But in all this, as in other aspects of the *Théorèmes*, can be discerned the interplay of two different dimensions of a world-view: the one is 'horizontal', linear, and rational, as in narration or argument; the other is 'vertical' and relates the similitudes of a symbolic universe.

(ii) *Formal divisions.* The first part of the *Théorèmes* is divided into three 'livres', each of which contains 100 sonnets, the whole being concluded by a 'vœu pour la fin de cet œuvre'. The Trinitarian implications of the triad of 'livres' and of the century of sonnets have not escaped notice.[27] Part II, however, has in general been neglected on the grounds that it was a mere afterthought, and is less harmoniously constructed than Part I.[28] Both these points stand in need of qualification. If the three books of Part I are assumed to be symbolic, then there is no reason why the four books of Part II should not be similarly regarded. It is worth considering the evidence for the use of Renaissance numerological principles in the composition of the *Théorèmes*.

The tradition of number symbolism was supported in the Renaissance by biblical and patristic allegorizations, and by Platonic and Pythagorean sources. La Ceppède was familiar with the principal mediators of this tradition: Augustine, Nicholas of Cusa, Vitruvius, Valeriano, and, perhaps most significantly, Du Bartas; and he explicitly refers to symbolic numbers in both sonnets and annotations. But caution is necessary in arguing from the presence of this 'substantive' number symbolism to 'formal' numerological and non-linguistic patterns in the organization of the work.[29]

The sole mention of the triad in Part II occurs in the context of Jesus's threefold prayer in Gethsemane (I. i. 34). The fact that

---

[27] See Rousset, *Intérieur et extérieur*, p. 27; Donaldson-Evans, *Poésie et méditation*, p. 39.

[28] Rousset, op. cit., p. 27, n. 12; Donaldson-Evans, *Poésie et méditation*, p. 39, n. 4.

[29] On literary numerology see Curtius, *Europäische Literatur*, pp. 493 ff.; Fowler, *Spenser and the Numbers of Time*; on the distinction between 'substantive' and 'formal' numerology see Fowler, p. 250.

there is only one explicit reference in Part I to the triad may be surprising in view of La Ceppède's concern with the Incarnation and Trinity, and in view of the tripartite division of the work. In general Part II is richer in explicit reference to symbolic numbers. In II. i. 19 there is a verbal allusion to I. i. 34: 'Vous estes tres-parfaict, O grand nombre ternaire.' La Ceppède's acknowledged source here is Aristotle, on the basis of whose opinions he goes on to show that the number is also 'de ce tout le vray dénombre-ment' (l. 4), and a symbol of the fulfilment of the divine plan, the Resurrection symbolizing the third era of grace (following those of the Law and before the Law).[30] Similarly, the number 7, though not mentioned in Part I, receives a universalist interpretation in Part II. La Ceppède's authorities state that 'pource que tout le temps est comprins vniuerselement en sept iours, le nombre septenaire figure l'vniuersalité' (II, p. 37). This explanation is offered with respect to an allusion to 'sept traistres Demons', and can only be used indirectly as a justification for interpreting the seven books of Parts I and II together numerologically.

Other symbolic numbers in the *Théorèmes* have less general application. The number 40 in II. iii. 2, and more especially in II. i. 38, merely provides the third term of comparison for a list of types and antitypes, and is not represented as having any intrinsic mystery. A more elaborate case is the numerological interpretation of the miraculous haul of 153 fishes in II. ii. 85, which is based on the account of Maldonado: the component 100 is 'grand & parfaict', and represents the redeemed Gentiles; the 50 represents the smaller number of Jews, and the 3 the Trinity. For alternative interpretations La Ceppède refers the reader to Augustine's treatise on the Gospel of St. John, but adds that they are beyond his comprehension (II, p. 371). This remark suggests that it is unwise to look for complex symbolic patterns beyond the major threefold and sevenfold divisions with their biblical and theological significance.

But it is reasonable to consider each of the seven books in turn, and ask whether the internal subdivisions display any numerical symmetry. Much depends on the criteria used for establishing breaks in the continuum of sonnets. But if it is assumed that the Gospel text provides the foundation, then symmetrical or near-

[30] Other Trinitarian interpretations of the triad occur in II. ii. 89 and 90; cf. also II. ii. 11, 60; II. iii. 29.

symmetrical subdivisions can be postulated for certain of the books. Book i of the first part divides into the most aesthetically satisfying proportions of the seven:

I. i. 1–14 (total 14):   initial invocation (sonnet 1) and the journey to Gethsemane after the Last Supper;

I. i. 15–42 (total 28):   arrival at Gethsemane and the Agony;

I. i. 43–100 (total 58):   arrest of Jesus and departure from the garden.

These three subdivisions correspond to clearly marked transitions in the narration. Further, it can be seen that the total number of sonnets in the second subdivision doubles the total in the first, and the total in the third approximately doubles that in the second. This schema necessitates taking incidents such as the flight of the adolescent not as separate narrative sections but as subordinate sections of a larger whole. The approximation in the proposed third subdivision is of course inevitable, given the fact that a total of 100 seems to be a prerequisite.[31]

If the same subordinating principle is assumed for the incidents of Peter's denials and Judas's suicide, taking Jesus's trials to be the main story line, then it is possible to discern the same geometrical progression in the sonnet totals of the subdivisions of I. ii. In spite of the difficulty of grouping the multiplicity of episodes, which themselves are clearly delimited by La Ceppède, the following arrangement seems plausible:

I. ii. 1–14:   initial invocation; the sending of Jesus to Annas; Peter's first denial as a simultaneous subordinate action outside the palace;[32] and the actual examination of Jesus by Annas.

I. ii. 15–43:   trial of Jesus before Caiaphas (15–25); the parallel sub-action of Peter's second and third denial and repentance (26–31), which seems to have considerable thematic importance, although its subordination to the main narrative is indicated;[33] the trial by the Sanhedrin (32–7); and Judas's remorse

---

[31] Since it is 'grand & parfaict' (II, p. 371).

[32] The return to the main narrative is indicated in the linking phrase 'Cependant le Pontife . . .' (I. ii. 6).

[33] It is contained between the 'tandis' of I. ii. 26 and the 'tandis' of I. ii. 32.

and suicide (38–43), which can be seen as a
subordinate action taking place while Jesus is
being transferred to the next major stage of
narrative, and coinciding with part of this next
stage.[34]

This gives one group of fourteen sonnets and a group approximately twice as long. Although divisions are certainly less clear than in
the case of I. i they can to some extent be supported on the grounds
of the symmetry of the subordinate actions. In 1–14 the subordinate
action is simultaneous with and in the narration interrupts the
action of the first trial. It is this that makes this group appear to
stand apart from the point of view of the composition. By contrast in 15–43 the sub-actions act as transitions, and overlap
temporally with the second and third trials, while alternating
thematically with them. The second trial is followed by Peter's
remorse, which is followed by the third trial, which in turn is
followed by the parallel remorse of Judas.

The Judas episode concludes the trial of Jesus by the Jews, and
the remainder of the book (sonnets 44–100) is concerned with the
trial by the Romans and the beginning of the Crucifixion. Within
this section there seems to be no further formal organization of
the episodes: Jesus's first appearance before Pilate (sonnets 44–51);
his appearance before Herod (51–4); his second appearance before
Pilate (55–9); the scourging (60–9); the *Ecce Homo* sequence (69–
73); Pilate's capitulation to the Jews (74–89); the preparation of
the cross (90–100). There is a linear continuity in the action in
this part of the book which the earlier sections do not have, and
which may justify regarding it as a distinct section of the composition. If this is so, then Book ii is very similar in its numerical
divisions and proportions to Book i. There are three main
groups of sonnets: 1–14 (14 sonnets), 15–43 (29 sonnets), 44–100
(57 sonnets).

However, Book iii defies this kind of analysis. There are certainly
clearly indicated narrative episodes, but it is impossible to reduce
them to any formal groupings within the book. The distinct
episodes would seem to be the following:

1–9   initial invocation and journey to Golgotha;
10–13: Jesus is stripped by the Jews and veiled by the Virgin;

---

[34] I. ii. 44 begins 'Les Prestres cependant . . .'

14–17:   he is nailed to the cross;
18–31:   elevation of the cross;
32–6:   crucifixion of the thieves; titles fixed to cross; the seamless robe;
37–47:   the Jews' mockery and first word from the cross;
48–56:   second word;
57–64;   third word;
65–71:   fourth word;
72–6:   fifth word;
77–81:   sixth word;
82–4:   seventh word;
85–92:   death of Jesus and sympathetic reaction of nature;
93–5:   Jesus's side is pierced;
96–100:   deposition and burial.

The most unified section here would be the seven words from the cross (48 sonnets). This leaves two other possible groupings—the first 36 sonnets constituting a preparation to the central drama on the cross, and the last sixteen sonnets which recount the death and burial. However, it is by no means certain that a narrative framework of this kind can be imposed on Book iii. It has been seen that 10–31 can be regarded as a coherent meditation, and it may be the meditative influences behind what is the earliest portion of the *Théorèmes* to have been composed that explain why Book iii differs in its internal organization from Books i and ii.

In outward appearance Part II resembles Part I in being divided into two books covering separate stretches of coherent narrative. But the books are now four in number, contain fewer sonnets, and are each followed by a 'vœu pour la fin de ce liure'. Book i, containing 50 sonnets, falls into two parts clearly marked within the body of the book by the title 'La Resurrection', which comes between the fourteenth and fifteenth sonnets. The round number of 14 sonnets devoted to the descent into hell recalls the fact that this total is also found in the first subdivision of I. i and I. ii. There are no relevant narrative divisions in the remaining 36 sonnets, although it has been argued above on other grounds that they are divided into two approximately equal parts.[35] Book iii also contains 36 sonnets, including the 'vœu', which is here linked with the sonnets preceding it .

[35] See p. 203 f.

Book ii is the only book of Part II to contain a century of sonnets (101 including the 'vœu'). As in I. ii there is a multiplicity of short narrative episodes, some of which are simultaneous with and subordinate to the main action. Sonnets 1–4 include an initial invocation to the Virgin and the account of Jesus's first appearance to her; 5–20 recount the finding by the women of the deserted tomb; 21–30 describe the appearance of Jesus to the Magdalen; 31–3 constitute a sub-action—the suborning of the guards by the Jews that takes place, 'Tandis qu'elles s'en vont' (II. ii. 31). It is the explicit temporal link that justifies the grouping of 31–3 with what has preceded, although it is also true that they form a transition to the next major narrative unit—the appearance of Christ to the apostles. The change becomes clear in II. ii. 34:

> AYant donque le Christ de l'aspect gracieux
> De son visage aymé rasserené ces femmes,
> Il veut, auant la fin de ce iour precieux,
> Ses vnze resiouyr comme il a fait ces Dames. (ll. 1–4)

This initiates the sequence 34–52 in which first the appearance to Peter is fleetingly narrated (II. ii. 34, ll. 5–8), and then in much more detail the appearance on the road to Emmaus. Sonnet II. ii. 53 begins a section in which Christ appears in the upper room and delegates divine power to the apostles. The section ends in II. ii. 70 with an exhortation to magistrates, to whom the power of the monarch is said to be similarly delegated. Sonnets 71–7 centre on Thomas's absence from this gathering, his return, his doubt, and his encounter with the risen Christ one week later, when the apostles are assembled behind closed doors at Jerusalem. The two assemblies of the apostles linked by the Thomas episode could be said to form a single unit of 25 sonnets (53–77). Sonnet 78 starts a different phase in the narration of the appearances to the apostles:

> APres céte entreueüe il fut temps de partir:
> Les Disciples ioyeux s'en vont en Galilee. (II. ii. 78, ll. 1–2)

The section 78–86 then recounts the miraculous haul of fishes: sonnets 87–96 take place after the meal of fishes and recount Jesus's delegation of Peter; sonnets 97 to the 'vœu' constitute a temporally separate episode ('APRES, & tous les vnze, & maint autre se rendent Sur le Mont . . .', II. ii. 97, ll. 1–2), but are thematically related to the preceding sonnets, since they are still concerned with the mission of the apostles. The group 78 to the end, therefore, has a certain continuity. This analysis gives one major division of 33 sonnets (the appearances to the women) and one of 68 (the appearances to the apostles). In other words, the second half is approximately twice as long as the first. In addition, the second half can be seen to be divided into three roughly equal sections; one of 19 sonnets (34–52, the road to Emmaus), one of 25 (53–77, the appearances to the assembled apostles and to Thomas), and one of 24 (the haul of fishes and the mission of the apostles).

Book iii (35 sonnets) can also be considered as two sections: sonnets 1–8, which narrate Jesus's instruction of the disciples in the interpretation of the Old Testament; and sonnets 9 to the end, which narrate the Ascension. This second major section can be further subdivided into two phases: 9–24, in which Jesus rises from the earth, and the nature of this motion is debated; and 25–35, in which the entry into heaven is discussed.

Book iv, which has 30 sonnets and is followed by a 'Vœu pour la fin de ce Liure & de tout cet œuure', has three main sections based on the short passage of Acts 2: 1–4. Sonnets 1–7 include the opening invocation and the appearance of the Holy Spirit in the form of wind; sonnets 8–19 deal with the descent of the Spirit as fire; and sonnets 20–7 represent the gift of tongues, which leads to a concluding discussion of the procession of the Spirit from the Father and the Son (28–30).

It seems, then, that if narrative (rather than meditative, exegetic, or other) units are taken as the principle of composition, certain plausible symmetries appear in the grouping of the sonnets. The most striking of these are the geometrical proportions of I. i, I. ii, and possibly II. ii. The effect is of a gradual opening-out of the preoccupations of the book concerned, namely, the humanity and humiliation of Christ in the case of I. i, his trials in I. ii, and his transfigured appearances in II. ii. The tripartite, progressively expanding structure serves to reiterate the principal themes with increasing richness and reflective breadth. The bipartite structure of II. ii simply serves to repeat the theme of the manifestations of the risen Christ with reference to different groups of people.

But the uniqueness of these particular books of the *Théorèmes* only raises the question of the unity of the two parts of the work. If the above description is accepted, then Part I consists of two formally similar books followed by one that is quite different in composition. The first is open-ended, and in its final sonnet, which narrates the flight of the disciples towards Jerusalem, prepares the scene for the action of I. ii. Similarly, I. ii expands and opens up into I. iii, the final sonnet forming a transition by narrating the procession from Jerusalem to Golgotha. Book iii, with its two long subdivisions followed by a shorter one, is more static and reflective: it constitutes a culmination of the dynamic construction of Books i and ii.

The internal unity of Part II is more problematic. By the nature of the source material the sequential narrative is less prominent than in Part I. There are two ways of looking at the general plan of the second part. In the first place, it can be regarded as having a roughly symmetrical plan, with the 100 sonnets of Book ii at its centre. On one side of this block would be Book i with its 50 sonnets and distinct divisions into two groups of 14 and 36 sonnets; on the other side would be the two separate Books iii and iv, with 35 and 30 sonnets respectively. The centrality and length of II. ii may be significant in such a scheme, since it is concerned, unlike the other books of Part II, with the presence of Christ on earth, and since it is clear from Part I that the humanity of Christ and the manifestation of the divine in the human sphere is a constant preoccupation. However, this scheme depends on an asymmetrical break within II. i. A second way of looking at it is to retain the four books as they stand, in which case the final book appears not as part of a static symmetry, but as an asymmetrical extension. The first three books have their own narrative structure and logic: descent to hell, resurrection from hell, appearance on earth, and ascension from earth to heaven. Book iv then has the role of an epilogue with the particular theological theme of the continuation of the divine presence and redemptive grace on earth. This produces an open-ended effect that coincides with the closing argumentative exposition of the outgoing of the Spirit from the Godhead. Thus the structure of Part II may be ambiguous: there seems to be a combination of a static symmetrical form with one that is progressive and dynamic.

As for the relationship between the first two parts of the work, it is not enough to dismiss the second part as an afterthought composed after the success of the first. Although there is no evidence that the second part was an integral component in La

Ceppède's original plan, it is clear that when he came to write it he attempted to incorporate it in some formal literary unity. The principal of round-number composition in the individual 'livres' is apparently common to both, even if the numerical totals are not equal; the quasi-epic ornamentation is continued in Part II— indeed, the opening sonnet is manifestly intended to recall the Virgilian paraphrase of the first part:

> IE chante les amours, les armes, la victoire . . . (I. i. 1)

> I'AY chanté le Combat, la Mort, la sepulture
> Du Christ . . .
> Ie chante sa descente aux antres stygieux. (II. i. 1)

In addition, the annotations to the sonnets provide the reader with frequent cross-references to the sonnets of Part I. But it would be possible to say *a priori* that the unity of the Christian myth on which they both depend will ensure the compatibility of the two parts. The Resurrection and Ascension of Jesus in the second part are naturally complementary to his suffering and death in the first; more generally, the humanization of Jesus in Part I is followed by his divinization in Part II. These inherent relationships have been seen most clearly represented in the images and typologies that inform the *Théorèmes* as a whole and give the work's themes their cyclical rhythm.

A certain rhythm is also inherent in the way the numerical divisions of the *Théorèmes* correspond with significant narrative phases. Obviously the seven divisions of the *Théorèmes* represent seven biblically and theologically distinct phases (Agony, trials, Crucifixion, Resurrection, appearances, Ascension, and Pentecost). But the transition points between these phases, that is, the beginning and end of each of the work's seven Books also suggest a certain symbolic pattern. It is a pattern inherent in the biblical narrative, but it is brought into focus by the formal organization of the *Théorèmes*.

One of the noticeable features of the selection of material in I. i is the scant attention given to the Last Supper (I. i. 2, ll. 9–11), whereas the exit from the city and the journey to the garden are given a comparatively detailed treatment (I. i. 2–14). The reason for this becomes clearer if it is related to the fact that the exit, the expulsion from the garden of Gethsemane, is given some weight at the end of I. i. In other words, I. i can be seen as incorporating a pattern of exit from the city, penetration to the sacred site of the Agony,[36] with its several typological parallels in the rest of the *Théorèmes*, and finally the exit from Gethsemane. The opening of I. ii depicts the return to the city, that is, the reverse of the beginning of I. i, and it concludes with the narration of the procession out of the city towards Golgotha and the mystery of the cross.[37] Moreover, within the body of Book ii there is a constant and scrupulously indicated ingress and egress from one location of the trial of Jesus to the next until the trial by Pilate is reached (I. ii. 44–100). And while the sacred enclosure of the natural grove is emphasized in I. i (e.g. in I. i. 6 and 7), in I. ii the enclosure of the city becomes a symbol of the sinful world. It is the temptations of the city, for instance, that in I. ii. 26 are said to contribute to Peter's sin. Just as I. i opens with the arrival at the sacred grove, and just as I. ii opens with the arrival at the palace of Annas, so I. iii opens with the arrival of the procession at Golgotha. The movement of penetration by the individual *dévot* to the central mystery reinforces this theme:

> QVI m'ouurira les rangs? Qui me fendra la presse
> Pour t'approcher, Seigneur?   (I. iii. 1)

Book iii, as the conclusion of the triad of Part I, is relatively static; even so, the last two sonnets initiate the movement away from the place of crucifixion with the narration of the Deposition and the transportation of the body to the tomb.

In Part II a similar rhythmic alternation is present between the beginnings and ends of the four books; but instead of entrance and exit the symbolic motion is now primarily ascent and descent. The two divisions of II. i are concerned with the descent into hell and then the rising of Christ; Books iii and iv are concerned respectively with the ascension of Christ into heaven and the descent of the Holy Spirit. This leaves II. ii as a central narrative of events acted out between Christ and the disciples on earth, rather than between hell and earth or between earth and heaven. Consequently, the rhythm reverts to a horizontal movement of entrance and exit. In the first major subdivision (1–33)

---

[36] See above, p. 120 f., on the images associated with the garden.

[37] The correspondence between the exit from the garden and the exit from the city is reinforced by rhyme: see above, p. 199 f.

the women leave the city for the tomb (II. ii. 5), while the guards to the tomb return to the city (31–3). In sonnets 34–100, which concern Christ's appearances to the disciples, the basis of the narrative is still the journey to and from the city. The journey from Jerusalem to Emmaus (34–52) is followed by the return to Jerusalem and the subsequent events (53–77); the rest of the section narrates the journey to Galilee and the encounters by the lake (78–96), and the final mission of the disciples from Mount Tabor (97–100). In II. iii there is a return to the city both at the beginning and the end of the book; but the central portion, taking place outside Jerusalem, is dominated by the movement between earth and heaven. In Book iv the city is no longer such a precise point of reference: all movement is now in the spiritual dimension between earth and heaven.

These patterns are yet another aspect of the dynamic cyclical organization of the *Théorèmes*. The constant motion from interior to exterior, or between underworld, world, and heaven, coincides with the numerical divisions of the work, thus creating a symbolic form embracing the whole of the *Théorèmes* and giving it unity. It is a form which symbolizes a notion that lies at the heart of the work: the mediation between man and God, the penetration and divulgation of closed mysteries. It is in fact in terms of the spatial metaphor of inner and outer that La Ceppède speaks of the communication of mysteries explicitly in his *Avant-propos*, and implicitly in his imagery. In the formal composition of the work, therefore, as well as in the style and the imagery, there is embedded a problem and its symbolic resolution—the problem of the opposition and the communication between what is concealed and sacred and what is open and profane.

CONCLUSION

THE sonnet form has been called 'une machine à penser'.[1] Similar things have been said of mythological imagery. The *Théorèmes* use conventional literary forms to explicate and reformulate meanings already implicit in the corpus of Christian and pagan myth. Hence perhaps the title: *Les Théorèmes*. One should not rule out the possibility of a deliberate ambiguity, in which 'théorème' is associated with 'théorie' with its sixteenth-century meaning 'contemplation'.[2] However, 'théorème' is etymologically distinct, having the dominant sense of 'logical demonstration'. It is found in this sense as the title of theological and apologetic works in the Middle Ages and Renaissance.[3] In so far as a theorem is the demonstration of a non-self-evident proposition, this understanding has particular relevance to the nature of La Ceppède's work: the exposition of mysteries, paraphrastic commentary on the Bible, the concern with revelation and communication, the desire to make the world intelligible and ordered. The imagery and the formal coherence of the work constitute an unfolding analogue of the basic material, opening it up and clarifying it by interpretative restatement.

What, then, is the relationship between this poetry and the meditative tradition? As far as sources are concerned, La Ceppède's explicit references to the early Fathers, to the scholastics of the Middle Ages, and to the neo-scholastics of the sixteenth century far outweigh his references to contemplative or meditative writers. While the orthodoxy of these authors may reflect the Tridentine climate, he does show some independence in his utilization of versions of the Bible, just as he freely draws on pagan and con-

[1] Louis Aragon, 'Du sonnet'.

[2] Cf. de Mourgues, *Metaphysical, Baroque and Précieux Poetry*, pp. 49 f. For 'théorie' Cotgrave gives 'Theory, contemplation, deep study; a sight, or beholding, speculation'; 'théorème' is not mentioned. Cf. Huguet, *Dictionnaire*, who cites 'la théorie et contemplation des choses divines' from Guevara, *Épîtres dorées*.

[3] E.g. Duns Scotus, *Theoremata* (attributed); G. F. Pico della Mirandola, *Theoremata de fide et ordine credendi* (1521); J.-B. Morin, *De vera cognitione Dei, ex solo naturae lumine; per Theoremata adversus Ethnicos et Atheos mathematico more demonstrata* (1657).

temporary secular authors. The theological element is certainly less marked than the exegetic, but is at least as important in certain parts of the work as the meditative. La Ceppède continues to discuss dogmatic questions (at least, those which are not too controversial), especially Christological dogma, in some technical detail. As for the form, the model of the classic meditative exercise is far from providing a comprehensive account of the structure of the *Théorèmes*. This is not to say, of course, that the *Théorèmes* are not part of the sixteenth-century devotional movement, nor is it to deny that the meditative literature played a part in the constitution of the devotional climate. Naturally, there will be similarities between the various manifestations of this climate. This does not mean there is any kind of causal relationship between parallel manifestations. More generally, the point is that the hypothesis of the influence of meditative method is no doubt necessary to illuminate the context and certain features of the text of the *Théorèmes*, but is not sufficient to account for the most striking characteristics of the work as a whole.

The dominant factor appears rather to be La Ceppède's interest in the biblical text and in the range of exegetic sources from Origen to Maldonatus. It is with the discovery of underlying significance that he is concerned, and with the moral response to it: a devotional attitude, certainly, but not *necessarily* one associated with the formal or stylistic influence of meditative tracts. It is the exegetic basis that accounts for the meticulous presentation of the Gospel narrative and the exhaustive commentary and (in the prose annotations) self-commentary, which includes the analogical levels of interpretation, as well as the discursive *quaestio*. It is exegesis that provides the fund of typological correspondences which inform the *Théorèmes* and whose prime significance for La Ceppède may well be that they represent the participation of history in a divine scheme. It is also this basis that helps to explain the resistance to the Malherbian conception of language and the affinity with Pléiade assumptions about the poet and poetic language. The Pléiade notions, based on exegetic conceptions, were inherently capable of specific religious interpretation: the poet is an inspired interpreter of signs, his poetry a revelatory commentary on them, while imitating a model. The difference is that Ronsard failed to capture the theory in practice.[4] The Christian poet, however, does

---

[4] Cf. Cave (ed.), *Ronsard*, pp. 184 ff., 207 f.

not add mythical ornament to his theme, but draws themes out of the sacred myth. Moreover, he is in possession of a coherent total philosophy of man, the world, and history.

It has been claimed that the *Théorèmes* are a 'retour sur soi', a personal meditation that seeks to abolish time through the contemplation of myths and mysteries, and an actual escape from contemporary upheavals into transcendence.[5] The intricate coherence of the work certainly creates an aesthetic effect, which as such transcends the historical conditions of its production. But it would be arbitrary to neglect the possible relationship between the work's structure and its situation, and its possible function in that situation.

The *Théorèmes* are a *machine à penser* with their own logic built into the poetic fabric. It is a logic of relationships between separate domains. The relationships are of opposition or of analogy between, for instance, sacred and profane, God and man, sun and earth, inner and outer, signified and signifier, non-literal and literal. Similarly, there is a paradigm of mediating terms between these oppositions: the incarnate Christ, the sun's heat and light, the garment, and, ultimately, the 'théorèmes' themselves.

If one postulates a connection with the historical milieu, certain correspondences suggest themselves, for, as has been seen, the situation in Provence from about 1580 to 1630 can be considered in terms of its conflicts and attempts to resolve them. There was an implicit opposition between province and court, reflected on the cultural level in the revival of the dialect and in the local sense of historical destiny. These tendencies were indistiguishable at times from the Ligue revolt. Associated with these tensions between province and State, therefore, was the tension between State and Church. After Henry IV's victory and a period of collective guilt and penitence, manifest in contemporary penitential literature, Provence resolved these conflicts in an era of increasingly monarchist and Gallican sentiment.

In the symbolic network of the *Théorèmes* the concern with a *tertium quid*, with themes of renewal, mediation, conversion, and communication, epitomizes some of the crucial social and intellectual problems of the Counter-Reformation. The problem of communicating mysteries through the priesthood was implicit in the hierarchical organization of the Catholic Church; it was the

---

[5] Donaldson-Evans, *Poésie et méditation*, pp. 111 ff.

problem of reforming the clergy as an effective educating, proselytizing, and propagating body that was the object of attention of men such as de Bus, Romillon, Bérulle.

Further, it is impossible to ignore the fact that the author of the *Imitation* and the *Théorèmes* was a magistrate, socially and culturally associated with the local Provençal nobility, as well as with the Valois court through his links with Henri d'Angoulême's circle. The Provençal magistracy and nobility were torn between acceptance of the legitimacy of the French monarch and a local loyalty to an independent Provence that was compounded with Ligueur Catholicism. Although one can say nothing categorically of La Ceppède's personal position, it is reasonable to suppose that his poetry plays a role within the historical context of the civil wars in Provence. The *Imitation* with the accompanying 'Douze meditations' (as also the penitential paraphrases of Gallaup) seems to represent a collective act of penitence, akin to the ritual acts of public repentance widespread in France during the wars, but reflecting the particular moral confusion of the divided Aixois magistrates and poets. The first part of the *Théorèmes* was largely composed during this period, and in fact displays a certain thematic congruence—first in the portrayal of the suffering and destruction of Jesus, and second, perhaps, in the treatment of the archetypal magistrate, Pilate, torn between conscience and political expediency. Once it is accepted that Part I relates to the war years, the significance of Part II, which belongs to the period of national reconstruction (and reassimilation of Provence), and which deals with rebirth and ascension, becomes obvious.

If the *Imitation* was a local act of penitence, the *Théorèmes* (according to the Preface) have a national role. It is clear that there is a moral, social, and political function in the mind of the author, for what he envisages is the re-establishment of order and law, and the harmonization of nation and devotion. That in part is why the *Théorèmes* are a search for and a demonstration of the existence of significant order in the universe. In poetic terms these functions are manifest in the rhetorical resources and in the symbolic and hermeneutic use of language. Rhetoric itself is both the interpersonal, persuasive use of language and a symbolic mode. La Ceppède's rhetoric embraces both the sacred language of the Bible and the secular domain of the law court. Its persuasive function operates in the devotional aim of converting and emotionally involving the reader in the recitation of the sacred narrative. Prayer, too, is rhetoric, serving to plead a spiritual cause, or to influence the deity's actions. But the verbal repetitions of rhetoric operate also within the formal structure of the sonnet, reinforcing the world of repetitive correspondences that the *Théorèmes* seem to seek to create.

Indeed, the work as a unity could be said to have a persuasive, even quasi-magical function. The *Théorèmes*, whose narrative symbolism is that of the eucharistic rite, have the characteristics of ritualistic representation: the obsessional concern with the correct presentation of the action, exhausting of possibilities of interpretation, the accumulation of authoritative justification, the repetition of symbolic patterns. The work seeks to restore a fragmented world by means of the representation of destruction and resurrection. La Ceppède's poetry is not, then, merely a 'reflection' of the contemporary situation, and not flight from it. It is the most coherent cultural response of the Aixois élite to the problems of the day, a response which seeks to transcend these problems through a poetic representation of the recovery of unity. The mere act of publication and public dedication to the monarch of the work affirms the integration of a francophone Provençal culture into the nation-state.

It is the remarkable structural coherence and stylistic complexity that give La Ceppède's poetry its importance in literary history. The *Imitation* pinpoints a stylistic turning-point: the clash between the aesthetic of the biblical paraphrase and urbane secular styles. It is partly a matter of the clash between a provincial style and a court style (represented by Malherbe), but also perhaps of a clash between two distinct modes of sensibility. La Ceppède travels only part of the way with Malherbe, as the versions of the *Imitation* and the *Théorèmes* testify. There was no doubt a limit beyond which the stylistic peculiarities of the sacred model could not be further 'refined'. But, at a deeper level, a whole conception of reality and language seems to be involved. La Ceppède's poetry, founded as it is on the hermeneutic mentality, implies belief in words and things as natural signs awaiting commentary, and is in practice based on principles of analogy and restatement.[6] The probability that the advent of the 'new science' amongst other

---

[6] Cf. Foucault, *Les Mots et les choses*, p. 48; Dubois, *Mythe et langage*, pp. 19 ff.

factors led to a shift in attitudes towards literary language (especially figurative language) is well known.[7] Along with the analogical universe is lost the pervasive notion of intrinsic, 'natural' correspondences between signifier and signified; language ceases to have the objective character of a text to be interpreted, and becomes ideally an actively organized means of designation.[8] La Ceppède, steeped in the biblical and exegetic tradition, may well have been less receptive to the wider implications of the Malherbian trend than to a more superficial, and in any case congenial, aspect like rhyme. As Foucault has indicated, the transition can be seen as a clash between an inherently religious and exegetic spirit and an inherently profane and critical attitude. Commentary, interpretation, and repetition are the essence of the earlier conception, whereas the classical conception is essentially instrumental or utilitarian. The opposition is between the sacred and the profane.[9] It seems reasonable to think that it is the religious foundation in its conceptual and stylistic aspects that helps to perpetuate the older manner in La Ceppède.

The *Théorèmes* are more than merely a specimen in the wave of devotional poetry of late sixteenth-century France. The work constitutes one of the most remarkably wrought poetic texts produced by a Catholic loyalist in that disturbed period. True, it speaks the 'language' of several deeply-rooted Christian and humanist traditions: but it is a unique creative utterance with its own meaning and historical significance. That meaning is only apparent in a context—the context of religious commitment, political conflict, and intellectual and cultural change. It is a context which, as well as the *Théorèmes*, includes—and this is a measure of La Ceppède's stature—the *Semaines* of Du Bartas and the *Tragiques* of d'Aubigné. All three in their varying degrees are the product of religious divisions, seek to transcend the contradictions of their time, and strive to endow the universe with meaning.

[7] See Klein, 'La pensée figurative de la Renaissance'; Koyré, 'Attitude esthétique et pensée scientifique'; Lenoble, *Mersenne*; Rousset, 'La querelle de la métaphore' in *Intérieur et l'extérieur*.

[8] Cf. Foucault, pp. 60 ff.   [9] See Foucault's remarks, op. cit., p. 95.

APPENDIX I

COMPARISON OF RHYMES IN THE 1594 AND 1612 VERSIONS OF THE *IMITATION*

Rhyme	Rich				Non-Rich				Over-all total
	A	B	C	Total	A	B	C	Total	
1594 retained 1612	68	17	12	97	6	20	25	51	148
1594 subsequently changed	17	3	3	23	8	22	85	115	138
1612 introduced	37	9	80	126	1	4	7	12	138

A—masculine polysyllables, or feminine polysyllables without final mute *e*
B—monosyllables
C—feminine polysyllables ending in mute *e*

C-rhymes offer the best indication of La Ceppède's closeness to Malherbian practice. From the above it can be seen that 15 out of 125 C-rhymes are rich in 1594. In 1612 this rises to 92 out of 124. The significance of this can be brought out by comparison with Bertaut, whose own attention to technical detail is well known. According to Fromilhague's count for dateable poems by Bertaut with at least 40 C-rhymes (*Technique*, pp. 526 ff.), 143 out of 715 C-rhymes are rich, i.e. 1 in 5, which is inferior to the final totals for La Ceppède's *Imitation* (approximately 1 in 1·3).

APPENDIX II

STRUCTURE OF IMAGERY

Hierarchy \ Cycle	Obscurity winter/night	←Mediation→	Revelation summer/day
God sun fire	O.T. eclipsed destroys		N.T. lights, recreates, cleanses, sublimates
king		vanquishes rebels	triumphal entry
hero		kills monster	
lover		marriage	
Jesus	types	Incarnation, cross (centre, tree, ladder, garment, etc.)	Resurrection, Ascension
Man	flesh	Redemption	spirit
animals	wolves, vipers, etc.		lion, stag, phoenix, etc.
water	flood		cleanses, fertilizes
vegetation	sterile		fertile
ice, earth	inert	melts	sublimated
God	obscurity		revelation
Jesus		Incarnation	
	meaning obscure (inside)	symbolic text & symbolic world	meaning revealed (outside)
poet		inspiration exegesis & expression	
	meaning obscure (inside)	symbolic text (*théorèmes*)	meaning revealed (outside)
Man reader		inspiration & exegesis	

The upper block is labelled "Mediation" (vertical) and "Hierarchy". The lower block is also labelled "Mediation" (vertical).

The vertical axis is the axis of analogies and influences, the horizontal that of repetitive sequences. The lower half of the diagram should be thought of as superimposed on the upper: the notion of the poetic process is intimately bound up with ideas clustering around the Incarnation.

BIBLIOGRAPHY

A. MANUSCRIPTS

I. *La Ceppède*

Letter to Henry IV (19 March 1594), BN MS., ancien petit fonds français, 23194, fos. 445–6.

Truncated sonnet in Louis de Gallaup, 'Imitation et paraphrase des pseaumes de la pénitence royalle', 1595, p. 31.

Letter to Henry IV (13 October 1601), BN MS., ancien petit fonds français, 23196, fos. 425–6.

Letter to the Duke of Guise (4 November 1617), BN MS., ancien petit fonds français, 20560, fo. 87.

Four letters to Peiresc (1617–18), Ing. MS. 1878, fos. 413–16.

Letter to the consuls of Marseille (31 August, 1616), Archives de la ville de Marseille, cc. 2051.

II. *Other Writers*

Du Périer, François, *Recueil de poésies*, Ing. MS. 391.

Gallaup, Louis de, sieur de Chasteuil, *Poésies de L. de Gallaup*, Ing. MS. 386.

—— *Cahiers of L. de Gallaup*, Ing. MS. 193.

—— *Imitation et paraphrase des pseaumes de la pénitence royalle au treschrestien roy de France et de Navarre Henri IV*, 1595, Ing. MS. 17.

Henri d'Angoulême, *Les Œuvres poétiques de Monseigneur le Grand Prieur de France Henry d'Angoulesme* . . . BN MS., ancien fonds français, 482.

L'Hôpital, Paul Hurault de, Letters from Aix, BN MS., ancien fonds français, 23195.

B. PRINTED BOOKS

I. *La Ceppède*

Imitation des pseaumes de la penitence de David Par M.M.J. De la Ceppede Docteur es droictz, Conseiller du Roy, & President en la cour des Comptes, Aides & Finances en Provence.

Lyon, Jean Tholosan, 1594.

Copies: Arb. R312; Bibliothéque municipale de Versailles, G167; Bibliothèque de la ville de Lyon, t. 2, 329800–329806.

Imitation des pseaumes de la penitence de David, par Messre. J. De la Ceppede Chevalier, Conseiller du Roy en ses Conseils d'Etat & Privé, & premier President en la Cour des Comptes, Aydes, & Finances de Provence. Seconde edition Reveüe & augmentée de quelques Paraphrases d'autres Pseaumes, & pieces de devotion.

Toulouse, Colomiez, 1612.

Copies: bound with *Theoremes*, q.v. The Marseille copy lacks title-page (A1).

Les Theoremes de Messire Jean De la Ceppede, seigneur d'Aigalades, chevalier, conseiller du Roy en ses Conseils d'Estat & Privé, & premier President en sa Cour des Comptes, Aides, & Finances de Provence, sur le sacré mystere de nostre redemption, Divisez en trois Livres, & enrichis de trois Tables tres-amples du sujet des Sonnets, des Matieres, & des Autheurs: suivis de l'Imitation de quelques Pseaumes, & autres Meslanges spirituels.

Toulouse, J. and R. Colomiez, 1613.

Copies: Arb. R582; Arsenal, 4° B3133; BN D5460; Bibliothèque Méjanes, Aix, G2484; Bibliothèque de Marseille, Rés. 26714.

La seconde partie des Theoremes de M. J. De la Ceppede, seigneur d'Aigallades, Conseiller du Roy en ses Conseil privé & d'Estat, Chevailler & premier President en sa Cour des Comtes, Aides & finances de Provence. Sur les mysteres de la descente de Jesus-Christ aux Enfers, de sa Resurrection, de ses apparitions apres icelle, de son Ascension, & de la Mission du S. Esprit en forme visible. divisée en quatre livres.

Toulouse, R. Colomiez, 1621.

Copies: Arb. R185; BN D5460.

All copies of Part I listed also have on a separate leaf a variant title within an ornamental frame. The Marseille copy of Part II is the only copy of Part II seen to use the same frame for the title. The date is different, and the title-page transcribed above for the Arbaud and BN copies of Part II is not present:

Seconde partie des Theoremes de Mre. J. De la Ceppede Chevalier, Conseiller du Roy en ses Conseils d'Estat & Privé, & Premier President en la Cour des Comptes, Aides & finances de Provence. Sur les mysteres de la descente de Jesus-Christ aux Enfers, de sa Resurrection, &c. Divisée en quatre livres.

Toulouse, R. Colomiez, 1622.

Sonnet in Louis de Gallaup, *Imitation* (1596), p. 18, q.v.

11. *Other sixteenth- and seventeenth-century writers*

Bellarmine, Robert (Saint), *Explanatio in Psalmos*, Lyon, H. Cardon, 1611.

—— *Institutiones linguae Hebraicae, postremo recognitae, ac locupletatae,* F. Fabrum, 1619; 1st edn. 1578.

Bellarmine, Robert (Saint) (*cont.*) *The Soul's Ascent to God, by the steps of Creation*, trans. H. Hall, London, 1705.

Bellaud de La Bellaudière, Louis, *Obros et rimos prouvenssalos de Loys de La Bellaudiero* . . ., Marseille, P. Mascaron, 1595; second issue 1595, National Library, 839. h. 29.

Colletet, G., *Traitté de l'epigramme et traitté du sonnet*, ed. P. A. Janini, Geneva, 1965.

Desportes, Philippe, *Les CL Pseaumes de David mis en vers français par Ph. Des-Portes Abbé de Thiron*, Paris, A. L'Angelier, 1603.

Du Bartas, *The Works of Guillaume de Salluste, sieur Du Bartas*, ed. U. T. Holmes *et al.*, 3 vols, Chapel Hill, University of North Carolina Press, 1935–40.

Du Bellay, Joachim, *Œuvres poétiques*, ed. H. Chamard, 6 vols., Paris, 1908–31.

—— *La Deffence et illustration de la langue françoyse*, ed. H. Chamard, Paris, 1948.

Du Perron, Jacques Davy, *Perroniana et Thuana, ou pensées judicieuses, bons mots, rencontres agreables & observations curieuses du Cardinal du Perron, et de Mr. le President de Thou*, Cologne, 1694.

Ficino, Marsilio, *Divini Platonis opera* . . ., 5 vols., Lyon, 1550.

François de Sales, S. *Œuvres. Édition compléte d'après les autographes et les éditions originales*, ed. B. Mackey and P. Navatel, 26 vols., Annecy–Lyon, 1892–1932.

Gallaup, Louis de, sieur de Chasteuil, *Imitation des pseaumes de la pénitence royale. Au tres-chrestien roy de France et de Navarre, Henry IV*, Paris, A. L'Angelier, 1596. Ars. 8° 843.

—— *Imitation des pseaumes de la pénitence royale. Au tres-chrestien roy de France et de Navarre Henry IV*, 2nd edn. (expanded), Paris, A. L'Angelier, 1597; Ars. 8° T844.

Génébrard, Gilbert, *Psalmi Davidis, vulgata editione, calendario Hebraeo, Syro, Graeco, Latino, hymnis, argumentis, & commentariis* . . . *a G. Genebrardo* . . . *instructi*, Paris, O. P. L'Huillier, 1581.

—— *Psalmi Davidis Variis calendariis et commentariis genuinum sensum* . . . *aperientibus a Gil. Genebrardo* . . . *instructi*, Lyon, H. Cardon, 1600.

Granada, Luis de, *Devotes contemplations et spirituelles instructions sur la Vie, Passion, Mort, Resurrection, & glorieuse Ascension de nostre Sauveur Jesus Christ*, trans. F. de Belleforest, Paris, 1589.

Guez, Jean-Louis, sieur de Balzac, *Socrate Chrétien* . . . *et autres œuvres* . . ., 2 vols., Paris, 1657.

Ignatius de Loyola, *Les Vrais exercices spirituels* . . . *ensemble la guide ou directoire pour ceux qui font faire lesdits exercices. Edition seconde, reveue, corrigée et augmentée.* Paris, 1620.

Laval, A. de, *Paraphrase des Pseaumes de David tant literalle que mystique. Avec Annotations necessaires, le tout fidellement extraict des saincts Docteurs receuz et approuvez en la saincte Eglise Catholique, Apostolique et Romaine*, Paris, A. L'Angelier, 1610.

Le Fèvre de La Boderie, Guy, *L'Encyclie des secrets de l'éternité*, Antwerp, 1570.

L'Estoille, P. de, *Journal pour le règne de Henri III (1574–1589)*, ed. L.-R. Lefèvre, Paris, 1943.

Malherbe, F. de, *Œuvres* recueillies et annotées par L. Lalanne, 5 vols., Paris, 1862–9.

—— *Œuvres poétiques*, ed. Fromilhague and Lebègue, 2 vols., Paris, 1968.

Marguerite de Navarre, *Les Marguerites de la Marguerite des Princesses*, ed. F. Frank, Paris, 1873.

Marot, Clément, *Pseaumes de David* in *Œuvres complètes*, ed. A. Grenier, vol. ii, Paris, n.d.

Montaigne, M. de, *Œuvres complètes*, ed. A. Thibaudet and M. Rat, Paris, 1962 (Bibliothèque de la Pléiade).

Nostredame, César de, *Les Perles, ou les Larmes de la saincte Magdalene, avec quelques rymes sainctes dédiées à Madame la comtesse de Carces*, Toulouse, 1606.

—— *Pièces héroïques et diverses poesies dediees à Messeigneurs les Archevesques et Princes d'Arles et D'ambrun*, Toulouse, 1608.

—— *L'Histoire et chronique de Provence*, Lyon, S. Rigaud, 1614.

—— *L'Entrée de la Reine Marie de Médicis à Salon*, ed. Boy, Marseille, 1855 (reprint of Aix, 1602).

Nostredame, Jean de, *Les Vies des plus célèbres et anciens poètes provençaux*, ed. J. Anglade, Paris, 1912.

Peletier Du Mans, Jacques, *L'Amour des amours, vers lyriques*, ed. A. van Bever, Paris, 1926.

Racan, H. de Bueil, marquis de, *Mémoires* in Malherbe, *Les Poésies*, ed. Martinon and Allem, Paris, 1926.

Richeome, Louis, *Les Œuvres du R. Pere Louis Richeome provençal, religieux de la compagnie de Jesus. Reveues par l'autheur avant sa mort et augmentées de plusieurs pièces non encore imprimées*, 2 vols., Paris, 1628.

Ronsard, P. de, *Œuvres complètes*, ed. P. Laumonier, completed by Silver and Lebègue, Paris, 1914–67.

Sebillet, Thomas, *Art poétique françoys*, ed. F. Gaiffe, Paris, 1932.

Soliers, N. Jules Raimond de, *Les antiquitez de la ville de Marseille* . . . *où il est traicté de l'ancienne république des Marseillois* . . . *translatées de latin en françois par Charles Annibal Fabrot*, Cologny, A. Pernet, 1615.

Sponde, J. de, *Méditations avec un essai de poèmes chrétiens*, ed. A. Boase, Paris, 1954.

Tallemant des Réaux, G., *Historiettes*, ed. Mongrédien, 8 vols., Paris, 1932–4.

Tyard, Pontus de, *Solitaire premier*, ed. S. F. Baridon, Geneva, 1950.

Vauquelin de la Fresnaye, *L'Art poétique*, ed. G. Pellissier, Paris, 1885.

III. *Historical, critical, and reference works*

(a) *On La Ceppède*

Balmas, E., 'Jean de La Ceppède', *Lingue straniere*, vol. viii, no. 5 (1959).

Braunschweig, R., 'Petites découvertes sur La Ceppède dans Gallaup', *BHR* 28 (1966), pp. 672 ff.

Buffum, I., 'A Religious Sonnet Sequence: the *Théorèmes* of Jean de La Ceppède' in *Studies in the Baroque from Montaigne to Rotrou*, New Haven, 1957.

Castan, F., 'The Realm of the Imaginary in Du Bellay/Ronsard and Du Bartas/La Ceppède', *Yale French Studies*, 47 (1972), pp. 110 ff.

Clarac, P., 'Jean de La Ceppède, poète de la Passion', *Cahiers du Sud*, 42 (1956).

—— 'Un ami de Malherbe: le poète Jean de La Ceppède, *XVIIᵉ siècle*, 31 (1956), pp. 332 ff.

—— 'Jean de La Ceppède', *Quatrième centenaire de la naissance de Malherbe*, Aix, 1956, pp. 59 ff.

Donaldson-Evans, L. K., 'L'édition de 1594 de l'*Imitation des Pseaumes* de la Ceppède', *Australian Journal of French Studies*, 2 (1965), pp. 279 ff.

—— 'Notice biographique sur Jean de La Ceppède', *BHR* 28 (1966), pp. 123 ff.

—— *Poésie et méditation chez Jean de la Ceppède*, Geneva, 1969.

Du Bruck, E., 'Descriptive Realism in the *Théorèmes* of Jean de La Ceppède', *MLN* 80 (1965), pp. 596 ff.

—— 'Three Religious Sonneteers of the Waning Renaissance: Sponde, Chassignet and Ceppède', *Neophilologus*, 54 (1970), pp. 235 ff.

Evans, A. R., 'Figural Art in the *Théorèmes* of Jean de La Ceppède', *MLN* 78 (1963), pp. 278 ff.

Evans, A. R. and Evans, C., 'Two sonnets of Jean de La Ceppède', *The Month*, 28 (1962).

Lawrence, F., 'The Renaissance Theory of Poetry as Imitation of Nature and the *Théorèmes* of Jean de La Ceppède', *Journal of Medieval and Renaissance Studies*, 3 (1973), pp. 233 ff.

Lawrence, F. L., 'La Ceppède's *Théorèmes* and Ignatian Meditation', *Comparative Literature*, 17 (1965), pp. 135 ff.

—— 'Nature Imagery in the *Théorèmes* of Jean de la Ceppède', *L'Esprit créateur*, 6 (1966), pp. 248ff.

Lebègue, R., 'L'influence des romanciers sur les dramaturges français de la fin du XVIᵉ siècle', *BHR* 17 (1955), pp. 74 ff.

Nugent, R., 'La Ceppède's Poetry of Contemplation', *French Review*, 36 (1963), pp. 450 ff.

Pingaud, B., 'La Ceppède, poète et magistrat aixois', *L'Arc*, 7 (1959).

Probes, C. McCall, 'La Ceppède's *Théorèmes* and Augustinian Sources', *BHR* 32 (1970), pp. 409 ff.

—— 'La Ceppède's Discriminatory Use of St. Augustine as *Garent*', *BHR* 34 (1972), pp. 65 ff...

Quenot, Y., 'Un discours inconnu de Jean de La Ceppède', *BHR* 36 (1974), pp. 354 ff.

Rousset, J., *Jean de La Ceppède. Choix de textes et préface par Jean Rousset*, Paris, 1947.

—— Préface to *Les Théorèmes* . . . *Reproduction de l'édition de Toulouse, 1613–1622*, Geneva, 1966.

—— 'Jean de La Ceppède et la chaîne des sonnets' in *L'Intérieur et l'extérieur*, Paris, 1968.

Ruchon, F., *Essai sur la vie et l'œuvre de Jean de La Ceppède, poète chrétien et magistrat (1548–1623)*, Geneva, 1963.

Saulnier, V.-L. and Worthington, A., 'Du nouveau sur Jean de La Ceppède', *BHR* 17 (1955), pp. 415 ff.

Wilson, E. M., 'Notes on a Sonnet by La Ceppède', *FS* 22 (1968), pp. 296 ff.

(b) *General*

Allais, G., *Malherbe et la poésie française à la fin du XVIᵉ siècle (1585–1600)*, Geneva, 1969 (reprint of Paris, 1891).

Allen, J. W., *A History of Political Thought in the Sixteenth Century*, London, 1957.

Aragon, L., 'Du sonnet', *Les Lettres françaises*, 506, (1954), pp. 1 ff.

Aude, E., 'La Poésie en Provence au temps de Malherbe', *Cahiers d'Aix-en-Provence*, hiver 1923–4, pp. 3 ff.

Auerbach, E., *Scenes from the Drama of European Literature*, New York, 1959.

Backer, Augustin, Backer, Aloys, and Sommervogel, C., *Bibliothèque de la Compagnie de Jésus*, 11 vols., Brussels and Paris, 1890–1932.

Baker, C. D., 'Certain Religious Elements in the English Doctrine of the Inspired Poet during the Renaissance', *English Literary History*, 16 (1959), pp. 300 ff.

Baldwin, C. S., *Medieval Rhetoric and Poetic*, New York, 1928.

Barr, J., *The Semantics of Biblical Language*, Oxford, 1961.

Barthes, R., 'Comment parler à Dieu', *Tel Quel*, 38 (1969), pp. 32 ff.

Berger, S., *La Bible au seizième siècle*, Paris, 1879.

—— *La Bible française au Moyen Âge*, Paris, 1884.

Boase, A., 'Poètes anglais et français de l'époque baroque', *Revue des sciences humaines*, 86 (1949), pp. 155 ff.

—— *The Poetry of France*, 4 vols., London, 1964–9.

Braudel, F., *La Méditerranée et le monde méditerranéen à l'époque de Philippe II*, Paris, 1949.

Braunschweig, R., 'Une source profane de la "Sainte Pécheresse" ', *BHR* 28 (1966), pp. 670 ff.

Bray, R., *La Formation de la doctrine classique en France*, Paris, 1927.

Bremond, H., *Histoire littéraire du sentiment religieux en France depuis la fin des guerres de religion jusqu'à nos jours*, 11 vols.. Paris, 1921–36.

Brun, A., *Bellaud de La Bellaudière, poète provençal du XVIᵉ siècle*, Gap, n.d.

—— *Recherches historiques sur l'introduction du français dans les provinces du Midi*, Paris, 1923.

—— *Poètes provençaux du XVIᵉ siècle*, Gap, 1957.

Bruneau, Ch., 'L'image dans notre langue littéraire' in *Mélanges de linguistique offerts à Albert Dauzat*, Paris, 1931.

Brunot, F., *La Doctrine de Malherbe d'après son 'Commentaire sur Desportes'*, Paris, 1891.

—— *Histoire de la langue française des origines à nos jours*, 11 vols., Paris, 1966–9.

Bruyne, E. de, *L'Esthétique du Moyen Âge*, 3 vols., Bruges, 1946.

Buffum, I., *Studies in the Baroque from Montaigne to Rotrou*, New Haven, 1957.

Busson, H., *Le Rationalisme dans la littérature de la Renaissance en France*, Paris, 1957.

Cambridge History of the Bible, 3 vols., Cambridge, 1963–70.

Campbell, L. B., 'The Christian Muse', *Huntington Library Bulletin*, 8 (1955), pp. 30 ff.

Castor, G., *Pléiade Poetics*, Cambridge, 1964.

The Catholic Encyclopedia, ed. C. G. Herbermann *et al.*, 15 vols., London, 1907–14.

Cave, T. C., 'The Protestant Devotional Tradition: Simon Goulart's *Trente tableaux de la mort*', *FS* 21 (1967), pp. 1 ff.

―― *Devotional Poetry in France, c. 1570–1613*, Cambridge, 1969.

Cave, T. C. (ed.), *Ronsard the Poet*, London, 1973.

Certau, M., 'Crise sociale et réformisme spirituel au début du XVIIᵉ siècle: une "nouvelle spiritualité" chez les jésuites français', *Revue d'ascétique et de mystique*, 41 (1965).

Charity, A. C., *Events and their Afterlife: the Dialectics of Christian Typology in the Bible and in Dante*, Cambridge, 1966.

Cioranesco, A., *Bibliographie de la littérature française du seizième siècle*, Paris, 1959.

Clements, R. J., *Critical Theory and Practice of the Pléiade*, Cambridge, Massachusetts, 1942.

―― 'Iconography on the Nature and Inspiration of Poetry in Renaissance Emblem Literature', *PMLA* 70 (1955), pp. 781 ff.

Colish, M. L., *The Mirror of Language. A Study in the Medieval Theory of Knowledge*, New York, 1968.

Copleston, F., *A History of Philosophy*, vols. i–iii, New York, 1962–3.

Cotgrave, R., *A Dictionarie of the French and English Tongues*, London, A. Islip, 1611.

Curtius, E. R., *Europäische Literatur und lateinisches Mittelalter*, Berne, 1948.

Dagens, J., *Bérulle et les origines de la restauration catholique, 1575–1611*, Brussels, 1952.

―― *Bibliographie chronologique de la littérature de spiritualité et de ses sources, 1501–1610*, Paris, 1953.

Daniélou, J., *Sacramentum Futuri*, Paris, 1950.

Darlow, T. H. and Moule, H. F., *Historical Catalogue of the Printed Editions of Holy Scripture in the Library of the British and Foreign Bible Society*, 2 vols., London, 1903–11.

Dawson, J. C., *Toulouse in the Renaissance*, New York, 1923.

Demerson, G., *La Mythologie classique dans l'œuvre lyrique de la Pléiade*, Geneva, 1972.

Dictionnaire de théologie catholique, ed. A. Vacant, E. Mangeot, and E. Amann, 15 vols., Paris, 1930–50.

Droz, E., 'Bibles françaises après le concile de Trente', *Journal of the Warburg and Courtauld Institutes*, 28 (1965), pp. 209 ff.

Dubois, C.-G., *Mythe et langage au seizième siècle*, Bordeaux, 1970.

Dunbar, H. F., *Symbolism in Medieval Thought*, Yale, 1929.

Eliade, M., *Le Mythe de l'éternel retour: archétypes et répétition*, Paris, 1949.

—— *Images et symboles*, Paris, 1952.

—— *Mythes, rêves et mystères*, Paris, 1957.

—— *Traité d'histoire des religions*, Paris, 1964.

Elwert, W. T., *Traité de versification française des origines à nos jours*, Paris, 1965.

Eys, W. J. van., *Bibliographie des Bibles et des Nouveaux Testaments en langue française des XVe et XVIe siècles*, 2 vols., Geneva, 1900–1.

Foucault, M., *Les Morts et les choses. Une archéologie des sciences humaines*, Paris, 1966.

Fowler, A., *Spenser and the Numbers of Time*, London, 1964.

Fromilhague, R., *La Vie de Malherbe, apprentissages et luttes (1555–1610)*, Paris, 1954.

—— *Malherbe. Technique et création poétique*, Paris, 1954.

Gilson, E., 'La scolastique et l'esprit classique', *Les Idées et les lettres* (1932), pp. 243 ff.

—— *History of Christian Philosophy in the Middle Ages*, London, 1955.

Glaire, J.-B., *Dictionnaire universel des sciences ecclésiastiques*, 2 vols., Paris, 1868.

Gordon, A. L., *Ronsard et la rhétorique*, Geneva, 1970.

Goujet, abbé, *Bibliothèque françoise*, 18 vols., Paris, 1741–56.

Graham, V. E., 'The Pelican as Image and Symbol', *Revue de littérature comparée*, 36 (1962), pp. 235 ff.

Griffiths, R., 'The Influence of Formulary Rhetoric upon French Renaissance Tragedy', *Modern Language Review*, 59 (1964), pp. 201 ff.

—— 'Some Uses of Petrarchan Imagery in Sixteenth-century France', *FS* 18 (1964), pp. 311 ff.

Haitze, Pierre-Joseph de, *Histoire de la ville d'Aix, capitale de la Provence*, 6 vols., Aix-en-Provence, 1880–94.

Hatzfeld, H., 'Christian, Pagan and Devout Humanism in Sixteenth-century France', *Modern Language Quarterly*, 12 (1951), pp. 337 ff.

—— 'The Role of Mythology in Poetry during the French Renaissance', *Modern Language Quarterly*, 13 (1952), pp. 392 ff.

—— 'Imbrie Buffum: Studies in the Baroque' (review), *MLN* 72 (1957), p. 631.

Hautecœur, L., 'Le Concile de Trente et l'art', *La Table ronde*, 190 (1963), pp. 15 ff.

Henkel, A. and Schöne, A., *Emblemata, Handbuch zur Sinnbildkunst des XVI. und XVII. Jahrhunderts*, Stuttgart, 1957.

Huguet, É., *Dictionnaire de la langue française du seizième siècle*, 7 vols., Paris, 1925–67.

Hurter, H., *Nomenclator literarius theologiae catholicae*, 5 vols., Innsbruck, 1903–13.

Jackson, R. A., 'The Sleeping King', *BHR* 31 (1969), pp. 525 ff.

Janelle, P., *The Catholic Reformation*, London, 1971.

Jasinski, M., *Histoire du sonnet en France*, Douai, 1903.

Jeanneret, M., 'Marot traducteur des psaumes entre le néo-platonisme et la réforme', *BHR* 27 (1965), pp. 15 ff.

—— *Poésie et tradition biblique au XVIe siècle*, Paris, 1969.

Joukovsky-Micha, F., *Poésie et mythologie au XVIe siècle: quelques mythes d'inspiration chez les poètes de la Renaissance*, Paris, 1969.

Joüon, P., *Grammaire de l'hébreu biblique*, Rome, 1923.

Jung, M.-R., *Hercule dans la littérature française du XVIe siècle*, Geneva, 1966.

Kantorowicz, E. H., *The King's Two Bodies*, Princeton, 1957.

—— 'Oriens Augusti — Lever du Roi', *Dumbarton Oaks Papers*, 17 (1963), pp. 119 ff.

—— 'Dante's Two Suns', in *Selected Studies*, New York, 1965, pp. 325 ff.

Klein, R., 'La pensée figurative de la Renaissance', *Diogène* (1960).

Kovach, F. J., *Die Ästhetik des Thomas von Aquin*, Berlin, 1961.

Koyré, A., 'Attitude esthétique et pensée scientifique', *Critique*, II (1955).

Lafont, R., *Renaissance du Sud*, Paris, 1970.

Lausberg, H., *Handbuch der literarischen Rhetorik*, 2 vols., Munich, 1950.

Lebègue, R., 'Nouvelles études malherbiennes' *BHR* 5 (1944), pp. 135 ff.

—— 'L'influence des romanciers sur les dramaturges français de la fin du XVIe siècle', *BHR* 17 (1955), pp. 74 ff.

Lebègue, R. *et al.*, *Malherbe et son temps*, *DSS* 31 (1950).

Leblanc, P., *La Poésie religieuse de Marot*, Paris, 1955.

—— *Les Paraphrases françaises des psaumes à la fin de la période baroque (1610–1660)*, Paris, 1960.

Lefranc, A., *Grands Écrivains français de la Renaissance*, Paris, 1914.

Legré, L., 'Le Grand Prieur Henri d'Angoulême', *Revue de Marseille et de Provence* (1861), pp. 18–36, 78–97, 196–203.

Lemaire, H., *Les Images chez saint François de Sales*, Paris, 1962.

—— *Étude des images littéraires de François de Sales, avec un florilège*, Paris, 1969.

Lenoble, R., *Mersenne ou la naissance du mécanisme*, Paris, 1943.

—— *Histoire de l'idée de nature*, Paris, 1969.

Levi, A. H. T., *French Moralists: The Theory of the Passions 1589–1649*, Oxford, 1964.

L'Hôte, J., 'Malherbe et la Provence', *Mémoires de l'Institut historique de Provence*, 10 (1953), pp. 109 ff.

Lubac, H. de, *Exégèse médiévale, les quatre sens de l'Écriture*, 2 parts in 4 vols., Paris, 1959–64.

Mâle, É., *L'Art religieux de la fin du Moyen Âge en France: étude sur l'iconographie du moyen âge et sur ses sources d'inspiration*, Paris, 1949.

—— *L'Art religieux après le concile de Trente*, Paris, 1932.

Malherbe et la Provence [catalogue of the exhibition for the fourth centenary of Malherbe's birth held in Aix], Preface by P. Colotte, Aix-en-Provence, 1955.

Malherbe et les poètes de son temps [catalogue of the exhibition for the fourth centenary of Malherbe's birth held at the Bibliothéque nationale], Preface by J. Cain, Paris, 1955.

Maritain, J. A. H., *Art et scolastique*, Paris, 1947.

Marty-Laveaux, Ch., *La Langue de la Pléiade*, 2 vols., Paris, 1896–8.

Martz, L., *The Poetry of Meditation*, Yale, 1962.

McGowan, M. M., 'Prose Inspiration for Poetry: J.-B. Chassignet' in *The French Renaissance and its Heritage: Essays Presented to Alan M. Boase*, ed. D. R. Haggis *et al.*, London, 1968.

Mesnard, J., 'La théorie des figuratifs dans les *Pensées* de Pascal', *Revue d'histoire de la philosophie et d'histoire générale de la civilisation*, 11 (1945), pp. 219 ff.

Migne, J.-P., *Patrologia Latina*, 221 vols., Paris, 1844–64.

Mönch, W., *Das Sonett, Gestalt und Geschichte*, Heidelberg, 1959.

Mourgues, O. de, *Metaphysical, Baroque and Précieux Poetry*, Oxford, 1953.

Müller, A., *La Poésie religieuse catholique de Marot à Malherbe*, Paris, 1950.

Nolhac, P. de, *Ronsard et l'humanisme*, Paris, 1921.

Oesterley, W. O. E., *The Psalms Translated, with Text-Critical and Exegetical Notes*, London, 1939.

Ong, W. J., *Ramus, Method, and the Decay of Dialogue. From the Art of Discourse to the Art of Reason*, Cambridge, Massachusetts, 1958.

Patterson, W. F., *Three Centuries of French Poetic Theory: a Critical History of the Chief Arts of Poetry in France (1328–1630)*, 2 vols., Ann Arbor, 1935.

Perrier, E., *Un Village provençal: Les Aygalades*, Marseille, 1919.

Pétavel, E., *La Bible en France*, Paris, 1864.

Picard, R., 'Aspects du lyrisme religieux au XVIIᵉ siècle', *DSS* 60 (1965), pp. 57 ff.

Poulet, G., 'Poésie du cercle et de la sphère, *CAIEF* 10 (1958), pp. 44 ff.

—— *Les Métamorphoses du cercle*, Paris, 1961.

Pourrat, P., *La Spiritualité chrétienne*, 4 vols., Paris, 1918–28.

Praz, M., *Studies in Seventeenth-century Imagery*, London, 1959.

Quatrième centenaire de la naissance de Malherbe 1555–1628, Publications des annales de la Faculté des Lettres, Aix-en-Provence, nouvelle série, 14, Gap, 1956.

Raymond, M., *L'influence de Ronsard sur la poésie française (1550–1585)*, 2 vols., Geneva, 1965.

—— *La Poésie française et le maniérisme*, Geneva, 1971.

Reichenberger, K., 'L'Uranie ou la Muse céleste. Eine Dichtungslehre aus der zweiten Hälfte des 16. Jahrhunderts', *Zeitschrift für französische Sprache und Literatur*, 71 (1961), pp. 38 ff.

Rousset, J., 'Les images de la nuit et de la lumière chez quelques poètes religieux', *CAIEF* 10 (1958), pp. 58 ff.

—— *L'intérieur et l'extérieur. Essais sur la poésie et sur le théâtre au XVIIᵉ siècle*, Paris, 1968.

—— 'Les recueils de sonnets, sont-ils composés?' in *The French Renaissance and its Heritage: Essays Presented to Alan M. Boase*, ed. D. R. Haggis *et al.*, London, 1968.

Saintsbury, G., *A History of Criticism and Literary Taste in Europe from the Earliest Texts to the Present Day*, 3 vols., Edinburgh, 1900–4.

Sayce, R. A., *The French Biblical Epic in the Seventeenth Century*, Oxford, 1955.

Schmidt, A.-M., *La Poésie scientifique en France au XVIᵉ siècle*, Paris, 1938.

Seznec, J., *La Survivance des dieux antiques*, London, 1939.

Smalley, B., *The Study of the Bible in the Middle Ages*, Oxford, 1941.

Spingarn, J. E., *A History of Literary Criticism in the Renaissance*, 2nd edn., New York, 1908.

Steele, A. J., 'Conversions', *CAIEF* 10 (1958), pp. 69 ff.

Svoboda, K., *L'Esthétique de saint Augustin et ses sources*, Brno, 1933.

Thomas Aquinas, St., *Summa theologiae. Latin Text and English Translation*, London, 1964.

Tortel, J. *et al.*, *Le Préclassicisme français*, Paris, 1952.

Trénel, J., *L'Élément biblique dans l'œuvre de d'Aubigné*, Paris, 1904.

Truchet, J. *et al.*, *Points de vue sur la rhétorique*, *DSS* 80–1 (1968).

Tuve, R., 'Imagery and Logic: Ramus and Metaphysical Poetics', *Journal of the History of Ideas*, 3 (1942), pp. 365 ff.

—— *Elizabethan and Metaphysical Imagery: Renaissance Poetic Imagery and Twentieth-century Critics*, Chicago, 1947.

Varga, A. Kibedi, 'La poésie religieuse au xvie siècle. Suggestions et cadres d'études', *Neophilologus*, 46 (1962), pp. 263 ff.

—— *Rhétorique et littérature: études de structures classiques*, Paris, 1970.

Vianey, J., *Le Pétrarquisme en France*, Montpellier, 1909.

—— 'La Bible dans la poésie française', *Revue des cours et conférences*, 23 (1921–2), *passim*.

Wadding, L., *Scriptores ordinis Minorum*, Rome, 1906.

Weber, J., *La Création poétique au XVIe siècle en France*, 2 vols., Paris, 1956.

Wickersheimer, C. A. E., *La Médecine et les médecins en France à l'époque de la Renaissance*, Paris, 1906.

Wilson, E. M., 'Spanish and English Religious Poetry of the Seventeenth Century', *Journal of Ecclesiastical History*, 9 (1958), pp. 38 ff.

Wind, E. R., *Pagan Mysteries in the Renaissance*, London, 1958.

Yates, F. A., *The French Academies of the Sixteenth Century*, London, 1947.

—— 'Dramatic Religious Processions in the Late Sixteenth Century', *Annales musicologiques*, 2 (1954), pp. 215 ff.

INDEX